ANALYZING RHETORIC

A Handbook for the Informed Citizen in a New Millennium

◆◆◆

Robert C. Rowland
University of Kansas

KENDALL/HUNT PUBLISHING COMPANY
4050 Westmark Drive   Dubuque, Iowa 52002

For Joan

Chapter Four ◆ Rational Argument   55

Chapter Five ◆ Narrative Forms of Rhetoric   77

Contents

Chapter Six   ◆   Credibility Strategies   93

Chapter Seven   ◆   Aesthetic Strategies   115

Introduction

The most common usage of the word "rhetoric" is negative. People often associate rhetoric with overblown language or with deception. For example, in a speech contained later in this book Mario Cuomo distinguishes between "rhetoric" and "reality." Cuomo's usage reflects the common perception that rhetoric is both unimportant and generally used to deceive or manipulate. It is for this reason that political commentators often place the adjective "mere" in front of the word rhetoric. They do so to distinguish "mere rhetoric," from something truly important like legislation.

The perception that rhetoric is unimportant, not worthy of serious consideration, is misguided. To make this point clear, it is first important to understand what the term rhetoric means. *Rhetoric is the use of symbols (primarily language) to persuade or inform.* Any time one person uses speech (or writing or an object or a film and so forth) to influence another person, he/she is relying on the resources of rhetoric. As long as the person presenting the rhetoric (the rhetor or rhetorician) relies on "symbol use" rhetoric is being presented.

A symbol is an object that means something to both the rhetor and the audience. Our most common symbol system is language, but tangible objects (a cross for example), places (such as the FDR memorial in Washington), songs, pictures, and so forth also may function as symbols. People engage in rhetoric whenever they use symbols to communicate with others.

Perhaps the most common use of the term "rhetoric" is to refer to a political speech. But rhetoric is found in other kinds of speeches as well. When a manager tries to motivate or explain a principle to employees, he or she is using rhetoric. When a doctor explains to a patient the importance of taking all of a certain prescription, that doctor is using rhetoric. Rhetoric is also found in other forms. A book that informs or persuades us is rhetorical, as are many newspaper, magazine and internet articles. Many television programs and films use symbols to make an important point. Steven Spielberg's award winning film, "Saving Private Ryan," made a powerful point about the heroism and sacrifice of soldiers in World War II. The movie was so powerful that the media reported instances of veterans overcome with emotion at the conclusion of the film. Music too may be rhetorical. Beethoven's "Ninth Symphony" has been treated as a symbol for international peace and is played every year at the United Nations on United Nations Day. And art may be rhetorical as well. A photograph or a drawing of a murdered child in Rwanda or Kosovo may bring home the horrors of genocide more powerfully than a thousand speeches.

The important point to remember is that any time we use symbols to persuade or inform, we are using rhetoric.

The Importance of Rhetoric

The foregoing analysis should make clear the importance of rhetoric. Any time people use "talk" to make decisions they are engaged in rhetoric. In this way, rhetoric is the primary vehicle through which all democratic decision making is made. In any democratic organization (from the church special events committee to the United States Congress), the business of the group gets done through the give and take of rhetoric.

In a fundamental sense, democracy might be understood as the "rhetorical form of government," for the most essential definition of democracy is that decisions are made via discussion and debate. In totalitarian organizations at all levels, by contrast, it is the "Big Boss" who decides; there is no place for rhetoric in such a society. This is true in organizations where one person makes all the decisions and it was true in Hitler's Germany and Stalin's Russia. In a sense, the very hallmark of totalitarianism is that there is *no need for rhetoric* in making decisions. After the decision is made, rhetoric may be used to motivate the public, but rhetoric will not be needed at the decision making stage.

In a sense, rhetoric can be understood as both the blood and bone in any democratic society. It is the bone, because it is our words (like the Constitution, the Declaration of Independence, and the Gettysburg address)[1] that hold us together. It is the blood, because it is through rhetoric that the work of any democratic society gets done. In any democratic organization, prior rhetoric acts as the skeleton holding the organization together and current rhetoric functions as the lifeblood, leading to action.

Rhetoric is also important because rhetorical failure means institutional failure, inaction, and gridlock. Over the winter of 1995–1996, the United States Government was shut down because President Clinton and the Republican-led Congress could not agree on a budget to fund government programs. Many attacked Clinton and the Republicans for various mistakes in this dispute, but what was not recognized was that the government shutdowns were failures of rhetoric. Our system of rhetoric had broken down to the point that Clinton and the Republicans could not talk through the budget issues in a sensible fashion. When rhetoric failed, the government was shut down and millions of ordinary people suffered.

Rhetorical failure is devastating. And this is just as true at the local level or in a business or other organization. Many organizations have failed because the boss couldn't effectively use rhetoric to motivate his/her employees to achieve a given aim.

Thus, rhetoric is anything but trivial. It is the means through which decisions are hammered out at all levels in our society. When rhetoric fails, so does the organization or society.

And yet, the critics of rhetoric are not completely off base in associating rhetoric with deception and manipulation. Many leaders use rhetoric not to facilitate rational decision making, but simply to get their way. The practice of using rhetoric to deceive an audience is so common that we have invented a special word to describe it—"spin." It is very common to hear political commentators discuss how one politician or another used "spin" to persuade an audience.

Even worse, sometimes rhetoric is used to create hatred or otherwise destroy a society. Hitler used rhetoric to take over Germany. He did not have vast wealth or power, but he had the resources of rhetoric to build a movement that eventually killed millions of innocent people and very nearly captured all of Europe. For every Winston Churchill who used rhetoric to warn of the Nazi threat, there is a Hitler using rhetoric to mislead, deceive and manipulate. And this is also true at every level of society. The leaders of cults are skilled rhetoricians who use their words to gather a group of followers. Rhetoric can be powerful (and dangerous) stuff.

The aim of this book is to provide students with a means of critically analyzing and evaluating rhetoric. The ability to break down a work of rhetoric—whether an essay, a speech, or Spike Lee's latest film—into its constituent rhetorical parts is an essential one for any informed and involved citizen. Therefore, this book provides the tools for the student to act as a rhetorical critic.

What is the role of the critic? To many a critic is someone who criticizes other people's creations. Criticism is therefore often thought of as inherently negative. In this view, artists create while critics criticize. To others, criticism is a simple yes/no judgment about quality. Does the film get a "thumbs up" or a "thumbs down"? Each of these meanings of "criticism" is partially correct, but inadequate.

Criticism (at least in the area of rhetoric) means critical analysis. The goals of rhetorical criticism are to understand what is being said, how it is presented, whether and why it is persuasive for an audience, whether it can be considered good or just or moral rhetoric, and what that rhetoric tells us about related issues, including historical, political, and sociological questions.

In the sense developed throughout this book, a rhetorical critic is an informed analyst, someone who is able to break a work of rhetoric into stylistic and substantive categories and fairly judge that rhetoric. To be a critic does not mean simply to criticize (in the negative sense), although there is much rhetoric that calls for negative criticism, but also to understand the way that rhetoric functions in any community.

Why is rhetorical criticism an important subject? Some might react to the description of criticism in the previous paragraph and label it a purely academic endeavor. They would doubt that real people need to be able to analyze or evaluate rhetoric. In fact, they are quite wrong. Skill at rhetorical analysis is one of the essential elements in becoming an informed and engaged citizen.

Functions of Rhetorical Criticism

Training in rhetorical analysis serves three important goals. First, skill at rhetorical analysis helps the individual understand how people use symbols to persuade. Rhetoric, like all arts, contains a number of different strategies. The third section of this book focuses on six main strategies for using rhetoric to persuade. But the strategies in a given work of rhetoric may not be immediately obvious to someone hearing, reading, or observing the rhetoric. Training in rhetorical analysis will help the individual understand the way the rhetoric functions.

An example may make this point clear. In their analysis of a 1980 debate between President Jimmy Carter and Republican nominee Ronald Reagan, the press almost universally concluded that Carter had better substance and Reagan better style. A *New York Times* reporter, said simply, "It was a contest of content against style."[2] Many others in the media came to a similar conclusion.[3] The problem is that a close analysis of the debate shows that it was not a contrast between Reagan's style and Carter's substance. Analyzed as an academic debate, Reagan clearly was more substantive. He did a better job of answering questions, presenting evidence, and countering the claims of the other side than did Carter.[4] Why did many in the press miss Reagan's substantive success? The answer seems to be that they saw what they expected to see. They knew that Carter was extremely bright and had been a hands-on manager of every detail of U.S. policy during his term as President. And they knew that Reagan was a former actor. So they expected Reagan to be stylish and Carter substantive. But that wasn't what happened in the debate. The press needed training in rhetorical analysis in order to understand how the debate really functioned.

How does this purpose apply to average people who aren't evaluating presidential debates? The ability to analyze rhetoric can help the individual in dealing with the school board, the city council, their boss, in fact anyone who uses rhetoric. You can't appropriately and effectively respond to rhetoric, if you don't understand both what is said and how it is said.

Second, skill at rhetorical analysis is essential to protect the individual from manipulative and deceptive rhetoric. There are many in politics, business, and everywhere in society who skillfully use rhetoric to get their way. Some lie or deceive in order to accomplish their aims. Others use rhetoric to create hatred or to attack some group in society. One of the essential skills needed to be an informed and empowered citizen is the ability to identify deceptive or manipulative rhetoric. Thus, rhetorical criticism serves a self-protection function for the ordinary person. Later in this book, I will develop what I call the "informed citizen" system for identifying deceptive and manipulative rhetoric. Through the application of that system, people can protect themselves from those who would manipulate or deceive them.

Third, skill at rhetorical analysis can help individuals become more skillful persuaders. I said earlier that democracy can be understood as a form of government in which people use rhetoric to make their decisions. There is a corollary to this definition. To be an effective citizen, one must be a skilled rhetorician. For it is through rhetoric, whether talking to the city council or testifying in front of a Congressional Committee, that people protect their rights and interests.

Training in rhetorical analysis can help one become a more skillful persuader. If you understand how other people use language to persuade, that understanding can help you develop effective (and ethical) strategies for building a persuasive case, whether you are asking your boss for a raise or giving an inaugural address.

Rhetorical criticism is, therefore, not merely an academic undertaking. It is a crucial skill and process which ordinary people use every day in conducting their business. A skillful critic will understand what others are saying to him or her, be able to distinguish between strong arguments and deceptive claims, and be capable of developing effective rhetorical strategies for use in any occasion.

It is instructive that when the Greeks first invented the Liberal Arts, they treated rhetoric as the first of those arts. They knew that the most fundamental skill needed by any person living in a democracy was the ability to use rhetoric to state a case. That remains true today.

Notes:

1. Gary Wills makes a similar argument in his recent book about the Gettysburg address. *Lincoln at Gettysburg: The Words That Remade America* (New York: Simon & Schuster, 1992).
2. Hedrick Smith, "No Clear Winner Apparent," *The New York Times* 29 October 1980: 1.
3. This literature is summarized in Robert Rowland, "The Substance of the 1980 Carter-Reagan Debate," *Southern Speech Communication Journal* 51 (Winter 1986): 142–165.
4. See my analysis cited above.

CHAPTER ONE

A System for Rhetorical Criticism

In order to understand the way a given work of rhetoric functions, one needs a system for breaking down that rhetoric into its constituent parts and for placing the rhetoric in a context. Fulfilling the self-protection function of rhetorical analysis further requires a means of testing rhetoric to see if it is deceptive or manipulative. In order to accomplish these aims, I have developed the "I Care" System.

The remainder of this book will develop the "I Care" system. In this chapter, I provide an overview of the system. Chapters two and three focus on the "analysis" and "research" stages in more detail. Chapters four through nine then examine the six main strategies for persuading an audience. In chapter ten I discuss how some groups of rhetorical acts are best understood as aspects of a broader category of rhetoric called a "genre." Finally, in chapter eleven, I discuss how an *"Informed Citizen,"* can use standards for identifying deceptive or manipulative rhetoric.

The "I Care" System

The "I CARE" system of rhetorical analysis includes a series of stages through which the critic (remember, we are all critics any time we analyze something) proceeds in carrying out a piece of rhetorical criticism.

The "I" in the "I CARE" system refers to each individual. "I" (and you) should care about rhetorical analysis because of the central role played by all forms of persuasion in our society. We are all rhetorical critics (or at least we should be). Every time we listen to a politician, or a manager, or a salesperson or anyone else who wants us to act in a certain way, we implicitly are acting as rhetorical critics. One goal of rhetorical criticism as a discipline is to make individuals more informed critics in order that they can understand, appreciate, and protect themselves from other people's use of rhetoric. Therefore, rhetorical criticism is our foremost tool for understanding and evaluating why and how people persuade each other.

CARE

In order to analyze any work of rhetoric, whether a speech by Lincoln or a rock video by Madonna, the critic must move through four research stages prior to the final analysis. These four stages are represented in the acronym "CARE." CARE stands for:

Choice
Analysis
Research
Evaluation

Choice

The first stage in any rhetorical analysis is *choice,* which entails the selection of an appropriate work of rhetoric for analysis. There are four possible principles that can be used for choosing a work to analyze. The first and most important principle is *immediacy.* The critic analyzes the work because it has been presented (or assigned) to him or her. It is immediately in front of you. You are at the city council meeting and a developer argues for changing zoning to put in a bowling alley near your home. The rhetoric of the developer is immediately in front of you and you must respond. The same is true when you hear a politician give a speech or listen as a doctor advises a friend concerning therapy. In most cases in the classroom and real life, immediacy guides our choice of works for analysis.

In some instances, however, the critic is not faced with a work of rhetoric immediately in front of him or her. For example, a person might want to analyze the rhetoric of a politician (whether a national figure like Ronald Reagan or a local leader) in order to understand or evaluate that person's effectiveness. In that situation, you cannot analyze all of the politician's rhetoric, so you must consider a selection of that material. How should the critic choose works to analyze? The second, third, and fourth principles of choice provide the tools to make that choice.

The second principle of choice is *representativeness.* If you want to understand someone's rhetoric, the most obvious method is to choose representative works that reflect the entire volume of the person's rhetorical output. Using this principle, the critic should attempt to choose works that are in some sense normal or average and avoid those that clearly are atypical. If you were looking at the rhetoric of former President George Bush, for example, you would want to choose works that broadly represented everything that he said during his presidency.

The third principle of choice is *distinctiveness.* Here, the critic chooses a work of rhetoric, because it is distinctive in its composition or effect. The distinctiveness principle is in a way the opposite of the representativeness principle. Sometimes the critic should choose to analyze a work of rhetoric, precisely because it is so different from the norm. This explains why rhetorical critics focus on major speeches by Lincoln, or Reagan or Franklin Roosevelt. These major speeches may not in every case have been representative of all of the rhetoric of the person, but they are distinctive in what they contain and the effects they produced. Therefore, they merit analysis.

How should the critic balance the principles of representativeness and distinctiveness? There is no simple answer to this question. All the critic can do is recognize that both principles are important in some cases, but also recognize that either can be misapplied. For example, it probably would not make sense to choose works to analyze for a book on Ronald Reagan by selecting pages at random from his presidential papers. That approach would be representative, but it hardly seems likely to produce much insight. But then again it also wouldn't make sense to focus only on his most important speeches.

The final principle of choice is *relevance*. In some cases, the critic chooses to analyze a given work, not because of that work's intrinsic importance, but because it helps him or her get at another question. The rhetorical historian Barnet Baskerville makes the point that rhetoric is not only an instrument that humans use for persuasion, but also a "window" on the society in which the rhetoric was presented.[1] One way to understand the United States in the 1950s, for example, would be to focus on rhetoric of the time. Looking at speeches from that era undoubtedly would reveal a much more conservative moral climate than in the United States today. It also would reveal a public sphere in which almost all of the actors were white males. In other words, by looking at the rhetoric of the 1950s, we might be able to learn a lot about the entire society.

A study of rhetoric might be used to get at other questions as well. For example, some theorists argue that all rhetoric in one way or another tells a story.[2] If a critic were interested in testing this claim, he or she would pick rhetoric that is "relevant" to the theoretical issue under debate. The critic probably would analyze several works on the same topic (in order to hold that issue constant), only one of which explicitly told a story. The critic then would consider whether all of the works on the topic really could be considered stories.[3]

In sum, the principle of relevance is most important when the critic uses rhetorical analysis to answer questions relating to a purpose other than explaining or evaluating the particular piece of rhetoric, for example, using rhetorical analysis to illuminate history.

The four principles of choice have been listed in descending level of importance. For most citizens, the principle of immediacy is far and away the most important. You need to understand what your boss is saying so that you can write a persuasive letter asking for a raise. In many cases, we need to analyze a work of rhetoric, because if we do not do so we may not be able to understand what is being said, or, worse, we may be manipulated by that rhetoric. In some circumstances, however, the principles of representativeness, distinctiveness, and relevance also are important.

Analysis

The second stage in rhetorical criticism is *analysis*. Here, the goal is to see clearly what is being said and how the rhetor is saying it. The analyst identifies the explicit and implicit message, the supporting reasoning and evidence, the role played by the speaker or writer (the rhetor), the implied relationship between the rhetor and the audience, and all of the various strategies present in the rhetoric.

Why is such a system needed? The short answer is that humans tend to see what they expect to see. Take the 1996 presidential election as an example. Republicans tended to think that Senator Dole did a better job than President Clinton in various debates while partisans of President Clinton drew the opposite conclusion. The same is true everywhere that rhetoric is used. A system of rhetorical analysis is needed to help us break through the "rhetorical blinders" that we all wear in order to see clearly what is being said.

The two most important principles operating in the analytical stage are *critical distance* and *completeness*. Critical distance means that the critic should try to be as objective as possible in putting aside his/her feelings and prior experience relating to the rhetoric. The goal is to see as clearly as possible what was in the words and other symbols used by the rhetor.

Loss of critical distance often leads to misunderstanding the rhetoric. At the analytical stage, a critic takes off his/her badge as a Republican or Democrat, liberal or conservative, and so forth and becomes as much as is possible a pure analyst. This is a hard principle to meet, but especially important.

Some people argue that objectivity is impossible or even unimportant.[4] They note that everyone has biases and assert that achieving perfect objectivity is a pipe dream. Some even argue that attempting to be objective is a bad thing because it privileges "reason" over feelings.

On that last point, the critics of objectivity are clearly right. The idea of "critical distance" does assume that human reason is the best available tool for discovering the strategies in any work of rhetoric. It is in their judgment that reliance on "reason" is a bad thing that the critics of objectivity go wrong. Of course, the ideals of objectivity and critical distance are impossible to achieve in a perfect sense. Everyone has their biases. But we should strive to put aside those biases as much as possible. Would you want your worst enemy evaluating your job performance? Would it be fair for the prosecution in a criminal trial to pick all the jurors? These simple questions make clear the danger posed by bias. It is because that same danger exists in rhetorical analysis that critics should strive for critical distance.

Completeness is also a crucial goal of the critic at the analytical stage. Oftentimes people see part of the message or part of the strategy, but miss other parts. For example, in the 1992 presidential election, many in the media noted that Ross Perot relied on charts and "plain Texas talk." And Perot did use charts and he did talk like a Texan. But Perot did other things as well. He drew on enormous public displeasure with government. He also appealed to the populist sentiment that ordinary people could fix things if they only could get into office. And Perot also built strong arguments that the budget deficit threatened the economic well-being of this nation.[5] An analysis that focused on Perot's charts and his "Texas talk," but ignored the anti-government, anti-deficit, and pro-populist appeals, would have been an incomplete analysis. In order to see clearly what is present in rhetoric, the rhetorical critic needs to see "completely." That requires the critic to identify all of the important components in a given work of rhetoric.

How can the critic achieve both critical distance and completeness in carrying out the analytical stage? The answer is to systematically apply a set of overlapping and in some cases inconsistent descriptive categories. The use of these categories can "force" the critic to put aside his/her blinders and conduct a complete analysis of all facets of the rhetoric. I will present a detailed system of analysis categories in the next chapter.

Research

The third stage in preparing a rhetorical critique is research. Here, the critic is concerned with learning as much as possible about the situation in which and audience to whom the rhetoric was presented. It might seem that the research stage should come before the analytical one. Other than spoiling the acronym, however, there is one good reason that analysis should come before research. The problem is that research may act as a set of blinders limiting what the critic sees. If research reveals that several experts have written about the emotional appeals in a given speech, this data could cause the critic to miss other aspects of the speech. He or she would see the emotional rhetoric, because he/she expected to see it. Recall the example cited in the introduction of the 1980 Carter-Reagan debate. In their analysis of the debate, the media saw what they expected to see: Carter was better on the facts and Reagan better in his delivery. Of course, that was not what actually happened in the presidential debate.

Research should be conducted after a preliminary analysis in order to avoid the risk that previous research will bias your consideration of the message, as it biased the media analysts of the Carter-Reagan debate. You should look for yourself before reading what others have written about the rhetoric.

There is one exception to the rule that analysis should come before research. There are rare cases in which it is impossible to understand the rhetoric without some knowledge of the context in which it was presented. This situation occurs most frequently when the rhetoric was presented in a culture or at a time radically different than present day America. In that case, the critic has to do enough research to understand the rhetoric prior to carrying out the analysis.

Goals of the Research Stage

In the research stage the critic has four main goals. First, research often is necessary to understand the time/place/culture in which the rhetoric was presented. The greater the difference in time/place/culture from our own, the more that the critic needs to do adequate research in order to place the rhetoric into perspective. So, for example, more research would be needed to understand a speech presented in medieval France than a speech given in the 1996 presidential campaign.

Second, the research stage is important for discovering as much as possible about the mindset of the audience to whom the rhetoric was presented. In order to explain and evaluate why a given work of rhetoric was or was not effective, the critic has to be able to see through the eyes of the audience. One of the most fundamental principles in rhetoric is that the successful rhetor must begin with where the audience already is. You persuade them to change their views by starting with where they are. In order to apply this principle, the critic must understand the mindset of the audience at the time the rhetoric was presented.

In accomplishing the first two goals the most important theoretical concepts are rhetorical barriers and rhetorical advantages. A "rhetorical barrier" *is an attitude, belief or other problem that a rhetor must overcome in order to persuade an audience to accept a given position.* For example, in the 1996 presidential campaign, Republican nominee Robert Dole had to overcome the perception of some that he was too old to run for President.

A "rhetorical advantage" is precisely the opposite of a rhetorical barrier. A "rhetorical advantage" *is an attitude, belief or other position that gives the rhetor assistance in persuading an audience.* For example, immediately after the Gulf War, General Colin Powell was immensely popular. That popularity functioned as a "rhetorical advantage" that helped him every time he spoke to an audience.

In the research stage the critic should be concerned with gathering adequate information to explain the barriers and advantages that the rhetor faced in attempting to persuade a particular audience. By focusing on rhetorical barriers and advantages, the critic will be able to get a good idea of both the context in which the rhetoric was presented and the mindset of the audience. In chapter three, I will develop a category system for describing the various types of rhetorical barriers and advantages.

Third, the critic needs to be able to place him/herself in the place of the rhetor. For example, research might reveal that a given political candidate did not seriously expect to win a particular election, but instead wanted to use his or her rhetoric to rouse public interest in an issue. Some argue that this was the case in Ross Perot's two campaigns for President. This discovery might cause a critic to judge the candidate's rhetoric as successful, where otherwise it would have been labelled a failure. Even if the candidate only received ten or fifteen percentage points of the vote, he/she may have accomplished his/her aim, which was to bring an issue to the attention of the public. Precisely that judgment could be made about the influence of Ross Perot in the 1992 election.

Finally, the critic needs to gather all data relevant to the evaluation of any work of rhetoric. As I will explain in chapter three, in nearly all cases, the rhetorical critic should base evaluation of the effectiveness of the rhetoric upon the rhetoric itself. That is, the critic asks whether the rhetor did as good a job as possible of responding to the audience in a given situation. In some cases, however, external data on audience reaction or some other aspect of the issue can be very useful in supporting an evaluation of a given work. For example, there was vast public reaction to the testimony of Oliver North before Congress during the Iran-Contra affair. North was called a national hero.

There were Ollie North for President bumper stickers, Ollie North drinks, Ollie North sandwiches (a hero of course), and many other events illustrating strong support for North. This material is strong evidence that the main question in relation to North's rhetoric was not "whether" it was effective, but "why" it was so effective.[6]

As the North example illustrates, it is important to gather any available external data on the impact of a given work of rhetoric. Oftentimes, there will be no such data. But in some cases there may be opinion polls, press reports on audience reaction to a speech, newspaper editorial responses to a statement, letters to the editor, or other information that gives a strong hint about public reaction.

Four Functions of the Research Stage

1. Clarify the context in which the rhetoric was presented;
2. Gather information on the mindset of the audience;
3. Discover the motives of the rhetor;
4. Gather information on public response to the rhetoric.

In order to fulfill these four aims, the critic needs to research material relating to the rhetoric as fully as is relevant. If the rhetoric comes from the present day, the research required may not be very much, only enough to support claims about audience attitudes and values. If, however, the rhetoric comes from another time/place/culture then large amounts of research may be required. For example, the rhetorical practices in the United States in the 19th century were different in important ways from today. Research would be needed in order to understand the cultural norms of the time, among other reasons.

There is a general rule in regard to research. The farther away in time, place, culture, or issue from the present day, the greater the research burden.

The key to the research stage is to recognize that the goal is not to research the person's biography per se or all aspects of the issues involved in the rhetoric. Rather, the critic should look for material in that biography, in information about the issue, and elsewhere that helps him or her understand, explain, and evaluate the rhetoric. The research process is discussed in more depth in chapter three.

Evaluation and Explanation

The final stage in rhetorical analysis is evaluation. Here, the critic takes the materials gathered in the previous three stages and uses them to evaluate the rhetoric.

The goals of the evaluative stage are to judge the effectiveness, truth, or ethical quality of the rhetoric. Here, the primary aim is to focus on the quality of the *rhetoric,* as opposed to the positions advocated in the rhetoric.

In relation to effectiveness, the critic asks whether the rhetor did as good a job as possible in developing strategies to persuade an audience in a particular situation. In relation to truth and the ethical quality of the discourse, the critic asks whether the rhetor built a strong case for his/her position or whether he/she used ethical means of persuasion. Principles for evaluating effectiveness are developed in chapter three. Standards for evaluating truth and ethics are found in chapter eleven.

In all of these three types of evaluation, the critic is concerned with the rhetoric and not primarily the position being advocated in the rhetoric. In considering a speech about gun control, for example, the issues would not be whether gun control is a good idea, but whether the rhetor did as good a job as possible of supporting the issue and did so in an ethical manner.

Conclusion

The "I Care" system of analysis provides a systematic approach for rhetorical criticism. It can be used to critique a speech by President Clinton, a music video advocating aid to the poor, an editorial in the *New York Times*, a feminist science fiction novel, or any other work of rhetoric. The next chapter lays out in more depth the analysis stage in the system.

Notes

1. See Barnet Baskerville, "Must We All Be 'Rhetorical Critics'?" *Quarterly Journal of Speech* 63 (1977): 107–116.
2. Walter Fisher makes this argument. See "Narration as a Human Communication Paradigm: The Case of Public Moral Argument," *Communication Monographs* 51 (1984); 1–22.
3. I carried out this project in "On Limiting the Narrative Paradigm: Three Case Studies," *Communication Monographs* 56 (1989): 39–54.
4. The view that objectivity is unimportant and impossible to achieve is quite common in the philosophical movement called postmodernism. I explain and refute that position in "In Defense of Rational Argument: A Pragmatic Justification of Argumentation Theory and Response to the Postmodern Critique," *Philosophy and Rhetoric* 28 (1995): 350–364.
5. See Ross Perot, *United We Stand: How We Can Take Back Our Country* (New York: Hyperion, 1992).
6. See Robert C. Rowland, "The Strange Case of Ollie North: Rhetoric, Politics, and Criticism," paper presented at the Iowa Scholars Workshop on the Rhetoric of Political Argumentation, Spring 1991.

◆ CHAPTER TWO ◆

Tools for Analyzing Rhetoric

In order to understand the way that any work of rhetoric functions, the analyst needs two sets of tools. The first set of tools is used to break the rhetoric down into constituent parts. A system of analysis is needed that can be applied systematically to any work of rhetoric. That system is developed in this chapter.

The second set of tools is a system for placing a given work of rhetoric in its context. Any work of persuasion exists in a particular context and cannot be understood apart from that context. For example, Franklin Roosevelt's advocacy of the "New Deal" must be understood in the context of the Great Depression. And Ronald Reagan's conservative rhetoric opposing large government is only understandable as a response to the expansion of Federal social programs, beginning with Roosevelt and continuing for almost five decades. Even the very meaning of words may change over time. The word "gay" had a very different meaning in the 1930s, when it primarily was used as an adjective to describe someone who was full of fun, than it does in the 1990s. Tools for describing the context in which rhetoric is presented are explained in the following chapter.

Analysis

The second stage in the "I CARE" system of rhetorical criticism is "analysis." The purpose of this stage is to see clearly all of the main elements present in the rhetoric, while putting aside any predispositions. In order to fulfill this purpose it is important systematically to apply a broad set of categories designed to reveal the significant features in the rhetoric.

To carry out the analytical stage, the critic initially should familiarize him/herself with the "I CARE" categories. Then, he or she should carefully go over the rhetoric making appropriate notes. These notes then should be integrated into the system. An outline of the analysis categories is included at the end of the chapter. This outline can be used to analyze any work of rhetoric, from a film by Spike Lee, to a speech by Al Gore, to a political cartoon or a rhetorical work of art.

The following section defines each category and cites an example of how to apply it, drawing from the essay "Stop Serbia Now," that originally was published in *The New*

Republic on May 10, 1993. I have chosen this essay as an illustration because it deals with an issue that is both quite important and that recurs in different forms. The *New Republic* editorial concerned Serbian "ethnic cleansing" in Bosnia and the proper response of the United States and other Western nations. Although the specific issue considered was Bosnia, it could just as easily have been war crimes in Kosovo, Rwanda, or a host of other places on the planet.

◆◆◆

Stop Serbia Now

At the beginning, there was confusion. A state that was not a state was cut loose from an empire and convulsed itself in ancient hatreds. A civil war or an ethnic implosion? A religious feud or an imbalance of power? The status of Bosnia was, after all, historically problematic. It was not a "nation" as such; and the Europeans, with a long history of caution in such matters, advised caution. Besides, were not all the parties—Croats, Muslims, Serbs—morally tainted? 1

So the United States, exhilarated by the end of the cold war and consumed with an election campaign in which the arguments of retrenchment outweighed the passion for entanglement, let it be. The Europeans revealed themselves to be Europeans, incapable of united action, guided by separate historic and cultural temperaments, fearful of the larger truths that the Serbian war revealed about Europe's intolerance of tolerance and addicted to the process of peace, which soon became the management of war. The United Nations, through it's humanitarian efforts, indirectly facilitated the incursions of the Serbs, and by placing Western troops on the ground, provided a perfect excuse for the British and French to oppose military escalation. The U.N. thus assumed the role of the expediter of invasion, escorting the evacuees, shepherding the wounded, ushering in the victors. They do not wish to resist the Serbian conquest, they wish only to take the pain out of it. They are the cleansers of the cleansing, struggling to believe in decency in the face of unvarnished evil. 2

There may have been a point when the United States, confronted by what seemed to be an intractable internecine war, was right to pretend to stay aloof. We say pretend, because the United States has long been indirectly involved in the war. By upholding the arms embargo against Bosnia, we engineered a one-sided massacre; by halfheartedly supporting the Vance-Owen plan, we allowed the Serbs diplomatic space in which to pursue their military aims; by the policy of food air drops to those about to be slaughtered, we gave notice that we would do nothing to end the slaughter itself. Slobodan Milosevic, who follows the logic of force, rightly calculated that all the cards were his. 3

What we face now, however, is a new drama: the possibility not merely of new Serbian progress into Bosnian Muslim territory (and Macedonia and Kosovo), but the horrific possi- 4 bility of genocide in those areas that the Serbs already control. The threat is thus both moral and strategic. Those who argue that this region is of no strategic importance are simply wrong. The entanglement of Russia and Greece, the mobilization of Islamic states in defense of the Muslims, the destabilization of Turkey, the possibility of mass migration on the edge of Europe, all are threats to European stability as a whole. But the moral signal that is now being sent by the American government (which, in the other side of its brain, is busy congratulating itself for its ethical activism in Somalia) is even more worrying: that international borders are movable by force of arms; that racial and religious terror will go unchecked.

As so often before, the fixation on multilateralism is restraining credible action. The U.N.   5
has shown itself to be toothless; the British and French are as pusillanimous now as they were in a far greater but similar crisis in the 1930s. Russia's Serbian sympathies preclude helping Bosnia. (There is something really unpleasant about this sudden renewal of the great Russian people's tenderness toward the great Serbian people. Is this what the end of the cold war was supposed to accomplish?) If the United States can only act in concert with other powers, it simply will not act at all.

So we must act alone: but we must act. President Clinton should deliver an ultimatum to   6
Milosevic and his strutting surrogates: that, by a certain date, all incursions are to cease; that genocidal actions must immediately cease (including what might be called "strategic rape"); that negotiations should begin on constructing a defensible and credible Bosnian state out of the ruins of Bosnia-Herzegovina; and that, if these actions are not taken, the arms embargo on the Bosnians will be unilaterally lifted and unspecified military action against Serbian military targets from the air and sea will begin. This declaration should be made after the April 25 referendum in Russia and should be a unilateral declaration that can give Yeltsin complete deniability. (We owe Yeltsin that much in this matter, but not more.) If the Western allies and the U.N. can agree to this, so be it. But if they cannot, Clinton should summon the will to go ahead without them. There are times when America, alone of nations, has an obligation to take a stand, and act where the self-styled angels fear to tread.

◆◆◆

Application of Analysis Categories

I.   Goal—The goal refers to the aim either stated or implied in the rhetoric. The critic infers the goal from the rhetoric itself and not from any knowledge of the subject or the rhetor. Within the goal it is important to consider the themes that are presented and the action that the rhetor requests from the audience.

A.   Themes

Themes are the main points made in the work. There may be multiple themes presented in a work of rhetoric or there may be a single main point (the thesis of the work) that is backed up by supporting themes. In this case, the thesis of *The New Republic* editorial is that the United States has a moral responsibility to act to "Stop Serbia Now." In the concluding paragraph, the editorial notes that there are times "when America, alone of nations, has an obligation to take a stand." In this statement and others, the editorial suggests that the United States has a unique moral responsibility to prevent genocide.

In support of the thesis, the editorial develops two additional themes. First, it argues that the actions of Serbia are indefensible. In the opening paragraph, the editorial discusses initial "confusion" over who was right and who was wrong in the Balkans. Much of the remainder of the piece is spent explaining how that confusion has been eliminated. The Serbs are characterized as "unvarnished evil" (para 2). They are also accused of using "strategic rape" and "genocide" (para 6) and the entire essay attacks them as invaders, who have carried out a slaughter.

The other theme in the essay refers to the possibility of multi-lateral action, either by a combination of the United States and various European nations or by the United Nations. The editorial consistently argues that such multi-lateral action cannot work. In the second paragraph, the piece sarcastically refers to the Europeans as "Europeans, incapable of united action," a point that is echoed in paragraph 5 where the actions (or rather inaction) of the French and British are referred to as "pusillanimous" (cowardly) and compared to the failure to stop Hitler prior to the Second World War. Similarly, the essay labels action by the U.N. as "toothless" (para 5) and claims that it actually has "expedite[d]" the Serbian invasion (para 2).

The two themes combine to support the thesis that I already have identified. That thesis might be rephrased: If the actions of the Serbs are immoral and multi-lateral action cannot succeed then, the United States must act.

B.   Requested Action

The requested action concerns what the rhetor wants to be done and what he/she wants the audience to do in order to achieve that aim. In many cases, the rhetoric explicitly will call on the audience to take some action. A fund-raising letter will conclude by asking for money. In others, the action that should be taken by the audience is implied, but not explicitly stated. An editorial attacking gun violence might imply that strengthened gun control laws are needed, without ever stating that point explicitly.

In rare cases, the requested action may be the opposite of what is actually stated in the rhetoric. Imagine a situation in which a politician has been accused of misconduct. A speaker might lay out all of the reasons why the politician has every right to fight the charges, despite the harm to his/her career. In so doing, the speaker explicitly would be saying that the politician has the right to fight to the end, but implicitly would be saying that the sensible thing to do would be to resign. Such rhetoric, where the implied conclusion is the opposite of what is stated, is uncommon.

In this case, the requested action is both explicit and implicit. *The New Republic* clearly wants to influence policy makers to support intervention.

The final paragraph seems aimed directly at President Clinton and also at Vice President Gore, who is a friend and former student of the owner of the magazine. The essay directly encourages Clinton to act.

At the implicit level, the piece is aimed at readers of the magazine who might facilitate U.S. intervention via public pressure. The editorial implies that they should write letters and otherwise put pressure on the administration to act.

II.   Organization—It is very important to lay out the organizational pattern found in any work of rhetoric. In some cases, the organization itself may be one of the characteristics defining the rhetoric. In a speech comparing the situation in Europe in 1993 with that just before World War II, the movement back and forth between the two times might be the essence of the presentation. The organization of the speech by John Anjain, which is considered in chapter five is the core of his rhetoric.

Even when the organizational pattern does not fully dominate the work, it is important to lay out the organization in order to reveal the emphasis that the rhetor places on different points. By carefully outlining the development of the rhetoric paragraph by paragraph, the critic can discover the main points in the rhetoric and determine what receives the most emphasis.

The key to identifying the organization of any work is to go through it paragraph by paragraph, listing the main points in each section. If the rhetoric is film, then the critic would go through it scene by scene. A song could be broken down verse by verse. And a picture could be described from top to bottom or side to side, depending on what was most convenient.

After the critic has identified the points in each unit of the rhetoric, he/she should then place those points in the following sub-categories.

A.   Introduction—Introductions are important for leading into the main body, establishing the credibility of the rhetor, and gaining the attention of the audience. As a general rule, the introduction (along with the conclusion) is proportionally more important than the main body of the rhetoric. It is therefore, important for the rhetorical critic to identify the illustrative devices in the introduction and also where the rhetor moves into the main body of his/her rhetoric.

In this case, the introduction is clearly the first paragraph, which sets up the remainder of the essay by laying out arguments that were made against U.S. involvement in what used to be called Yugoslavia. The remainder of the essay then shows that the effect of following those arguments has been to produce genocide in Bosnia.

The introduction sets up this argumentative progression with a series of enthymematic statements and rhetorical questions. An enthymeme is an argument in which either the conclusion or some aspect of the reasoning is implied but not clearly stated. The audience then fills in the remainder of the argument. In this case, *The New Republic,* uses references to Yugoslavia as "A state that was not a state" and so forth to call on the audience to fill in the various arguments made against intervention by the United States. If the audience does not fill in this material, the essay will not work as it is designed.

The editorial also uses rhetorical questions to fulfill the same function. A rhetorical question is one that is asked not to produce dialogue, but to imply a conclusion. A conservative politician might ask his/her audience: "Do we want more taxes?" That politician is not curious about what the crowd thinks about taxes. Rather, he/she uses the question to incorporate audience participation in the speech.

In this case, the editorial asks "A religious feud or an imbalance of power?" This question is used exemplify the confusion that once existed in the case of conflict in Bosnia. The editorial then explains that this confusion no longer exists.

B. Conclusion—In general, the function of a conclusion is to summarize the main points that have been made, call upon the audience to act, and use some form of illustrative material to keep the attention of the audience. Conclusions are very important.

In this case, the conclusion is clearly the final paragraph, which begins by calling on the United States to "act alone." The middle portion of the final paragraph then explains details of how the United States should act and the paragraph concludes with a call to action by alluding to the words of the poet Alexander Pope who said that "For fools rush in where angels fear to tread." Ironically, the reference to Pope seems to go against the thesis of the editorial, for it implies that U.S. intervention might be quite "foolish." Of course, only those who recognize the allusion will see the inconsistency between the conclusion and the essay.

C. Main Body—While the introduction and the conclusion are proportionally more important than the main body, the main body can be considered the core of the rhetoric. It is in the main body that the dominant themes of the rhetoric are developed. People remember speeches and other rhetoric with good introductions and conclusions, but without an effective main section they do not act on them.

In relation to the main body, it is important to identify the overarching organizational pattern that dominates the work in order discover the evolution of the claims made in the rhetoric. This also will help reveal the strategies that dominate the work. In some cases there may not be a clear organizational pattern. That is also a revealing discovery. If the organizational pattern is not clear that implies strongly that the rhetoric either is argumentatively flawed *or* that it works through non-argumentative strategies.

There are many possible organizational forms: topical, problem-solution, problem-cause-solution, chronological, geographical, and so forth. In this case, the organization is largely topical. In paragraphs 2–5 the essay develops the position that multilateralism has failed to stop the evil actions of the Serbs. Close inspection does not reveal a clear argumentative development within these paragraphs. Rather, the various paragraphs support the themes that I identified earlier without any clear argumentative progression.

III. Role of the Rhetor—Humans play many roles. For example, a President of the United States may speak to the nation as a grandfather figure (Uncle Sam), as a partisan politician, as leader of all the people, as a cheerleader, as Commander in Chief, and so forth. Ordinary people also assume roles in their rhetoric. For example, there is a major difference between the roles of teacher and priest.

Role identification is important for two reasons. First, the role that one assumes strongly limits what you can say. A person playing the role of minister or priest will be expected to act and speak accordingly. If he/she violates those role assumptions, his/her rhetoric is likely to fail. Second, the choice of a role is important, because it may influence the audience's evaluation of the rhetor's credibility. We would not necessarily find it credible if a politician who had been convicted of some ethical wrong-doing attempted to play a role of "political priest" and judged others in the political system. The role of the rhetor would not be consistent with our knowledge of the person and we would doubt his/her honesty. In general, skillful rhetors assume only those roles that they credibly can play.

There are two sub-parts of the role of the rhetor. As a first step in discovering this role it is important to consider the *implied relationship* between the rhetor and the audience. There are three possible general relationships: peer to peer, superior to inferior, and inferior to superior. First, a rhetor may speak to an audience as a peer. President Clinton often assumes this relationship when he attends Town Hall Meetings and talks to ordinary people, citizen to citizen. As a peer, he is able to "feel their pain" and "hear where they are coming from." Second, in the relationship of superior to inferior, the rhetor tells an audience what to think or what to do. When a General issues orders, he/she assumes a superior to inferior relationship with his/her troops. The General is not seeking input, he/she is simply telling the troops what to do. The third possible relationship is inferior to superior. Sometimes rhetors speak to an audience more powerful than they are. When the convicted criminal speaks to the jury, he/she is an inferior (a convicted felon) speaking to superiors (citizens on the jury).

There are two key signs in rhetoric that help the critic identify the *implied relationship* in the rhetoric. The first relates to the evidence cited. If the rhetor seems to assume that his/her audience is well-informed on a subject that indicates that he/she is not acting as a superior. In contrast, if the rhetor seems to be teaching the audience about the subject that is a strong indication of a superior to inferior relationship. Second, a similar point can be made about the moral tone of the rhetoric. If the rhetor tells his/her audience how to think that indicates a superior to inferior relationship. On the other hand, if the rhetor either assumes that the audience agrees with a point or actually asks for their assistance that indicates either a relationship as a peer or even an inferior speaking to a superior.

It is important to identify the general relationship between the rhetor and the audience because that relationship places limits on other aspects of the rhetoric. For example, it may be difficult for a leader to move from the role of peer to a more commanding role. Some have argued, for instance, that President Clinton was much better at playing the role of peer in a campaign situation than at assuming the relationship of a superior instructing an inferior. In their view, this partially explains difficulties that he had in mobilizing support for programs, such as the health care initiative.

The second sub-part of the role of the rhetor is the *specific role* played in the rhetoric (if any). After the general relationship is identified, it should be possible to nail down more specifically the role or roles being played by the rhetor. For example, the President of the United States often plays roles such as "Commander in Chief," Moral Leader, First Mourner, Uncle Sam (or America's Cheerleader). Again, identification of the specific role is important because that role limits other rhetorical choices. And choice of an inappropriate role may doom a work of rhetoric to failure.

In this case, the editorial can be broken down in relation to both the *implied relationship* and *specific role* played by the rhetor. In relation to the *implied relationship,* the editorial in some way treats readers as peers and in others as inferiors. The editorial clearly assumes wide knowledge of the conflict in Bosnia and world history on the part of readers. This is obvious in the enthymematic references throughout the piece to actions of Serbia. In that way, the editorial seems to assume that all moral and intelligent people (like readers of *The New Republic*) must support U.S. intervention. It thus speaks to peers. However, the tone of the essay, especially in the final two paragraphs, sounds like "intellectual elites" speaking to their followers. This reflects a superior to inferior tone.

In terms of the particular role played by the anonymous editorial writer, it might best be characterized as that of a foreign policy moral leader. The essay assumes that the United States has a special moral role to play in the world. This is most obvious in the final sentence where the editorial notes that "There are times when America, alone of nations has an obligation to take a stand." In this role as moral teacher the editorialist does not feel the need to fill in all the details of his/her argument. He/she is not so much developing a strong argument as "preaching to the saved."

IV. Linguistic or Aesthetic Tone—Linguistic tone refers to the "feel" of the language (or the other symbols) in a given work of rhetoric. In a speech on gun control a rhetor could be sarcastic, professorial, angry, or even satirical. The tone that is chosen limits the other options available to the rhetor. An inappropriate tone may prevent a work from being effective. Many people are offended by a sarcastic or satirical tone on issues of grave public concern.

Non-linquistic works of rhetoric also have a tone, which I label aesthetic tone. A song may sound romantic or militaristic or even sarcastic. Similarly, a film, a TV show, or a painting also may possess a specific aesthetic tone.

In this case, the tone is sarcastic and harsh, but within the context of a work of policy analysis. If the context for the rhetoric were a personal conversation then the tone would be considered objective or mild. But in the context of an editorial in a magazine of opinion the tone is clearly quite caustic. I already have noted the almost nasty references to the French and British. In paragraph 5 there is also a sarcastic reference to the "sudden renewal of the great Russian people's tenderness toward the great Serbian people," which is followed by a cynical rhetorical question "Is this what the end of the cold war was supposed to accomplish?" In addition to being harsh and sarcastic, the tone reflects an assumed American moral superiority over the rest of the world. Again, this is obvious in the final paragraph.

In regard to the tone of moral superiority, the allusion to Pope is ironic, since it implicitly places America in the role of the "fool" who will "rush in where angels fear to tread."

V.   Implied Audience—The idea of an "implied audience" at first may seem silly. After all there is a real audience for any rhetoric, in this case readers of *The New Republic*. The real audience will be considered in the next chapter.

The implied audience consists of those people for whom the rhetoric is best adapted as a work of persuasion. The critic thinks of the rhetoric as an arrow and asks, "Who would be the perfect target group for this arrow?" For example, if a scientist spoke about complex mathematical formulas and referred to material known only to those who read obscure scientific journals then the implied audience for that speech would be other experts in the field. If that same scientist relied on comparisons and homey examples to make his/her point then the implied audience would be the general public. The implied audience is a useful concept for identifying the target group at which the rhetor was aiming.

In discovering the implied audience, the critic should consider the complexity of the message, the knowledge that the rhetor assumes the audience to possess, any values or principles that the rhetor takes for granted that the audience accepts, and the language (or aesthetic) patterns in the rhetoric. The way that the rhetor presents his/her message in regard to those points tells us a great deal about the implied audience of the rhetoric. For example, if the rhetor cites complicated information without explaining it, this indicates that he/she assumes that the audience already understands the material. He/she may not be correct in that assumption or even may not have made it consciously, but that is what is indicated by the way the material is presented.

After the implied audience has been discovered it can be compared to the actual or empirical audience. Major inconsistency between the implied and the actual audience in almost every case will doom the rhetoric to failure. One common problem in many speeches, editorials, and other works of rhetoric is that the rhetor assumes the audience has knowledge about (or even interest in) a subject, when in fact the audience lacks that knowledge or interest. In that situation, the rhetoric is unlikely to be successful.

In this case, the implied audience and the actual audience are quite consistent. The editorial clearly assumes an audience of well-informed, well-educated people, who are quite concerned with foreign policy. This is obvious in the vague references to world history and actions in the Bosnian conflict. In paragraph four, for instance, the essay alludes to the danger of war in Macedonia and Kosovo, but does no more than mention the two places. It is obvious that such a reference can have no meaning, except for those who are already aware of the potential for conflict in these areas. Only those who were very well informed and quite interested would have had that knowledge in 1993. By 1999, Kosovo had become the focus of public discussion about conflict in what used to be Yugoslavia, but when the editorial was written that was not the case.

In political terms, the implied audience for the essay is one that is willing to use military force for moral purposes. The essay does very little to build a case for the view that use of military force by the United States is morally acceptable. Thus, isolationists and other opponents of force would not be persuaded and are not included in the implied audience.

The actual audience for editorials published in *The New Republic* is probably quite similar to the implied audience. *The New Republic* is a moderately liberal magazine of opinion that is read by people who are extremely interested in public policy and the arts. Given the editorial policies of the magazine, most of its readers probably would be willing to support use of military force in at least some circumstances.

VI. Strategy Categories—The most important category in this analytical system is "strategy." A strategy is a major plan of attack. In rhetoric, strategies are the way that the rhetor persuades the audience.

How can a critic identify strategies? In sports, the coach often will tell us what his/her strategy was. In rhetoric, however, we do not have access to the mind of the speaker/writer and, even if we did, there is no guarantee that he or she consciously could identify the main strategies in the work. This means that the critic must identify the strategy from the work itself.

Two clues for identifying main strategies are emphasis and distinctiveness. If a given appeal is really important then the speaker/writer is likely to spend a substantial amount of time or space on it. For example, if a speaker refers once to a given metaphor then that comparison may not be very important. But if as in the case of Martin Luther King's "I Have a Dream Speech," a given metaphor recurs throughout the rhetoric, then it is likely to be quite important. In addition, the more distinctive that a given component of rhetoric is, the more likely it is that the component reflects an important strategy in the work.

Rhetorical strategies can be placed in one or more of the following strategy categories: rational argument, narrative, aesthetic strategies, appeals to values, needs, or symbols, credibility, and confrontation. These strategies will be considered in much more detail in chapters four through nine.

In carrying out the sixth sub-stage in the analysis system, the critic carefully should consider whether one or more of these strategy types is present. Here, the critic should remember the general rule that rhetoric rarely contains more than three or four main strategies. In the next section, I first will define the six categories and then apply them to the editorial.

A.   Rational Argument—If the rhetor relies heavily on evidence and reasoning then he/she is utilizing a rational argumentative strategy for persuading the audience. There are three sub-types of rational argument. Evidence-oriented argument relies on the citation of evidence to persuade the audience. The main types of support are authoritative evidence, statistics, examples, and comparisons. The second sub-type is enthymematic argument, in which the rhetor hopes that the audience will fill in evidence and/or reasoning in support of a claim. The third sub-type is refutative argument. Refutative argument occurs when the rhetor explains why his/her position is superior to that of the other side. He/she "refutes" the views of the opposition with argument.

Where a rational argumentative strategy is present the critic should identify the main arguments present in a piece, note the different types of reasoning used, and identify the kinds of support materials used to back up the arguments.

B.   Narrative—If the rhetoric either directly tells a story or draws upon commonly known stories of one type or another, then it is built around a narrative strategy. Narratives work rhetorically because of the normal human pleasure in a good story and also because narrative form can create a strong sense of identification between the characters in the story and the audience, thus bringing home the message.

C.   Aesthetic—Aesthetics is the theory of beauty. In rhetoric, an aesthetic strategy relies upon the power of language or other aesthetic form to persuade the audience. In his Inaugural Address, which is included in the readings volume that goes with this book, John Kennedy used an aesthetic strategy to emphasize the importance of citizens aiding their government. Kennedy said, "Ask not what your country can do for you. Ask what you can do for your country." Here, Kennedy appealed to his audience with a strategy called antithesis in which two opposed ideas are juxtaposed against each other. It was not the power of Kennedy's idea which made this passage so important. After all, that idea was merely a conventional call to serve the community. It was the way he said it.

There are many sub-categories of language and other aesthetic strategies that will be considered later. In general language-based strategies rely on the appeal of a well-turned phrase or the capacity for rhetorical figures (metaphors, antithesis, and so forth), to both create interest and let us see the world in a different way. Other aesthetic strategies include physical objects, photographs, paintings, film, graphic formatting (such as bullet points), and so forth.

D. Values, Needs, and Symbols—The press often writes about politicians who appeal to our emotions. This is not as simple as it sounds. The emotions are not a spot in the brain at which a rhetor can aim. Rather, speakers and writers often create strong emotional reactions by appealing to basic societal values and attitudes or to essential human needs. Thus, a speaker might draw on patriotism as a value or the need for security in order to energize the audience. Alternatively, the rhetor could use symbols that indirectly energize the values or needs. Thus, in the United States the flag is a powerful symbol that taps into patriotism as a value.

E. Credibility—In some case, the strategy and the speaker are one. In other words, the rhetor relies upon his or her authority in order to persuade the audience to act. Credibility is crucial to persuasion.

In rare cases, we may be willing to act simply because someone tells us to. If Michael Jordan suggests a technique for shooting a jump shot, most of us will go along. In many other cases, credibility is a necessary precondition for persuasion. After his resignation, few would have listened to a speech by Richard Nixon on honesty in politics because he had lost all credibility on the subject.

F. Confrontation—More than two thousand years ago Aristotle noted that in order to persuade an audience, the speaker must start with where the audience already is.[1] He meant that in successful rhetoric the rhetor must begin with points of agreement in order to lead the audience to a new conclusion. In most cases, Aristotle is correct, but in some instances, the rhetor relies on disagreement in order to persuade the audience.

In confrontative rhetoric, the rhetor "confronts" the audience, often attacking them directly, in order to get their attention and change their views. Confrontation is a dangerous rhetorical strategy that is (and should be) rarely used. It is much less common than the other five strategies, precisely because it often produces backlash in the audience. Few people like to be attacked.

Strategies in the *New Republic* Essay

In the case of *The New Republic* editorial, *rational argument, aesthetic strategies,* and *appeals to values, needs, and symbols* are clearly the three dominant strategies. The most important strategy is the use of rational argument. The essay is built around three simple arguments leading to an ultimate conclusion: the Serbs are committing atrocities, multi-lateral action won't work, the United States has a special responsibility to prevent genocide, therefore the United States must intervene. While the piece is heavily argumentative, it does not present a lot of support materials. Rather, the essay seems to assume that the audience will fill in the supporting examples and other data from their knowledge. Again, this type of argument is referred to as an enthymeme.

The essay also relies on refutative argument. In refutation, the arguments of the other side are identified and denied. This essay sets up the refutation in the first paragraph by identifying the arguments against U.S. intervention. It then refutes those positions.

The second main strategy in the essay is aesthetic. Unlike many editorials, the essay relies on a number of language strategies to develop its persuasive message. For example, at several points the essay uses parallel structure and repetition. In paragraph two, the second sentence develops in a rhythmic repetitive pattern that is reminiscent of the rhetoric of John Kennedy. A similar example is present in paragraph three. The essay also uses harsh descriptive language to make its point. In paragraph five it refers to the British and French as pusillanimous," meaning cowardly. In paragraph six, it refers to the supporters of the president of Serbia as "strutting," which implies that they are concerned with power, not justice. At several points the essay relies on metaphor to make its point. For example, in paragraph five, the policies of the U.N. are labeled as "toothless" to make the point that they cannot be effective.

The final important strategy relates to values and needs. In this case, the need is obviously that of life itself. Implicitly the essay appeals to that need in reminding readers of the horrors of Serbian actions and in paragraph five comparing them to the Nazis. The essay combines this appeal to needs with references to the values for which the United States stands. This is again most obvious in the conclusion where the editorial refers to a special American responsibility to "take a stand."

Outline of Rhetorical Analysis Categories

I.   Goals
    A.   Themes
    B.   Requested Actions
II. Organization
    A.   Introduction
    B.   Conclusion
    C.   Main body—identify the organizational pattern
III. Role of the rhetor
    A.   Implied relationship
    B.   Specific Role

IV.   Linguistic Tone

V.   Implied Audience

VI.   Strategy Categories—use all that are relevant and identify sub-strategies as specifically as possible

    A.   Rational Argument

    B.   Narrative

    C.   Aesthetic

    D.   Values, Needs & Symbols

    E.   Credibility

    F.   Confrontation

Conclusion

The analysis system can be applied to any work of rhetoric. It can be used to discover the defining rhetorical elements of a speech, an editorial, a film, a television show, and so on. By applying the six categories, the critic (and that means all of us) can break the rhetoric down into its parts in order to better understand how it functions. In chapters four through nine, I will focus in detail on the six strategy categories to illuminate their functioning.

To illustrate the application of the system, I have included below a paid advertisement produced by the anti-gun organization "Handgun Control Inc.," and a sample outline showing how the advertisement would be described with the analysis system.

Note

1. See Aristotle, *The Rhetoric* in *The Basic Works of Aristotle*, ed. Richard McKeon (New York: Random House, 1941), pp. 1325–1451.

"The gunman, armed with several guns, including TEC-DC9 assault pistols, stalked John and me like we were human prey. John died while saving my life.

He had covered my body with his own as we tried to hide behind a file cabinet. He knew he was dying, and told me he loved me and to hug his family for him."—*Michelle Scully, who was wounded, and whose husband, John, was killed in the San Francisco high rise shooting, July 1, 1993.*

"December 7 began like any other day for my family. And it nearly ended like any other day. But because my husband Dennis and 26-year-old son, Kevin, were on the 5:33 Long Island commuter train,

December 7 changed our lives forever. Dennis and Kevin were among those who were senselessly and randomly gunned down by a hate-filled man wielding a semi-automatic pistol with a 15-round magazine. Dennis and five others lost their lives. Our son survived, but is paralyzed. Thankfully, Kevin continues to make progress."
—*Carolyn McCarthy, whose husband, Dennis, was killed and whose son, Kevin, was wounded in the Long Island Railroad massacre, December 7, 1993*

THE GUN LOBBY SAYS THAT ASSAULT WEAPONS ARE NOT A CRIME PROBLEM.

DREAMS SHATTERED. LIVES LOST. ISN'T THAT A CRIME?

"We were on our way to work, stopped at a traffic light, when a man with an AK-47 assault rifle calmly walked up and started shooting at our car. Bullets flew into the car. Bullets went

through the car and into other cars. And four of those bullets hit Frank, my husband of only three months. In a matter of seconds, my life went from heaven to the depths of hell."—*Judy Becker Darling, whose husband, Frank, was killed outside of CIA headquarters, January 25, 1993.*

"My wife, Jody, my daughter, Meghan, and I were a wonderful family, part of the fabric of American society. Our marriage was strong, our love was limitless, and creating the life of Meghan was the most special thing in both our lives. My wife was shot not once, not

twice, not three times, not four times, but five times. Imagine that trip to the coroner's office to look at the most important person in your life, lying there lifeless, with five bullets in her body."—*Steve Sposato, whose wife, Jody, was one of eight victims killed in the San Francisco high rise shooting, July 1, 1993.*

Analysis of Handgun Control Inc. Paid Advertisement

I. Goals
  A. Themes
       Assault weapons are used for murder.
       Assault weapons should be banned.
  B. Requested Actions
       Support efforts to ban assault weapons.

II. Organization
  A. Introduction
       The opening quotation and the story (and picture) in the upper left hand corner function as the introduction. The story is designed to grab the attention of the audience.
  B. Conclusion
       The conclusion is the question "Dreams Shattered. Lives Lost. Isn't That A Crime?" It implies that assault weapons should be banned.
  C. Main body—identify the organizational pattern
       The main body is organized around the four narratives in each corner of the piece. The four stories support the theme that assault weapons are used to murder ordinary people. In that way the organization is both narrative and topical.

IV. Role of the rhetor
   Implied relationship
       The narrative format indicates a role of one peer talking to another. The central statement and rhetorical question assume a role of superior to inferior.
   Specific Role
       The specific role is that of an innocent victim of gun violence.

V. Linguistic Tone
       The tone is angry and hurt.

VI. Implied Audience
       The implied audience is very broad. It includes anyone with a family. The only people excluded from the audience would be die-hard opponents of guns and especially NRA members.

VI. Strategy Categories—use all that are relevant and identify sub-strategies as specifically as possible
  A. Rational Argument
       The ad uses the four examples to support the argument that assault weapons threaten ordinary people.

B. Narrative

The four narratives are designed to grab the attention of the audience. The pictures help personalize the stories. The narrative is also linked to the appeal to values and needs.

C. Aesthetic

The large print and the rhetorical question make the theme hit home. Of course, the pictures are also an aesthetic strategy.

D. Values, Needs & Symbols

The dominant strategy in the piece is an appeal to the value of family and the need for life.

E. Credibility

Not an important strategy.

F. Confrontation

Not used in the ad.

CHAPTER THREE

Understanding Context and Judging Effectiveness

The third stage in the consideration of any work of rhetoric is research concerning the context in which the rhetoric was presented. No work of rhetoric can be understood or judged apart from its context.

The key point is that all rhetoric is presented at a specific time and place and cannot be understood apart from that time and place. Even our understanding of the meaning of words and phrases is shaped by the context in which they were presented. For example, a comment about Mr. Potato-Head in a speech in the 1970s would simply have been a reference to the children's toy, probably used to label someone as childish or stupid. But a reference to the same toy in the 1990s would have a totally different meaning, especially if the word potato were mis-spelled with an "e" on the end. In that case, the comment would be a reference to Vice President Dan Quayle's infamous misspelling of potato(e).

The focus of this chapter is on developing tools that the critic can use to illuminate the context in which a given work of rhetoric was presented. In the first section, I discuss the goals of contextual analysis. I then lay out the stages in the research process, develop a system for identifying rhetorical barriers and rhetorical advantages, and explain the proper method for evaluating the effectiveness of any work of rhetoric. I conclude the chapter with an analysis of Booker T. Washington's "Atlanta Exposition Address," to illustrate the principles discussed throughout the chapter.

Goals of Contextual Research

The contextual research stage has four goals. The first goal is to understand the cultural context in which the rhetorical interchange occurred. In order to fairly judge any speech, essay or other rhetorical artifact, one must understand the culture in which it was presented. Contemporary American culture is, for example, quite different from contemporary Japanese culture. It also is quite different from the culture found in this country in an earlier period. To understand any rhetorical artifact, the critic must have some understanding of the society in which it was presented. Obviously, this goal increases in importance in relation to works of rhetoric that come from cultural situations quite different from the United States today.

The second goal is to understand the mindset of the actual audience that heard/read/saw the rhetoric. In the analysis stage, the critic focused on the "implied audience" for a given piece of rhetoric. In the research stage, the focus shifts to the actual audience of people who heard a speech, read a magazine, saw a film, and so forth. It is important to understand the mindset of the audience, because of the general principle that effective rhetoric must be adapted to the views of the audience.

An illustration may make this point clear. Imagine that President Bill Clinton made a major speech calling for equal rights for all soldiers, regardless of their sexual preference. If that speech were presented at a meeting of the American Civil Liberties Union (ACLU), it is easy to predict that he would receive a standing ovation. The ACLU strongly supports equal rights for all Americans in general and gay rights in particular. On the other hand, if the speech were presented at one of the service academies, President Clinton might receive a very cold response, due to negative attitudes among many in the military about both homosexuality and President Clinton himself. The key point is that it would not be possible to evaluate the speech, without knowing the audience to which it was presented. The same speech would be effective in one case and ineffective in the other.

The third goal of the contextual stage is to gain an understanding of the goals of the rhetor. It is difficult to judge the effectiveness or ethics of a work of rhetoric without knowing what the person who created that work wanted to accomplish. For example, there is an important difference between protest rhetoric that is designed to rouse public attention and political campaign rhetoric that is designed to win an election. The former may be considered successful even if it does not persuade the people to support a given cause. But campaign rhetoric is successful only if the candidate wins the election. However, some candidates may be running for the purpose of "protest," rather than because they really expect to win the election. In that case, it is possible that their rhetoric might be considered successful, even if they only received a small percentage of the vote.

Ross Perot's 1992 presidential campaign illustrates this point. Was Perot's rhetoric successful? If his goal was to be elected President, clearly it failed. But if his goal was to focus attention on the budget deficit and other issues, then his campaign must be labeled a great success.

The key point is that it is important to discover the goals of the rhetor in order to adequately and fairly evaluate his/her rhetoric.

The final goal in the contextual research stage is to gather any relevant data concerning the actual influence that the work of rhetoric had on the audience. In some instances, there may be public opinion polls or other audience surveys indicating a strong reaction to a given speech, essay, or film. Alternatively, media reports may indicate how the actual audience responded to the rhetoric. In other cases, editorial reaction and letters to the editor may provide data indicating that a given work influenced (or failed to influence) a given audience. Film or book reviews may provide information about the impact of a movie or a novel.

In some cases there may be a wealth of information indicating that the audience was moved by a given work. For example, there is a great deal of data indicating that Ronald Reagan's "Star Wars" address, which advocated building a missile defense system to protect the nation, had vast influence both on the public and also on debate in Congress.[1] This data would be important in evaluating the rhetoric. In most instances, however, there probably won't be much, if any, external data indicating the impact of the rhetoric. Even when important figures present speeches, there is rarely significant media coverage. This means that there probably won't be any opinion polls, newspaper editorials, news stories, or other information indicating the effectiveness of the rhetoric.

Even if there is information, it may be difficult to tell what it means. For example, a newspaper might report that the audience responded to a speech by former President Bush by applauding twelve times. While this data is useful, it is not at all clear whether twelve rounds of applause means that Bush was especially effective or that the audience was polite to a former President.

While there often is no useful external data on the impact of a given work of rhetoric, that is not always the case. On occasion, external data tells us a great deal about the effect of a speech or other work, as well as how and why the rhetoric functioned.

Research Stages

In order to fulfill the four goals, the analysis should progress through four research stages. The first stage is to identify the necessary level of research on the subject. There is a simple rule in relation to this stage: the farther that one is in time, place, culture and so forth from the rhetoric, the more research that is needed. For example, someone who is active in local politics probably would not need to do any research in order to analyze and evaluate a speech by a city councilperson. At the opposite extreme, an enormous amount of research would be needed to analyze a work presented hundreds of years ago in a foreign culture.

Goals of Contextual Research

1. Gain an understanding of the cultural context.
2. Discover the mindset of the actual audience.
3. Isolate the goals of the rhetor.
4. Gather external data on the impact of the rhetoric.

The second research stage is immersion in the context concerning the rhetoric. This requires research on a number of subjects. First, all relevant material on the rhetoric itself should be reviewed. This means checking for articles or editorials about the work. If one were looking at a film, it would mean looking at all the reviews of the film, as well as press reports about ticket sales. If you were looking at a television series, you would look at both reviews of the series and information concerning ratings. Similar research should be done in source materials relevant to the particular type of rhetoric.

Second, the analyst should research the life of the person creating the rhetoric, if that is relevant. To understand Perot's rhetoric in 1992, it would be important to research Perot's life. On the other hand, if the subject of the analysis were an unsigned newspaper editorial then research on the author probably would not be necessary. It also might be impossible.

Third, the critic should look for relevant historical and cultural material to explain how the rhetoric worked for the actual audience that heard/read/watched the rhetoric. In particular, the critic should research the cultural situation in which the rhetoric was presented, the particular issue or issues that the rhetoric dealt with, and audience attitudes concerning those issues.

An example may make the three steps clearer. In order to evaluate a speech advocating a strong global warming policy, the critic would need to take the following steps. First, the critic would look for any articles or editorials on the speech. If Vice President Gore, or another famous environmentalist, gave the speech there might be press commentary. In the second step, the critic would research the life of the speaker. This research might turn up additional material on the speech. It also might tell the critic about the general ideas of the speaker and how people often respond to them.

The third research step is to gather information about the particular audience that heard/read/saw the rhetoric. The success or failure of a given work of rhetoric can be judged only in relation to a particular audience. This means that it is important to discover as much as possible about the audience that heard or read the rhetoric. In particular, it is important to discover information about the demographic characteristics of the audience and group membership. Demographic characteristics include age, sex, region of the country, educational and income status, and so forth.

Information about group membership is even more important. An example clarifies this point. If a critic knew that the audience for a given speech was composed primarily of highly educated white men, over sixty, with high incomes, he or she might leap to the conclusion that the audience was quite conservative and Republican. Each of the demographic characteristics I mentioned is an indicator that the audience member is more likely to be conservative than liberal and more likely to be Republican than Democratic. On the other hand, now imagine that one more piece of information is added to the mix: the audience members are all American Civil Liberty Union (ACLU) local chapter leaders. With this information, the critic would reason that most ACLU members are liberal Democrats and discount the importance of the demographic data.

The crucial point is that it is important to gather as much information as possible about the actual audience for the rhetoric, including demographic and group membership data.

Information about the audience can be discovered by considering where the rhetoric was presented and then reasoning to the nature of the audience that was present. If the rhetoric under consideration were an essay published in *Time,* then the critic would research the characteristics of readers of that magazine. This same process can be used to gain information about the audience for any work of rhetoric.

The fourth step is to research the cultural context and the particular issue. For a speech presented in the United States in the present day, research about culture probably wouldn't be very important. We all swim in the sea of our culture.

While in this case cultural research might not matter much, research on the issue could be very important. Global warming is a very complicated subject and research might be needed to clarify the message in the speech. Research on the issue also could reveal audience attitudes and values concerning the subject. In some cases, articles might summarize poll data on what Americans think about the environment in general and global warming in particular. In others, the article might indirectly tell the critic about the audience. So, for example, an article might report on the complexities associated with the debate over global warming. That article tells the critic that "complexity" is likely to be an important rhetorical barrier that a pro-environment speaker on global warming must overcome.

Gun control is another topic that illustrates the importance of issue research for identifying rhetorical barriers. For example, many Europeans find American public policy on gun control to be incomprehensible. Most European countries tightly regulate gun ownership and, consequently, given the epidemic of gun violence they do not understand the failure of the United States to implement similar laws. To understand why the NRA has been so successful in blocking gun regulation in this country, it would be necessary to research gun control as an issue. The goal of that research would be to discover audience beliefs, attitudes, and values that relate to gun ownership. This would require looking at research material that explains what people think about gun control

---

Summary of the Research Stage

1. Gather information relating to the particular rhetoric that was presented.
2. Gather information concerning the rhetor.
3. Gather information relating to the specific audience that was exposed to the rhetoric.
4. Gather information concerning the cultural context and the particular issue under consideration.

as an issue. After looking at that material, it should be possible to explain why pro gun control rhetoric only has been successful on a few issues.

Rhetorical Barriers and Advantages

Conducting the research stage, the rhetorical analyst should be particularly aware of material relating to *rhetorical barriers* and *rhetorical advantages* facing the rhetor. In chapter one, I defined a rhetorical barrier as *an attitude, belief or other problem that a rhetor must overcome in order to persuade an audience to accept a given position.* In contrast, a rhetorical advantage is *an attitude, belief or other position that gives the rhetor assistance in persuading an audience.*

An illustration may make these terms clearer. On an emotional issue like gun control, advocates of both sides face difficult rhetorical barriers, but also possess significant rhetorical advantages. For example, a pro gun control speaker must overcome barriers relating to public fear of crime and attitudes against government regulation of guns in order to persuade an audience to support strengthened gun control laws. On the other hand, an advocate of gun control also has certain rhetorical advantages, particularly on issues like assault rifles and concealed weapons. In relation to these policies, many in the public doubt that ordinary people need to carry either a concealed weapon or an assault rifle. Consequently, the pro gun control speaker starts out with a considerable rhetorical advantage.

How does the critic discover rhetorical barriers and advantages? The critic uses the material gained through the four steps and the category system developed in the following section to draw conclusions about the barriers/advantages that faced a rhetor in a particular situation. For example, in relation to gun control, knowledge that a particular audience was composed primarily of women *and* that women tend to support gun control more strongly than men, would suggest the presence of rhetorical advantages relating to the attitudes that guns are very dangerous and that gun regulations are sensible. It is through the combination of the four research steps and the category system for rhetorical barriers/advantages that the critic can isolate particular barriers/advantages for a given work of rhetoric.

In the next section, I lay out a system for identifying and understanding rhetorical barriers and advantages.

Types of Rhetorical Barriers and Advantages

There are four main types of rhetorical barriers/advantages: audience-related, situational, occasion-related, and those that are tied to the rhetor's reputation.

Audience-Related Barriers ◆ The most important barriers and advantages relate to the mindset of the audience. The mindset of the audience can be divided into three related categories: beliefs, attitudes, and values. A belief is a statement of fact that is in princi-

ple testable. A person might believe, for example, that many ho
protect their property. This belief could be tested against statist
tested in that manner, beliefs are difficult to change, even when t
by the best data.

An attitude is an evaluation of a belief. In this case, the attitud
such as, "I have a right to own a gun to defend myself" or "only criminals need assault
rifles." The first attitude is based on the belief that guns are an effective means of home
defense, but it also includes an evaluative component, in this case support for the right
to gun ownership. The second attitude is tied to a belief that ordinary people have no
use for assault rifles and the evaluation that we should not help criminals arm themselves with dangerous weapons. Attitudes are harder to change than beliefs because
they relate not only to factual material, but also to personal evaluation of those facts.
In common language, attitudes contain a strong emotional component.

Values are basic principles of right and wrong, good and bad. In a sense, a value is
a more basic version of an attitude. Basic values in the United States include support
for freedom, peace, prosperity, progress, and so forth. In relation to gun control, the
pro gun control speaker or writer faces barriers relating to public values concerning
limits on government regulation of the individual. Opponents of gun control tend to
value personal independence and de-value government control. However, the pro gun
control speaker has the advantage of being able to appeal to the value of life.

In relation to any work of rhetoric, the analyst should identify barriers/advantages
related to the beliefs, attitudes, and values of the audience. These barriers and advantages are generally the most important ones facing any rhetor. It is helpful to keep in
mind that of the three types, barriers/advantages related to values are the most powerful and those tied to beliefs the least powerful. Basic values are so ingrained in the individual that it is extremely difficult to change them. The rhetor either must adapt to the
values or recognize that he/she is unlikely to fully persuade the audience.

Beliefs are more easily changed because they are based on a factual understanding
of the world. With enough information (and time), one often can convince someone to
change their beliefs, although this is by no means an easy process.

The final barrier falling in the audience category is attention. On some issues it will
be difficult to gain or keep the attention of the audience because they do not care about
the subject or find it uninteresting. On the other hand, there are issues where it is easy
to get the attention of the audience. Far more press attention was focussed on the O.J.
Simpson murder trial than on the dangers posed by depletion of the ozone layer. Most
people find a discussion of the ozone layer to be difficult to understand and quite dull.
By contrast, tens of millions of Americans were fascinated by the Simpson trial. Of
course, there is no question that the threat of ozone depletion is vastly more important
to the world than the trial of O.J. Simpson, but a rhetor discussing this issue faces serious problems relating to attention. On the other hand, when a rhetor can link his/her
position to a subject about which there is intense public interest, that gives him/her a
rhetorical advantage.

Situational ◆ The second type of rhetorical barrier/advantage is tied to the situation in which the rhetoric is presented. There are three main types of situational barriers/advantages. The first relates to culture. Different cultures have varying expectations concerning rhetorical practice. This is most obvious in relation to foreign cultures, but is also true in this country. For example, greater formality is still the norm in the East and the South, as opposed to the Midwest or West. Culture also influences attitudes. There have been major controversies in recent years in several Southern states concerning displays of the Confederate flag. Obviously, there have been no such controversies in Minnesota.

Therefore, the critic should consider whether the culture either creates a barrier or provides an advantage for the rhetor.

The second situational barrier/advantage relates to complexity. If the topic of the rhetoric is complicated, then the rhetor faces a major barrier in persuading the audience. Nuclear power is a good example. Many experts believe that nuclear power is actually much safer than producing electricity in coal-fired plants.[2] In this view, the number of deaths from mining and transporting coal, when added to the deaths caused by air pollution coming from the coal plant, is much larger than a similar figure for nuclear power. But this argument is complex and runs up against fear of a nuclear accident. Many people somehow equate nuclear power and nuclear weapons as similar. In this case, the consensus of scientists that the most modern nuclear plants are extremely safe has not been enough to change public attitudes concerning the energy source. The result of this rhetorical situation has been to make it impossible for utilities to order new nuclear power plants.

On the other hand, if the issue is a very simple one that gives the rhetor a significant advantage. In relation to gun control, for example, both sides of the debate try to simplify the issue. The pro gun control advocates may reduce the issue to picture of a dead loved one killed in a gun accident. The pro NRA side, in contrast, will simplify the issue by focusing on horrible crimes that might have been prevented, if the homeowner had owned a gun.

The third type of situational barrier/advantage relates to specific events that sometimes occur immediately prior to or during a rhetorical interchange. In the Spring of 1996, Republicans in Congress were attacking President Clinton for accepting illegal campaign contributions from foreign sources. It then was discovered that the Republicans had accepted similar illegal donations. That discovery made it much more difficult for Republican leaders to maintain their attacks on the Democrats.

Occasion ◆ The third main type of barrier/advantage relates to the general occasion in which the rhetoric is presented. Barriers/advantages related to occasion are especially important for speeches. One sub-type relates to standards for appropriateness. For example, the standards of appropriateness in a church service and a political pep rally are somewhat different. Sometimes the rhetor is also limited by the expectations of the audience related to the category of the rhetoric. The expectations of an audience for the category "after dinner speech" are different than for the category "academic lecture." If a speaker presents an academic lecture in the after dinner situation, he or she is likely to bore the audience to tears. On the other hand, an after dinner speech might be perceived as mere fluff if the audience expected an academic lecture.

Reputation of the Rhetor ◆ The final category of rhetorical barriers/advantages relates to the audience's perception of the rhetor. In some cases, a main barrier may be that the audience does not trust the person creating the rhetoric. After his resignation from the Presidency, Richard Nixon always faced barriers related to the audience perception that he had lied to the American people and broken the law. Nixon had to overcome that perception before anyone would listen to him. In other cases, the rhetor may face an audience perception that he/she is not qualified to speak about the subject. It would be difficult for former President Bush to present a major speech on "Growing Up in Poverty," because he did not do so. On the other hand, former President Reagan would have no trouble on that subject because of his life experiences.

Just as there are barriers relating to the reputation of the rhetor, in some cases there are rhetorical advantages. Colin Powell is admired by nearly all Americans who know of his service in the military, in general, and his work during the Gulf War, in particular. He possesses a particular rhetorical advantage when he speaks to veterans or African Americans.

A Typology of Rhetorical Barriers and Advantages

A. Audience—
1. Beliefs
2. Attitudes
3. Values
4. Attention

B. Situational barriers
1. Cultural factors
2. Complexity of the issue
3. Specific events occurring immediately before or during the presentation of the rhetoric

C. The occasion—
1. Standards of appropriateness
2. Categorical expectations

D. The reputation of the rhetor

Summary of the Research Stage

At the end of the research stage, the critic should have a good understanding of the context in which the work of rhetoric was presented, the goals of the rhetor in presenting the work, and the barriers/advantages that he/she faced. The critic also would be aware of any data concerning the effect that the work had on the actual audience to which it was presented. The next step is for the critic to evaluate the effectiveness of the rhetoric as a work of persuasion.

Evaluating Effectiveness

One of the most important issues in rhetorical analysis concerns the effectiveness of a work of rhetoric. Rhetoric, unlike literature, is always concerned with persuasion. That makes it important to discover if a given piece of rhetoric was effective and why or why not. It might seem that evaluating effectiveness should be a very straight-forward process. The analyst simply would check to see if the rhetoric persuaded the audience. Unfortunately, it isn't that simple.

Here, the main problems relate to obtaining and interpreting "external" data on the effectiveness of a work of rhetoric. As noted earlier, in most cases, there will be no data relating to the impact of a particular work of rhetoric on an audience. Even in the case of speech by an important political figure, rarely will there be opinion polls directly bearing on the address. Nor are there likely to be newspaper articles or editorials on the speech. With the exception of the State of the Union Address and a few other speeches, even addresses by the President of the United States are largely ignored by the press.

Second, it is important to remember that even if there is data, it may be very difficult to tell what it means. Does the fact that three people wrote favorable letters to the editor about a given editorial mean that the editorial was effective? There is no clear answer to that question.

Of course, there are exceptions to this rule. In the last major section of this chapter, I evaluate Booker T. Washington's "Atlanta Exposition Address." There is an enormous amount of information proving that the speech was effective, but that case is the exception that proves the general rule that evaluation based on external data is rarely possible.

Therefore, since in most instances the critic will not be able to rely on external data concerning the effectiveness of a speech, essay, film, and so forth, another approach to evaluation must be taken. If evaluation based on "external" data is not feasible, then the alternative is an "internal" form of evaluation. In this view, the critic should ask a simple question:

Does the rhetor present strategies that are well-designed to overcome the rhetorical barriers (and maximize the rhetorical advantages) in order to achieve his/her purpose?

This question pulls together material gathered in the analysis and research stages in order to make an evaluation of the effectiveness of the rhetoric.

In answering this question, the critic first would outline the purpose of the rhetoric. This purpose would be identified in the goal section of the analysis stage and backed up with material gathered in the research stage. The analyst then would lay out the barriers/advantages that the rhetor faced. Of course, these barriers/advantages would have been discovered in the research stage. At that point, he/she would identify the main strategies present in the rhetoric, based on the outline created in the analysis stage. Finally, the strategies would be compared to the barriers/advantages in order to judge whether the rhetor did as good a job as possible in overcoming the barriers and using the advantages.

The key is for the analyst carefully to consider whether the strategies responded to each important barrier and maximized each advantage. If the rhetor accomplished these aims, that suggests the rhetoric was well-designed and should be judged as quite effective.

Judgment of effectiveness (or failure) based on the internal evaluating system I have outlined is not a scientific one. Rather, that judgment must be based on strong arguments for whatever conclusion is drawn.

One other point is important. The analyst should consider whether the internal evaluation of effectiveness is consistent with any data about the impact of the work, which was discovered in the research stage. In most cases, there will be no such data, but in a few instances, such as the Washington Address, there will be obvious external data. Clearly, the internal and external data should support the same conclusion. If they don't, something is seriously wrong.

Washington's "Atlanta Exposition Address"

Booker T. Washington's "Atlanta Exposition Address," has been praised as one of the greatest speeches ever presented by an American. An early biographer reports that "Journals of the North and South vied with each other in giving it [the address] praise" and concludes that "as a classic it passed into the realm of the world's famous orations."[3] Public reaction at the time was overwhelming. Washington himself reported that "I received so many and such hearty congratulations that I found it difficult to get out of the building."[4] The speech caused such a stir that Washington was offered $50,000 to go on a speaking tour.[5] Of course, in 1895 $50,000 was an enormous amount of money. Another sign of the influence of the speech is that President Grover Cleveland wrote a personal note to Washington in which he explained "I think the exposition would be fully justified if it did not do more than furnish the opportunity for its [the speech's] delivery."[6]

More recently, the speech has been widely criticized as a sell-out to the white establishment. Thomas Harris and Patrick Kennicott claim that Washington "told the majority what they wanted to hear" and consequently his rhetoric "disregarded many of the immediate social and political needs of the people for whom Washington spoke."[7]

If their judgment is correct then Washington's address merits criticism not praise. Robert L. Heath makes a similar judgment. He argues that "The hostile and bleak rhetorical atmosphere surrounding the race question in 1895 was not a time for Washington's Exposition address; it was a time for silence."[8] Harris, Kennicott, and Heath base their criticism of the address on passages in the speech in which Washington seemed to accept unequal treatment for Black Americans. In famous sections Washington emphasized the need for economic opportunity as more important than political and social rights.

Given the contrasting viewpoints, it is important to ask: Who is right about the Washington speech? This question cannot be answered without a careful analysis of the historical context in which the speech was presented. Clearly, if Washington's speech were presented in contemporary America, we would label him an "Uncle Tom," who had sold out to the white establishment. But Washington did not present his speech in 1990s America. He presented it in the deep South in 1895. In that time and place, Washington sensibly adapted to an impossible rhetorical situation.

The following analysis will show that Washington did not sell-out to Southern racists. I also will demonstrate the importance of judging any rhetoric in the context and time in which it was presented. In accomplishing these aims, I will illustrate the stages in the internal evaluation scheme described in the previous section. The Washington address is a good one to illustrate internal evaluation of effectiveness both because the context of the time played such a major role in the reaction to the speech and because the address is one of the very small group of rhetorical acts about which we have enough data to judge effectiveness externally.[9] There is no question that the address was successful for the immediate audience and the larger national audience. Internal evaluation should come to a similar judgment.

"Progress of the American Negro"
Atlanta Exposition Address

Booker T. Washington

Mr. President and gentlemen of the board of directors and citizens: One-third of the population of the South is of the Negro race. No enterprise seeking the material, civil, or moral welfare of this section can disregard this element of our population and reach the highest success. I but convey to you, Mr. President and Directors, the sentiment of the masses of my race when I say that in no way have the value and manhood of the American Negro been

1

Delivered in Atlanta on September 18, 1895.

more fittingly and generously recognized than by the managers of this magnificent Exposition at every stage of it's progress. It is a recognition that will do more to cement the friendship of the two races than any occurrence since the dawn of our freedom.

Not only this, but the opportunity here afforded will awaken among us a new era of industrial progress. Ignorant and inexperienced, it is not strange that in the first years of our new life we began at the top instead of at the bottom; that a seat in Congress or the state legislature was more sought than real estate or industrial skill; that the political convention or stump speaking had more attractions than starting a dairy farm or truck garden.

2

A ship lost at sea for many days suddenly sighted a friendly vessel. From the mast of the unfortunate vessel was seen a signal, "Water, water; we die of thirst!" The answer from the friendly vessel at once came back, "Cast down your bucket where you are." A second time the signal, "Water, water; send us water!" ran up from the distressed vessel, and was answered, "Cast down your bucket where you are." And a third and fourth signal for water was answered, "Cast down your bucket where you are." The captain of the distressed vessel, at last heeding the inunction, cast down his bucket, and it came up full of fresh, sparkling water from the mouth of the Amazon river. To those of my race who depend on bettering their condition in a foreign land or who underestimate the importance of cultivating friendly relations with the Southern white man, who is their next-door neighbor, I would say: "Cast down your bucket where you are"—cast it down in making friends in every manly way of the people of all races by whom we are surrounded.

3

Cast it down in agriculture, mechanics, in commerce, in domestic service, and in the professions. And in this connection it is well to bear in mind that whatever other sins the South may be called to bear, when it comes to business, pure and simple, it is in the South that the Negro is given a man's chance in the commercial world, and in nothing is this Exposition more eloquent than in emphasizing this chance. Our greatest danger is that in the great leap from slavery to freedom we may overlook the fact that the masses of us are to live by the productions of our hands, and fail to keep in mind that we shall prosper in proportion as we learn to dignify and glorify common labor and put brains and skill into the common occupations of life; shall prosper in proportions as we learn to draw the line between the superficial and the substantial, the ornamental gewgaws of life and the useful. No race can prosper till it learns that there is as much dignity in tilling a field as in writing a poem. It is at the bottom of life we must begin, and not at the top. Nor should we permit our grievances to overshadow our opportunities.

4

To those of the white race who look to the incoming of those of foreign birth and strange tongue and habits for the prosperity of the South, were I permitted I would repeat what I say to my own race, "Cast down your bucket where you are." Cast it down among the eight millions of Negroes whose habits you know, whose fidelity and love you have tested in days when to have proved treacherous meant the ruin of your firesides. Cast down your bucket among these people who have, without strikes and labor wars, tilled your fields, cleared your forests, builded your railroads and cities, and brought forth treasures from the bowels of the earth, and helped make possible this magnificent representation of the progress of the South. Casting down your bucket among my people, helping and encouraging them as you are doing on these grounds, and, with education of head, hand, and heart, you will find that they will buy your surplus land, make blossom the waste places in your fields, and run your factories. While doing this, you can be sure in the future, as in the past, that you and your fam-

5

ilies will be surrounded by the most patient, faithful, law-abiding, and unresentful people that the world has seen. As we have proved our loyalty to you in the past, in nursing your children, watching by the sick-bed of your mothers and fathers, and often following them with tear-dimmed eyes to their graves, so in the future, in our humble way, we shall stand by you with a devotion that no foreigner can approach, ready to lay down our lives, if need be, in defense of yours, interlacing our industrial commercial, civil, and religious life with yours in a way that shall make the interests of both races one. In all things that are purely social we can be as separate as the fingers, yet one as the hand in all things essential to mutual progress.

There is no defense or security for any of us except in the highest intelligence and devel- 6
opment of all. If anywhere there are efforts tending to curtail the fullest growth of the Negro, let these efforts be turned into stimulating, encouraging, and making him the most useful and intelligent citizen. Effort or means so invested will pay a thousand percent interest. These efforts will be twice blessed—"blessing him that gives and him that takes."

There is no escape through law of man or God from the inevitable:

The law of changeless justice bind
Oppressor with oppressed;
and close as sin and suffering joined
We march to fate abreast.

Nearly sixteen millions of hands will aid you in pulling the load upward, or they will pull, 7
against you, the load downward. We shall constitute one-third and more of the ignorance and crime of the South, or one-third its intelligence and progress; we shall contribute one-third to the business and industrial prosperity of the South, or we shall prove a veritable body of death, stagnating, depressing, retarding every effort to advance the body politic.

Gentlemen of the Exposition, as we present to you our humble effort at an exhibition of 8
our progress, you must not expect overmuch. Starting thirty years ago with ownership here and there in a few quilts and pumpkins and chickens (gathered from miscellaneous sources), remember the path that has led from these to the inventions and production of agricultural implements, buggies, steam-engines, newspapers, books, statuary, carving, paintings, the management of drug-stores and banks, has not been trodden without contact with thorns and thistles. While we take pride in what we exhibit as a result of our independent efforts, we do not for a moment forget that our part in this exhibition would fall far short of your expectations but for the constant help that has come to our educational life, not only from the Southern states, but especially from Northern philanthropists, who have made their gifts a constant stream of blessing and encouragement.

The wisest among my race understand that the agitation of questions of social equality 9
is the extremist folly, and that progress in the enjoyment of all the privileges that will come to us must be the result of severe and constant struggle rather than of artificial forcing. No race that has anything to contribute to the markets of the world is long, in any degree, ostracized. It is important and right that all privileges of the law be ours, but it is vastly more important that we be prepared for the exercise of those privileges. The opportunity to earn a dollar in a factory just now is worth infinitely more than the opportunity to spend a dollar in an opera-house.

In conclusion, may I repeat that nothing in thirty years has given us more hope and en- 10
couragement, and drawn us so near to you of the white race, as this opportunity offered by

the Exposition; and here bending, as it were, over the altar that represents the results of the struggles of your race and mine, both starting practically empty-handed three decades ago, I pledge that, in your effort to work out the great and intricate problem which God has laid at the doors of the South, you shall have at all times the patient, sympathetic help of my race; only let this be constantly in mind, that, while from representations in these buildings of the product of field, of forest, of mine, of factory, letters, and art, much good will come, yet far above and beyond material benefits will be that higher good, that, let us pray God, will come, in a blotting out of sectional differences and racial animosities and suspicions, in a determination to administer absolute justice, in a willing obedience among all classes to the mandates of law. Thus, this, coupled with our material prosperity, will bring into our beloved South a new heaven and a new earth.

◆◆◆

Internal Evaluation of the Atlanta Exposition Address

Internal evaluation of any work of rhetoric proceeds through four steps: purpose identification, outlining rhetorical barriers and advantages, strategy analysis, and comparison of strategies to the rhetorical barriers/advantages. In the following analysis, I illustrate the application of each stage via an analysis of Washington's address.

Washington's Purpose

The primary goals of Washington's address are quite clear. He wants to protect Black jobs in the South, obtain the good will of the white Southern audience, and seek assistance from Northern philanthropists. The most important of these goals relates to jobs. In the third paragraph, Washington uses a long figurative analogy based on the example of the crew of a ship lost at sea and running out of water being told to "Cast down your bucket" where you are. The ship was in the mouth of the Amazon and when the crew "cast" down their bucket, they came up with pure, clean water. Similarly, Washington argues that white Southerners should "Cast it [their metaphorical bucket] down in agriculture, mechanics, in commerce, in domestic service, and in the professions" (paragraph 4). In the next paragraph, he juxtaposes the "loyal" Black population with new foreign immigrants or labor. Clearly, Washington hopes that the white population will provide jobs to African Americans in the South.

The interpretation that Washington's primary concern was jobs is supported by Washington's emphasis upon "work" as the most important means of helping Black Americans. In paragraph 9, he both emphasizes the crucial value of work and suggests that having a productive job is more important than having complete equality with the white population. Washington says, "The opportunity to earn a dollar in a factory just now is worth infinitely more than the opportunity to spend a dollar in an opera house."

With this statement, Washington indicates that he believes work opportunity is far more important than social equality with white Americans.

The second goal in the speech clearly is to create good will with the white audience. Throughout the address Washington relies on a strategy of ingratiation. He praises the accomplishments of the white audience and sometimes puts down those of his own people. In the first paragraph, he refers to "this magnificent Exposition." A little later, he returns to a discussion of the Exposition itself stating, "Gentlemen of the Exposition, as we present to your our humble effort at an exhibition of our progress, you must not expect overmuch" (paragraph 8). Two paragraphs later, he concludes that "nothing in thirty years has given us more hope and encouragement and drawn us so near to you of the white race, as this opportunity offered by the Exposition." Clearly, Washington hopes that his rhetorical adaptation will produce a positive reaction among white Southerners.

Finally, Washington appeals to a very specific sub-audience—rich potential grant givers. In paragraph 8, he comments about the "constant help that has come to our educational life, not only from Southern states, but especially from Northern philanthropists. . . ." Here, his aim seems to be to generate additional revenues.

It is easy to see why some academics and others object to the tone and content of Washington's address. He praises the South and the Exposition shamelessly and demeans his own people. As I will note in the analysis of strategies, he also praises Southern history and rejects attempts to change the Southern system. From our vantage point today, his rhetoric is disgusting. But Washington did not have the luxury of living in a nation in which the African-American population has both significant political influence and legal restrictions that protect their rights.

The Situation Facing Washington in 1895

In 1895 Washington faced immense rhetorical barriers and possessed essentially no rhetorical advantages. In relation to barriers, the most important was extreme racism throughout our society. In his book, *Anti Negro Thought in America,* I. A. Newley explained that "Southerners and other Americans too were especially receptive to racist doctrine and accepted without question the whole complex of anti-Negro ideas."[10] It was a time in which terrible racism was the norm. Robert Brisbane puts it this way, "White people were united as never before in their determination to compel the Negro to begin from the bottom."[11] Brisbane also notes that even many Northern liberals supported strongly racist views.[12]

The second barrier Washington faced was the threat of white violence. In this period, Black Americans, especially in the South, often were beaten and sometimes lynched. According to Thomas Dye, "A virtual reign of terror began in the 1890s and extended to the beginning of World War I."[13] A study done for the NAACP found that in this "reign of terror" more than 3000 Black Americans were lynched.[14] Black men and women who seemed the least bit threatening to the white establishment often were simply murdered. In truth, at this time an African-American could be killed because a white person found offensive anything that he/she did. It was a very hard time to be a Black American.

The third primary rhetorical barrier was that Black Americans had essentially no political power. The Civil War had been over for thirty years and, as I noted earlier, many Northern Liberals had themselves become racists. To make matters worse, Black Americans were not allowed to vote. The distinguished historian August Meier writes that "By 1895 disenfranchisement had been pretty well accomplished by various devices . . . in most of the South."[15] It is difficult to appeal to people who strongly believe that you are inferior, when you lack the protections of law and have essentially no political power. It is also important to note that Black Americans could not effectively use violence to defend themselves against racism. Not only were Black Americans on average quite poor (and thus less likely to be armed than their white counterparts), but fighting back could provoke still worse racist violence.

As should be clear, Washington possessed no rhetorical advantages. He was coming "hat in hand" to ask for jobs and money to an audience that thought him and his people to be inferior. He had no power over his audience. It was in this context that Washington presented the "Atlanta Exposition Address."

Strategies in the Address

Washington's overall strategy was to adapt to the attitudes and values of the audience, but underneath the surface state a case for fair treatment for Black Americans. This last aspect of the address largely has been ignored by those who attack Washington.

Washington adapts to the Southern audience in several ways. First, as I noted earlier, he praises the exposition in the strongest terms. Of course, everyone loves to be praised. Washington pushes this about as far as he can, without making the strategy obvious. Second, and more fundamentally, Washington appeals to dominant attitudes of the age concerning the importance of business and hard work. The long "cast down your bucket" section of the introduction is both a wonderful use of metaphor, parallel structure and repetition, but also an appeal to the ideal of "work." This same strategic adaptation is also evident in Washington's negative comments about labor unions and foreign immigrants. With these statements, Washington appeals to business attitudes about labor and immigrants. He also is subtly suggesting to the audience that they would be better off with Black workers than the alternative.

Third, Washington adapts to Southern attitudes about race. Perhaps the most famous statement of the address occurs at almost exactly the midpoint. He uses the metaphor of the fingers and the hand to suggest that Blacks and whites can work together but still be separate. He says "In all things that are purely social we can be as separate as the fingers, yet one as the hand in all thing essential to mutual progress" (paragraph 5). With this statement, Washington clearly adapts to Southern racism. He returns to this theme in the conclusion, where he says that "The wisest among my race understand that the agitation of questions of social equality is the extremist folly, and that progress in the enjoyment of all the privileges that will come to us must be the result of severe and constant struggle rather than of artificial forcing" (paragraph 9). In these statements, Washington seems to accept segregation.

Washington also adapts to Southern attitudes about their history. In a long passage in paragraph 5, he depicts the past as a time in which the Black population of the South was extremely loyal to the white population:

> As we have proved our loyalty to you in the past, in nursing your children, watching by the sick-bed of your mothers and fathers, and often following them with tear-dimmed eyes to their graves, so in the future, in our humble way, we shall stand by you with a devotion that no foreigner can approach, ready to lay down our lives, if need be, in defense of yours, interlacing our industrial commercial, civil and religious life with yours in a way that shall make the interests of both races one.

In this statement, Washington almost seems nostalgic about the pre-Civil War period. Of course, in that time Washington and other African Americans were slaves in the South. One can imagine the satisfaction that the Southern audience would have with Washington's description. Even here, however, the strategic character of Washington's adaptation is obvious. He not only appeals to Southern history, but sneaks in a negative comment about foreign workers. Washington clearly was doing everything possible to generate jobs for Black Americans.

In addition to adaptation to Southern attitudes, Washington relies on a number of aesthetic strategies. I already have mentioned the two dominant metaphors of the fingers on a hand and the sailor casting down his bucket for water. Washington also relies on depiction in the passage concerning Southern history, as well as repetition, parallel structure, and rhythm. In this speech, Washington uses language strategies to make his message more appealing and memorable. The language strategies are not, however, the core of the speech.

Finally, Washington includes with the adaptive strategy an implicit call for justice and equality for all Americans. Recognizing the rhetorical situation, Washington does not make this conclusion explicit. Rather, he makes an implicit call for justice. The implicit call for justice takes two forms. The first is an implied threat that the South must help Black Southerners or face severe problems. After completing the introduction, Washington comments:

> Nearly sixteen millions of hands will aid you in pulling the low upward, or they will pull, against you, the load downward. We shall constitute one-third and more of the ignorance and crime of the South, or one-third its intelligence and progress; we shall contribute one-third to the business and industrial prosper-

ity of the South, or we shall prove a veritable body of death, stagnating depressing, retarding every effort to advance the body politic. (paragraph 7)

With this statement, Washington appeals to the self-interest of the audience. He warns them that they could be much worse off if they do not assist the Black population.

In the conclusion, he uses a somewhat different strategy. While rejecting demands for immediate social equality, Washington also emphasizes that eventually all rights must be guaranteed. For example, after downplaying the importance of social equality, Washington states "No race that has anything to contribute to the markets of the world is long, in any degree, ostracized" (paragraph 9). He then adds that "It is important and right that all privileges of the law be ours, but it is vastly more important that we be prepared for the exercise of those privileges" (paragraph 9). While he emphasizes the importance of responsibility in this statement, he also clearly says that Black Americans should have the same rights as others. Washington does not call for immediate action on civil rights, but he makes it clear that eventually change must come.

Washington's rhetoric has been labeled a rhetoric of compromise or even appeasement. While there is no doubt that his focus was on adapting to his audience, he also clearly warned them that ultimately society must change. There is a strong argument that under the circumstances this was the only strategy open to him. A more forceful address or outright confrontation certainly would not have worked with the Southern audience. And there was no caring national audience to which Washington could appeal. Moreover, a more forceful strategy very possibly could have caused white backlash, perhaps violence against the Black population. Given the situation, there is a strong argument that Washington went about as far as he could go in pushing his agenda.

Internal Evaluation

There is no question that Washington's address was a success with both the immediate audience and the larger audience. The secondary data on this is quite clear. The question then becomes: Does an internal evaluation of effectiveness yield the same judgment concerning the speech as an external evaluation? The answer is clearly yes. It is important to remember that the primary rhetorical barriers faced by Washington were intense racism, the complete absence of political allies, and lack of power in any form to influence his audience. He also lived in an extremely violent Southern culture in which lynchings were quite common. In that circumstance, adaptation was his only choice.

Washington brilliantly adapted to Southern history, the dominant attitudes of the age concerning work, and especially to Southern attitudes about race. He used metaphor, depiction and other aesthetic strategies to get and keep the attention of the audience. But he also included an implicit threat and implied that the day must come when equal rights are provided to Black Americans. In essence, he was willing to make a tactical retreat in order to protect Black Americans from violence and obtain jobs for them. It must have sickened him to say some of the things he said, but he had no alternative.

Washington's Address and Understanding Context

Booker T. Washington's "Atlanta Exposition Address," illustrates the importance of conducting adequate contextual research prior to judging any work of rhetoric. Today, a speech like Washington's rightly would be labeled a sell-out, but in 1895 it was an act of courage. The analysis of the address also illustrates the steps in the process of internal evaluation. By first identifying the goals of a work of rhetoric, then considering barriers (and advantages) to achieving those goals, next laying out the strategies in the work, and finally comparing the strategies to the barriers/advantages and making an on-balance judgment, the critic can evaluate the effectiveness of any work of rhetoric.

One final point is illustrated by the analysis of the Washington address and its later impact. Ethical evaluation also is dependent on the context. After presenting the speech, Washington became the most powerful Black American, until his death in 1915. For decades after his death, the conventional wisdom was that Washington had followed a policy of accommodating white America. Reasonable people differed on whether that policy was required by the times or was a sell-out. However, after Washington's private papers became available, a different picture emerged. It was discovered that while publicly seeming to accept segregation, Washington secretly attacked it. Louis Harlan writes:

> Washington in these circumstances decided to launch a secret but direct attack on racially restrictive laws. He secretly paid for and directed a succession of court suits against discrimination in voting, exclusion of Negroes from jury panels, Jim Crow railroad facilities and various kinds of exploitation of the black poor. In all of this secret activity it is clear that Washington was not merely trying to make a favorable impression on his militant critics or to spike their guns, for he took every precaution to keep information of his secret actions from leaking out.[16]

It would seem that Washington, who had been attacked for being too passive, a sort of rhetorical chicken, was in fact a rhetorical fox. He did what he could under very difficult circumstances. When he saw the chance to launch a legal attack, he did so, but secretly, so that he could maintain his other strategy of adaptation. In contemporary America, we would label what Washington did as deceptive, manipulative, and very possibly money laundering. But in the context of his time, his actions should be labeled as a wonderful example of rhetorical skill and moral courage.

Conclusion

In the previous section, I explained the process of contextual research, the goals which this research serves, the main and sub-categories of barriers (and advantages) facing rhetors. I also developed a system for evaluating the effectiveness of any work of rhetoric and applied that system to Booker T. Washington's "Atlanta Exposition Address."

The most important conclusion developed in this chapter is that a fair understanding of how any work of rhetoric works or a fair evaluation of that rhetoric requires an understanding of the context in which the rhetoric was presented.

Notes

1. See Robert C. Rowland and Rodger A. Payne, "The Effectiveness of Reagan's 'Star Wars' Address," *Political Communication and Persuasion* 4 (1987): 161–178.
2. See Bertram Wolfe, "Why Environmentalists Should Promote Nuclear Energy," *Vital Speeches of the Day* 1 November 1996: 52–56.
3. B. F. Riley, *The Life and Times of Booker T. Washington* (New York: Fleming H. Revell, 1916), pp. 206–207.
4. Booker T. Washington, *Up From Slavery* (New York: Doubleday, 1901).
5. Riley, p. 207.
6. President Cleveland is cited in Samuel R. Spencer, Jr., *Booker T. Washington and the Nergo's Place in American Life* (Boston: Little, Brown, 1955), p. 103.
7. Thomas E. Harris and Patrick C. Kennicott, "Booker T. Washington: A Study of Conciliatory Rhetoric," *Southern Speech Journal* 37 (1971), pp. 58, 59.
8. Robert L. Health, "A Time For Silence: Booker T. Washington in Atlanta," *Quarterly Journal of Speech* 64 (1978), p. 399.
9. A good description of the enormous impact of the speech is found in B.F. Riley, *The Life and Times of Booker T. Washington*.
10. I. A. Newley, *Anti Negro Thought in America 1900–1930* (Baton Rouge: LSU Press, 1965), p. 126.
11. Robert H. Brisbane, *The Black Vanguard* (Valley Forge: Johnson Press, 1970), p. 29.
12. Brisbane, p. 29.
13. Thomas R. Dye, *The Politics of Equality* (Indianapolis, The Bobbs-Merrill Company, 1971), p. 18.
14. Cited in Dye, pp. 18–19.
15. August Meier, *Negro Thought in America. 1880–1915: Racial Ideologies in the Age of Booker T. Washington.* (Ann Arbor: University of Michigan Press, 1964), p. 162.
16. Louis R. Harlan, "The Secret Life of Booker T. Washington," *Booker T. Washington and His Critics,* Ed. Hugh Hawkins (Lexington: D.C. Heath, 1974), p. 187.

Rhetorical Strategies

Introduction

In the next six chapters, I will discuss the six main strategy categories that were identified earlier. In each case, I will define the characteristics of the strategy category, identify sub-types of the strategy (if relevant), and lay out the strengths and weaknesses of the strategy type as a means of persuasion.

CHAPTER FOUR

Rational Argument

The most common meaning of "argument" is a verbal fight or disagreement. While that meaning is the most common, it is not the correct interpretation of the term, when it is considered a type of rhetorical strategy. As a strategy category, rational argument consists of the use of evidence and reasoning to persuade an audience with the power of the logic or facts.

Why is rational argument important? Why treat it as the first strategy category? The short answer is that while rational argument is not always the most effective strategy, it must be present if people are to use rhetoric to make effective decisions in a democratic society. Rational argument is based on the power of human reason. Through the give and take of argumentative discussion, people can come to a reasoned democratic decision. The alternative—an unreasoned decision—is certainly not very appealing.

In this chapter, I first lay out the functions of argument in any democratic society. I then discuss the formal components of argument and the three ways that argument can be used as a persuasive device. This section is followed by a consideration of the strengths and weaknesses of the four main types of supporting evidence. I then illustrate the way that argument functions as a strategy via analysis of a speech by former Speaker of the House Newt Gingrich. In the final section of the chapter, I consider the conflicting data on whether argument is a generally effective persuasive strategy.

The Functions of Rational Argument

Rational argument serves two primary functions. First, it is a method of persuasion. People often use argument to try and persuade each other to act in some way or believe in something. In the last section of the chapter, I will describe the somewhat conflicting research tradition on whether argument is an effective means of persuasion.

Second, argument is the preferred method of resolving disagreements and making decisions in a democratic society. Initially, it may seem odd to label argument as a key component of democracy. After all, we all hate having arguments. It is important, however, to remember that by argument I do not mean the common meaning of the term—

a verbal fight. Rather, I mean the use of data and reasoning to support a claim. Viewed in this manner, argument is not remotely similar to bickering.

Argument is essential in a democracy for two related reasons. First, argument is the primary method that humans have developed for solving problems of any kind. Through the give and take of argument, through testing evidence and reasoning, people can come to the best judgment possible about a given issue. Viewed in this manner, science, the law, and so on are merely specific types of rational argument. In argument of all kinds, we test each other's evidence and reasoning. This method is quite flawed, but a lot better than **not** testing our evidence and reasoning. Two rhetorical questions may make this point clear. What is the alternative to rational argument? Would it be better to rely on "irrational" means of persuasion?

Second, argument is at the core of democratic decision making at all levels because in argument all that matters is what you have to say. Rational argument values every individual the same, regardless of status. It doesn't matter if you are President of the United States, the Queen of England, or a janitor from Manhattan, Kansas. All that matters in argument is what you have to say. In addition, name calling and other divisive and unpleasant forms of rhetoric are not legitimate forms of argument. Thus, rational argument is valued not only because it is the basic human method for making reasonable decisions, but also because it consistent with democratic theory that values people for what they do and say and not their class or wealth.

The Defining Characteristics of Argument Form

A rhetor uses rational argument any time he or she backs up a claim with evidence and reasoning. Thus, the three defining characteristics of argumentative form are *a claim supported by evidence and reasoning.* It is important to understand how these three terms fit together. A claim is the conclusion that is drawn. The evidence is the supporting data the backs up the claim. And the reasoning is the premise that links the evidence to the claim.

Consider the following hypothetical argument:

Since Newt Gingrich was elected Speaker of the House, Republicans have succeeded in passing welfare reform and achieved an historic budget deal that was praised by several Nobel Prize winning economists. He forced Congress to consider 100% of the items in the Contract With America and in terms of his conservative legacy can only be compared to Ronald Reagan. The party should not forget this record in the year 2000.

On the surface, the claim in this argument is that Republicans should remember Gingrich in the year 2000. But because a Presidential election will occur that year, the obvious implication is that Gingrich deserves support for the Republican nomination for

President. Four types of evidence are cited to back up this claim: the expert opinion of Nobel Prize winning economists, examples of legislation passed under his leadership, a statistic about the legislation from the Contract With America that was passed, and a comparison to Ronald Reagan, who is, of course, a much admired figure for conservatives.

The reasoning linking the evidence to the conclusion is implied but not stated. In this case, the reasoning includes the principles that passing the listed legislation was a good idea as well as the assumption that the Speaker of the House deserves credit for legislation passed during the time of his/her service, and general rules for when statistics, examples, and other evidence types are acceptable forms of proof.

The Gingrich example illustrates both the simplicity and complexity of argument. Argument is simple in that it is built on three building blocks: evidence, reasoning, and claims. It is complex in that the relationship among those three elements can occur in many ways. Before considering the ways that argument can be used as a persuasive device, it is important to understand each component part.

Claims

A claim is the conclusion drawn from the evidence and reasoning. Newt Gingrich should be elected President is a claim, as is a statement such as "Katherine Hepburn is the greatest actress in the history of film." It is important to recognize that not all claims are explicitly stated. In some instance the conclusion may be *implied*, but not stated. When Republicans attacked President Clinton with statements such as "I'm not saying that he should be impeached, but we do have to weigh whether we want a perjurer in the White House," they really meant "Of course, he should be impeached." In rare cases, the real claim may be the opposite of what is explicitly stated.

Evidence

Evidence is the data that supports an argument, which explains why it is sometimes labeled as "support material." The architectural analogy in the words "support material" is on point. It is the evidence which supports any argumentative claim.

There are four types of evidence: examples, statistics, comparisons, and statements of authority. An example is a specific instance that is used to prove a broader conclusion. A statement—"I had wonderful risotto at Lidias. What a great restaurant."—is an argumentative claim supported by an example. A statistic is a compilation of examples into a category. When someone cites Michael Jordan's scoring average to support the claim that he was a great ballplayer, that person is using statistics to back up an obviously true conclusion. The third type of evidence—all forms of comparison, including metaphors, similes, analogies, and so forth—backs up a conclusion by noting the points of similarity between two objects, books, ideas, or whatever. Thus, when someone says that "We shouldn't send troops to Macedonia because it would be the new Vietnam," that person is supporting the conclusion that the United States should not send ground troops into Macedonia based on a claim that Macedonia today and South Vietnam in the 1960s and 1970s are similar. The final evidence type is a statement of authority. In argument from authority, the rhetor cites the expertise or experience of someone to support a claim. "Michael Jordan says eat your Wheaties" is an example of argument from authority.

Reasoning

Reasons serve a linking function between evidence and claims. There are three types of reasons. The first type is a simple rule for interpreting what evidence means. Consider the following statement "Joe Jones, of the National Weather Service, concludes that thunder storms are likely." The claim and evidence in this statement are readily apparent. What is the reasoning? The reasoning is so obvious that it is hard to see: "The opinions of experts in a given field function as strong evidence for claims within the field."

The second form of reasoning is as a rule for interpreting what evidence means in a context. Imagine the statement, "Sam Kelly is a great basketball player. He is hitting 37% of his three point shots." Clearly, the argument about Sam is based on the general principle that statistics are a valid form of evidence *and* the rule of thumb known by basketball fans that a 37% shooting percentage for three point shots is a very good one. That figure—37%—would not constitute a good completion rate for a football passer or a good conviction rate for a prosecutor. Thus, the second type of reasoning is a shared rule for what evidence means in a specific context.

The third form of reasoning is a value principle labeling something, someone, or some idea as good or bad. The statement—"Millions are dying in _____. We must act."—illustrates this point. This argument obviously depends upon the shared value assumption that genocide is not acceptable.

In sum, all arguments are made up of data, reasoning and claims and can be broken down into their component parts.

Three Ways that Argument Works as a Persuasive Strategy

There are three primary rhetorical forms that rational argument takes. The first form is evidence-oriented argument, in which the primary strategy is to provide information to persuade the audience to support a position. The second form is enthymematic argument. As noted earlier, an enthymeme is a kind of argument in which the audience fills in some portion of the evidence or reasoning or even the claim. In an enthymeme, the audience participates in creating the argument. The final form of argument, refutation, occurs when the rhetor identifies a claim made by someone with whom he/she disagrees and then systematically refutes that claim.

The three forms of argument have somewhat different persuasive purposes. Evidence-oriented argument is used primarily when the issue is factual and the presentation of new information can persuade the audience to take a particular stand. Enthymematic argument draws upon pre-existing audience knowledge. It works best when reinforcing a view already shared to some extent by the audience.

Refutation is used to deny the position of the other side. Refutation is most likely to be effective when appealing to an undecided audience that is considering two different perspectives. One is unlikely to be able to use refutation to change the mind of someone on the other side of an issue. For example, it is extremely unlikely that someone like Gingrich could use refutation to persuade someone like Ted Kennedy to change his mind on some issue. Kennedy's positions are too firmly established for him to change them easily. On the other hand, refutation may be quite effective when it is used with an undecided audience and when the arguer is refuting someone on the other side and not refuting the views of the audience.

Evidence Types

Earlier, I cited an example to illustrate each of the four main types of evidence. It is now important to consider the strengths and weaknesses of these evidence types as persuasive devices.

Examples ◆ Examples are individual instances of some larger category. Thus, I might cite examples of how homeowners had used guns to protect their homes to defend current gun laws. Examples have several strengths. In many cases, the example includes an interesting tidbit that helps keep the attention of the audience. In addition, examples can be used to personalize an issue. Citing an example of an AIDS victim might humanize the issue for people who knew intellectually about the horror of AIDS, but had not internalized that horror. Finally, examples may be cited to "bring home" an issue to someone. A detailed description of a particular homeless person might do more to bring home the fate of the homeless than a hundred statistics.

At the same time, examples also have weaknesses. For instance, a specific example may be perceived as atypical and thus not taken seriously. And since examples are specific instances, they easily may be refuted with counter-examples. There is also some

---

The Three Persuasive Functions of Argument

1. Evidence-oriented argument persuades people by giving them new evidence about an issue.
2. Enthymematic argument reinforces positions that an audience already accepts.
3. Refutative argument exposes the weakness in the views of the other side in order to support a particular position.

risk that a given example might be too interesting, causing the audience to miss the ultimate point.

Statistics ◆ Statistics are "bunches" of examples combined in a category. A batting average, for instance, is calculated based on the batter's total number of hits in relation to the total number of at bats. All statistics are simply compilations of examples.

One strength of statistics is that they show the size of a problem. It is one thing to cite an example of child abuse and quite another to show that there are many thousands of abused children. Another strength is the perception that statistics are both scientific and objective. Some people think that statistics are "hard facts" based on the best scientific research. Finally, by citing a number of statistics, the rhetor can add to his/her own credibility, since we tend to believe that someone who is aware of statistical data must be well informed on the subject.

Statistics also have weaknesses as a category of evidence. First, statistics are impersonal and dull. No one reads statistical analyses for entertainment. And because statistics reduce individual cases to a numerical representation, they remove any personal dimension from the rhetoric. It often is easier to ignore a statistic showing many people hurt by some problem, then a compelling example of a single victim. Third, statistics may be complicated and difficult to understand. Very few people understand the ins and outs of statistical analysis. Consequently, there may be problems getting an audience to understand exactly what a statistic means. Finally, while people perceive statistics as objective, some have nearly the opposite perception, that statistics can be cited to prove anything. The saying that there are "lies," and still worse, "damn lies," and worst of all, "statistics," is illustrative of that attitude.

Authoritative Evidence ◆ Authoritative evidence involves a citation of someone with either expertise or experience to support a point. An expert is someone who has extensive training in an area and thus can be quoted based on their knowledge. The other form of authoritative evidence is to cite someone with direct personal experience. In the area of prison reform, the expert might have an advanced degree in criminology or have worked in a prison for a decade. On the other hand, a former prisoner, while not an expert, could talk about prisons based upon his/her experience.

In general, experience is a more powerful form of authoritative evidence than expertise if the issue involves a specific event. The person with experience says "I saw it happen." It is difficult to deny such a statement. Expertise is the more powerful form if any kind of generalization is involved. In relation to a generalization, the expert is in a position to speak to the characteristics of the category. He/she has knowledge (expertise) on more than specific instances.

In terms of strengths as a general category of support, authoritative evidence may be used to simplify an issue. If a given position is difficult to explain, because of complexity, one way to deal with the problem is to simply quote an expert. A second strength is that citation of authoritative testimony again adds to the rhetor's credibility. The audience is likely to conclude that someone who can quote many experts, must him/herself be knowledgeable on the subject.

On the other hand, authoritative evidence can be dull. That is why so many more people watch tabloid news shows, rather than *The News Hour* with Jim Lehrer or any other news program that often brings in experts to discuss issues. Authoritative evidence also depends upon the knowledge base of the audience. If the audience doesn't have a minimum understanding of the issue, the expert evidence will be meaningless. And finally, authoritative evidence does not work very well if the audience is not aware of the identity of the expert. Citing the greatest expert in the world on a given subject will not persuade an audience if they do not both know who the expert is and are impressed by his/her qualifications.

Comparisons ◆ Comparisons occur in many forms. Analogies, metaphors, similes, and simple comparisons all fall into this category. There are two main dimensions for understanding all of these different types of comparisons: literal versus figurative and developed versus undeveloped. A literal comparison is used when two ideas, objects, people, etc. from the same category are compared. In a figurative comparison, in contrast, the two objects, ideas, or people being compared are from different categories. It would be a literal comparison to contrast President Reagan with President Clinton. It would be a figurative comparison to say that "Bill Clinton is the Michael Jordan of politics."

Comparisons also differ in terms of degree of development. Sometimes, all of the points of similarity are laid out in great detail. In such a developed comparison, the rhetor makes crystal clear the relationship between the objets being compared. In an undeveloped comparison, by contrast, the comparison is not developed in detail. The comparison of President Clinton to Michael Jordan would be an undeveloped comparison if an arguer simply stated it. On the other hand, if the arguer developed the comparison point by point then it would be a developed comparison. Obviously, undeveloped comparisons often are used in enthymematic argument. It should be remembered that undeveloped comparisons cannot be used effectively unless the audience already has a great deal of knowledge on the subject.

In terms of strengths, comparisons may be used to add interest to otherwise boring material. The comparison of Clinton to Jordan, for instance, draws on public knowledge of the two men and casts the President in a very different light from normal political analysis. Comparisons also are valuable as a way of taking an unfamiliar concept and making it clear. When people first started seeing UFOs, they called them "flying saucers" because everyone could imagine what a flying saucer would look like.

On the other hand, comparisons also have weaknesses. Comparisons are generally perceived as the weakest form of evidence, because they only "compare" two different objects. A second weakness is that a comparison may become trite. For example, the figurative comparison of "life is a journey" has been used so much that it no longer has any power. There is also a danger that a comparison will not "connect" with the audience. If a rhetor compares a contemporary scientist to J. Robert Oppenheimer, that

Figure 1 Strengths and Weaknesses of the Four Types of Evidence

Examples
  Strengths
- Add interest
- Personalize an issue
- Make the issue hit home

  Weaknesses
- May be perceived as atypical
- Easily refuted
- May be "too" interesting and distract from the main message

Statistics
  Strengths
- Show the magnitude of the problem
- Add to the credibilty of the rhetor
- Perceived as hard data

  Weaknesses
- Often are boring
- Impersonal
- Complicated and difficult to understand
- Perceived as a deceptive form of proof

Authoritative Evidence
  Strengths
- Can be used to simplify complicated material
- Adds to the credibility of the rhetor

  Weaknesses
- Often can be dull
- Depends upon the knowledge base of the audience
- Audience may be unaware of the identity of the expert

Comparisons
  Strengths
- Add interest
- Explain complex material in terms that are familiar to the audience

  Weaknesses
- Perceived as the weakest form of proof
- May become trite over time
- May not connect with the audience

comparison will be effective only if the audience knows that Oppenheimer was the head of the Manhattan Project, which developed the atomic bomb. Otherwise, they will say simply, "J. Robert-who?" Finally, as in the case of examples, there is some danger that a comparison can be too interesting. If the members of the audience becomes caught-up in the comparison, they may miss the point that is being made.

Summary of Evidence Types

Which of the evidence types that I have discussed is the strongest? The answer is that none of them is inherently stronger than the other. Rather, the skilled rhetor should use a variety of types of support material in order to keep the attention of his/her audience and should tie that evidence usage to the particular strengths of each of the four types of support. For example, it almost always is smart to combine examples and statistics in support of a claim. The statistics demonstrate the breadth of the problem being discussed, while the examples personalize the issue and add interest.

A good illustration of the strengths and weaknesses of the four types of evidence can be found in an address by Newt Gingrich, which he presented about three months into his service as Speaker of the House.[1] In the address, Gingrich, the first Republican to serve as Speaker in a generation, focused on the accomplishments of the Republican controlled House of Representatives. He commented in great detail about the "Contract With America," a document that he helped to create, which Republicans used as part of the 1994 campaign. In general, the "Contract With America," promised smaller government and cuts in Federal spending and taxation.

Address to the Nation

Newt Gingrich

Good evening. I want to thank you for joining me tonight and for this chance to give you, the American people, a report on the new Congress—what we've been doing, what we hope to do and how we're working to keep faith with what you sent us here to do.   1

But first let me thank the hundreds of thousands of Americans who've written me over the past few months. Your letters are full of good ideas and often moving words of encouragement. This letter, addressed to "Dear Mr. Newt" included a portrait of George Washington. It was sent to me by first grader Steven Franzkowiak from Georgia. And I thank each and every one of you.   2

Delivered in Washington, DC on April 7, 1995.

Last September the House Republicans signed a Contract with America. We signed this contract and made some promises to you and to ourselves. You elected us, and for the last 93 days we have been keeping our word. With your help we're bringing about real change. We made Congress subject to the same laws as everyone else, we cut Congressional committee staffs and budgets by 30%, and we voted on every item in the Contract. And I can tell you tonight we are going to sell one Congressional building and privatize a Congressional parking lot.

3

While we've done a lot, this contract has never been about curing all the ills of the nation. 100 days cannot overturn the neglect of decades. The contract's purpose has been to show that change is possible, that even in Washington you can do what you say you're going to do. In short, we've wanted to prove to you that democracy still has the vitality and the will to do something about the problems facing our nation. And it seems to me, whether you are conservative or liberal, that is a very positive thing.

4

And so I want to talk about the Contract tonight—our successes and our failures, but I also want to talk about something much larger. Because although I've spent the last six months of my life living and breathing and fighting for what's written in this Contract, I know the American people want more than these ten things.

5

So what I want to talk with you about tonight is not just what a new political majority on Capitol Hill has accomplished in 100 days, but how all of us together—Republicans and Democrats alike—must totally remake the federal government—to change the very way it thinks, the way it does business, the way it treats it's citizens. After all, the purpose of changing government is to improve the lives of our citizens, strengthen the future of our children, make our neighborhoods safe and build a better country. Government is not the end; it is the means.

6

We Americans wake up every morning, go to work, take our kids to school, fix dinner, do all the things we expect of ourselves and yet something isn't quite right. There is no confidence that government understands the values and realities of our lives. The government is out of touch and out of control. It is in need of deep and deliberate change. Now when that change is accomplished, then perhaps Americans will be able to sleep a little better at night and wake up feeling less anxious about their futures.

7

I represented the people who worked at the Ford plant in Hapeville, Georgia. The Ford Motor Company, like all of the domestic auto industry, faced the need to change in order to keep up with tougher competition. Today, they produce twice as many cars per employee at three times the quality. General Motors and Chrysler are doing the same thing. So are America's small businesses. They're all rethinking the way they operate. Should government be any different? . . . Of course not.

8

We sincerely believe we can reduce spending and at the same time make government better. Virtually every institution in America, except government, has reengineered themselves to become more efficient over the last decade. They cut spending, provided better products, better education and better service for less.

9

But I believe we must remake government for reasons much larger than saving money or improving services. No civilization can survive with 12-year-olds having babies, with 15-year-olds killing each other, with 17-year-olds dying of AIDS, with 18-year-olds getting diplomas they can't read. Every night on every local news we see the human tragedies that have grown out of the current welfare state.

10

And as a father of two daughters, I cannot ignore the terror and worry parents in our inner cities must feel for their children. Within a half mile of this capital, drugs, violence & despair threaten the lives of our citizens. We cannot ignore our fellow Americans in such desperate straits by thinking that huge amounts of tax dollars release us from our moral responsibility to help these parents and children. There is no reason the federal government must keep an allegiance to failure. With goodwill, with common sense, with the courage to change, we can do better for all Americans.   11

Another fact we cannot turn our head away from is this, no truly moral civilization would burden it's children with the economic excesses of the parents and grandparents. This talk of burdening future generations is not just rhetoric; we're talking about hard, economic consequences that will limit our children's and grandchildren's standard of living. Yet that is what we are doing. For the children trapped in poverty, for the children whose futures are trapped by a government debt they're going to have to pay, we have an obligation tonight to talk about the legacy we're leaving our children and grandchildren, an obligation to talk about the deliberate remaking of our government. This change will not be accomplished in the next 100 days, but we must start by recognizing the moral and economic failure of the current methods of government.   12

In these last 100 days, we have begun to change these failed methods. We outlined 10 major proposals in the Contract that would begin to break the logjam of the past; the House passed nine of them. First, we passed the Shays Act which makes the Congress obey all the laws that other Americans have to obey. The House passed it, the Senate passed it and the President signed it. So that's one law signed, sealed and delivered.   13

We passed a balanced budget amendment in the House with bipartisan support; it has been temporarily defeated in the Senate by one vote. Although constitutional amendments are harder to get through Congress because they require two-thirds vote rather than a simple majority, don't be discouraged. Senator Dole has said he will call it up for another vote. The momentum is with us and with your help and your voice I believe it is possible this amendment will pass later this Congress.   14

As promised, we introduced a constitutional amendment on term limits, but we failed even though 85% of House Republicans voted for it. Again, that two-thirds vote. There have been 180 bills introduced to limit congressional terms over America's history, but not one of them ever made it to the House floor . . . until last week. I pledge to you that term limits will be the first vote of the next Congress, so keep the pressure on, keep your hopes up.   15

In both the House and the Senate we passed a line item veto, just as you asked. It's remarkable that a Republican House and a Republican Senate are giving such a strong tool to a president of the other party. I believe it shows our good faith and determination to cut spending.   16

Other Contract proposals have passed the House and are being worked on in the Senate. We passed regulatory reform, legal reform and welfare reform. We passed a $500 tax credit per child. We passed an increase in the earning limit for senior citizens, so they won't have their social security checks cut if they earn extra money. We passed a capital gains tax cut and indexed these gains to spur the savings and investments that create jobs.   17

Even with all these successes and others, the Contract with America is only a beginning. It is the preliminary skirmish to the big battles yet to come.   18

The big battles will deal with how we remake the Government of the United States. The measure of everything we do will be whether we are creating a better future with more opportunities for our children.   19

New ideas, new ways and old-fashioned common sense can improve government while   20
reducing its costs. Let me give you an example. The United States Government is the largest
purchaser of vacuum tubes in the Western world. This is a Federal Aviation Administration
vacuum tube. Good solid 1930s technology. This is the updated mid-1950s version. When you
fly in America, vacuum tubes in the air traffic control system keep you safe. Our purchasing
rules are so complicated and so wasteful that our government has not been able in seven
years to figure out how to replace vacuum tubes with this. This is a microchip that has the
computing power of 3 million vacuum tubes. So today's government operates this way; after
we remake it, the government of the future will operate this way.

My point is this: this same reliance on the obsolete pervades most of the federal govern-   21
ment—not just in regard to computers but in regard to its thinking, its attitudes, its approaches to problems.

It's one thing if we're talking about vacuum tubes, but this backward thinking is entirely   22
something else if we're talking about human lives. The purpose of all this change is not simply a better government; it is a better America.

A truly compassionate government would replace the welfare state with opportunity.   23
The welfare system's greatest cost is the human cost to the poor. In the name of "compassion"
we have funded a system that is cruel and destroys families. Its failure is reflected by the violence, brutality, child abuse and drug addiction in every local TV news broadcast.

Poor Americans are trapped in unsafe government housing, saddled with rules that are   24
anti-work, anti-family and anti-property. Let me give you some statistics on this failure. Welfare spending now exceeds $300 billion a year. Yet despite all the trillions that have been
spent since 1970, the number of children in poverty has increased 40%.

On this chart, you'll notice that welfare spending goes up, and so does children born out-   25
side marriage. Year by year they track each other. The more tax money we spend on welfare,
the more children who are born without benefit of family and without strong bonds of love
and nurturing. If money alone were the answer, this would be a paradise.

Since money is not the answer, it should be clear we have a moral imperative to remake   26
the welfare system so every American can lead a full life. After all, we believe that all men and
women are endowed by our Creator with certain unalienable rights among which are life, liberty and the pursuit of happiness. We are determined to remake this government until every
child of every racial background, in every neighborhood in America, knows that he or she has
all the opportunities of an American.

I believe we have to do a number of things to become an opportunity society. We must   27
restore freedom by ending bureaucratic micromanagement here in Washington. As any good
business leader will tell you, decisions should be made as closely as possible to the source of
the problem. This country is too big and too diverse for Washington to have the knowledge
to make the right decision on local matters; we've got to return power back to you—to your
families, your neighborhoods, your local and state governments. We need to promote economic growth by reducing regulation, taxation and frivolous lawsuits. Everywhere I, go Americans complain about an overly complicated tax code and an arrogant, unpredictable and
unfair Internal Revenue Service. This summer we will begin hearings on bold, decisive reform
of the income tax system. We're looking at a simplified flat tax and other ways to bring some
sense to the disorder and inequity of our tax system. Another reason for optimism is the
tremendous opportunities being created by the information technologies. Tremendous is a
big word so let me show you an example. This is a traditional telephone cable. This is a fiber

optic cable. You can barely see it. This almost invisible fiber optic cable is equal to 64 of these big bulky traditional cables. Now that is a tremendous opportunity. With these break-throughs the most rural parts of America can be connected electronically to the best learn-ing, the best health care and the best work opportunities in the world. Distance learning can offer new hope to the present inner city neighborhood, the poorest Indian reservation and the smallest rural community. Distance medicine can bring the best specialist in the world to your health clinic, your hospital.

Furthermore, the breakthroughs in molecular medicine may cure Alzheimer's, eliminate many genetic defects and offer new cures for diabetes, cancer and heart disease. These breakthroughs combined with preventive care and medical innovations can create better health for all Americans. And we will pass a reform so that when you change jobs you can't be denied insurance even if you or your family have health problems. 28

We will improve Medicare by offering a series of new Medicare options that will increase senior citizens control over their own health care and guarantee them access to the best and most modern systems of health research and health innovation. My father, my mother, and my mother-in-law all rely on Medicare. I know how crucial the Medicare system is to senior Americans, and we will insure that it continues to provide the care our seniors need with more choices at less cost to the elderly. 29

All around us opportunities for a better life are being developed but our government all too often ignores or even blocks them. We need those breakthroughs which create new jobs, new health, and new learning, to give us the opportunity and growth to deal with our bud-getary problems. We must get our national finances in order. The time has come to balance the federal budget and to free our children from the burdens upon their prosperity and their lives. 30

This is a Congressional voting card. This card goes into a box on the House floor and the computer records the member's vote. The Congressional voting card is the most expensive credit card in the world. For two generations it has been used to pile up trillions in debt that our children and grandchildren will eventually have to repay. 31

Now a big debt has a big impact. To make such numbers real, let me give you an exam-ple. If you have a child or grandchild born this year, that child is going to pay $187,000 in taxes in their lifetime to pay their share of the interest on the debt. Yes, you heard me right, $187,000 in taxes, in their lifetimes—that's over $3,500 in taxes every year of their working lives just to pay interest on the debt we are leaving them. That's before they are taxed to pay for Social Security or Medicare, education or highways or police or the national defense. You know and I know, that's just not fair. It was once an American tradition to pay off the mort-gage and leave the children the farm. Now we seem to be selling the farm and leaving our children the mortgage. By 1997, we will pay more for interest on the debt than for the na-tional defense. That's right, more of our tax money will be spent to pay interest on govern-ment bonds than we'll pay for the Army, the Navy, the Air Force, the Marine Corps, the intelligence agencies and the defense bureaucracy combined. 32

Okay, Social Security. I want to reassure all of you who are on Social Security, or will soon retire, that your Social Security is fine. No one will touch your Social Security, period. But we must make sure that the baby boomers' retirements, which are coming up in the next cen-tury, are as secure as their parents'. Because the money the government supposedly has been putting aside from the baby boomers' Social Security taxes is not there. The government has been borrowing that money to pay for the budget deficit. The Social Security trust fund is 33 simply I.O.U.s from the U.S. Treasury. So when the baby boomers get set to retire, where's the money to pay them going to come from? Well, can't the government just borrow more money? The honest answer is no. No system, no country is wealthy enough to have unlimited borrowing.

But the answer is clear. The key to protecting the baby boomers' Social Security is to bal- 34 ance the budget. That way by the time the baby boomers retire the government will be financially sound enough to pay them. The problem is not Social Security. After all, Social Security would be fine if the federal government would stop borrowing the money. The government can stop borrowing the money when we balance the budget. It is just that simple.

Our goals are simple. We don't want our children to drown in debt. We want baby 35 boomers to be able to retire with the same security as their parents. We want our senior Americans to be able to rely on Medicare without fear.

These are the reasons why, as Franklin Delano Roosevelt said, "Our generation has a rendez- 36 vous with destiny." This is the year we rendezvous with our destiny to establish a clear plan to balance the budget. It can no longer be put off. That is why I am speaking to you so frankly.

Next month we will propose a budget that is balanced over seven years. The budget can 37 be balanced even with the problems of the federal government. It can be balanced without touching a penny of Social Security and without raising taxes. In fact, spending overall can go up every year. We simply must limit annual spending increases to about 3% between now and 2002.

The key is the willingness to change, to set priorities, to redesign the government, to rec- 38 ognize that this is not the 1960s or '70s but the 1990s and we need a government to match the times. As I've said, Social Security is off the table. But that leaves a lot on the table—corporate welfare, subsidies of every special interest. Defense is on the table. I'm a hawk, but a cheap hawk. As the budget battle rages over the coming months, you will hear screams from the special interest groups. I'm sure you've already heard the dire cries that we were going to take food out of the mouths of schoolchildren. That we were going to feed them ketchup. The fact of the matter is that all we did was vote to increase school lunch money four and a half percent every year for five years and give the money to the states to spend, because we thought they would do a better job than the federal government of ensuring that the children's meals were nutritional.

We believe that if local parents, local school boards and local state legislators visit their 39 children's local schools, they will know firsthand about their children's lunches. Our critics believe that if the school hires a clerk, who doesn't cook anything, to fill out a report to go to the state clerk, who doesn't cook anything but fills out a report so that the national clerk in Washington, who doesn't cook anything, can write you a letter about the school they didn't visit in the county they've never been able to reassure you about the lunch they've never seen. That is the difference in our two approaches.

All I ask is that as we work to balance the budget that you verify the facts on both sides. 40 And then you decide which approach is best.

Whatever the arguments this remains a country of unparalleled possibilities. I was talk- 41 ing the other day to a fellow who does business in Europe. He said what impresses people overseas is that the U.S. can change faster than anybody. That's why we're competitive once again in the world. We as a people have the natural ability to respond to change. That is what we do best when the government is not in the way. Our potential is as great and prosperous as it's ever been in our history. From now on all roads lead forward.

This job can't be done in Washington. We need your participation in a new dialogue. I   42
hope every high school and college student will spend some class time in April or early May
looking at the impact of the deficit on their young lives. We are making this speech and our
briefing on the budget available through the Library of Congress at Thomas on the Internet.
Both are also available from your Congressman or Congresswoman's office. We want every
American to have the facts and participate in the new dialogue.

If I had one message for this country on this day when we celebrate the act of keeping   43
our word, it would be a simple message: Idealism is American. To be romantic is American. It's
okay to be a skeptic, but don't be a cynic. It's okay to raise good questions, but don't assume
the worst. It's okay to report difficulties, but it's equally good to report victories.

Yes, we have problems, and of course it's going to be difficult to enact these things. That's   44
the American way. And of course, we're going to have to work hard, and of course we're going to have to negotiate with the President, and of course the American people are going to
have to let their will be known. But why should we be afraid of that? That is freedom.

I am here tonight to say that we're going to open a dialogue, because we want to create   45
a new partnership with the American people, a plan to remake the government and balance
the budget that is the American peoples' plan—not the House Republican plan, not the Gingrich plan, but the plan of the American people. And it is in that spirit of committing ourselves idealistically, committing ourselves romantically, believing in America, that we
celebrate having kept our word. And we promise to begin a new partnership, so that together
we and the American people can give our children and our country a new birth of freedom.

Thank you, and good night.   46

◆◆◆

Analysis of the Rational Argument in Gingrich's Speech

In his address to the nation, Gingrich utilizes all three of the sub-types of persuasive
rational argument. First, Gingrich clearly relies on enthymematic argument. In paragraph 7, he comments that for the American people "There is no confidence that government understands the values and realities of our lives. The government is out of
touch and out of control." This statement makes sense only if the audience fills in information on various failures of government. It also depends upon a general value position that "big government" is both ineffective and often restricts human freedom. A
little later, in paragraph 10, he notes that "No civilization can survive with 12-year-olds
having babies, with 15-year-olds killing each other, with 17-year-olds dying of AIDS,
with 18-year-olds getting diplomas they can't read." Clearly, Gingrich is claiming that
there are major social problems in our society, but he cites no specific evidence to back
up his claim. He obviously assumes that his audience will fill in examples from news
reports of the 15-year-olds killing each other and so forth.

As is often the case, Gingrich's use of enthymematic argument is designed to reinforce views that members of the implied audience already hold. It is clear that liberals

are not part of his implied audience. They would not accept the premises, which Gingrich seems to presume are true. On the other hand, conservatives and some moderates might find those premises quite credible, especially the assumptions he makes about the existence of serious social problems in this nation. Therefore, Gingrich's use of enthyematic argument is designed primarily to reinforce the views of that subset of his national audience that already agrees with him.

Gingrich also uses refutative argument, although it is not by any means a dominant strategy. In paragraph 25, he cites a chart to refute the liberal view that one problem with welfare spending is inadequate monetary support. According to Gingrich:

> On this chart, you'll notice that welfare spending goes up, and so does children born outside marriage. Year by year they track each other. The more tax money we spend on welfare, the more children who are born without benefit of family and without strong bonds of love and nurturing. If money alone were the answer, this would be a paradise.

With this statement, Ginrich implicitly states the liberal view of welfare spending and then refutes it.

As I explained earlier, refutation works best with an undecided audience. A strong proponent of increased social spending will not be convinced by Gingrich's chart. That person will admit that both welfare spending and the number of kids born out of marriage have gone up, but deny that there is any causal relationship between the two occurrences. The liberal, in all likelihood, will conclude that both increased welfare spending and increased illegitimacy are linked to social problems that demand more not less money.

On the other hand, Gingrich's refutation may work well for undecided viewers. For this group, his chart may indicate that more money is not the answer to the welfare problem. And the chart would reinforce the views of conservatives on that same point.

While Gingrich relies on both refutation and enthymematic argument, his dominant argumentative strategy is to present evidence to reinforce his message. In the next section, I discuss his use of each of the four evidence types in turn.

Examples ◆ Gingrich cites a host of examples in the speech. In paragraph three, he tells the audience that Congress already has made major progress in carrying out the Contract With America and cites the decision to "sell one Congressional building and privatize a Congressional parking lot" as proof of this claim. In paragraph 8 he refers to the example of a Ford auto plant in his district that has dramatically increased productivity. He also cites examples of action on various bills in Congress and assumes that his audience fills in specific examples related to drugs, crime, and so forth in the passage I cited earlier.

Gingrich's use of examples illustrates the strengths and weaknesses of examples as a type of evidence. The Ford Motor example is a particularly good one because it brings home the point that even very large organizations can change to adapt to the new age. This example also adds interest to his speech. On the other hand, Gingrich does not do a good job of using examples to personalize the issues. He could have cited specific people to personalize the issues that he cares about, but he does not do that. Moreover, some of his examples may seem either atypical or frankly trivial. For instance, the examples of the Congressional building to be sold and the parking lot that will be privatized are both weak. Viewers might respond by saying "big deal."

Overall, Gingrich does not fully utilize the power of examples in his speech. He does not use them to personalize complex issues or do much in the way of adding interest to his remarks. Additionally, several of his examples may seem atypical.

Statistics ◆ Gingrich does not rely heavily on statistics. He does cite the fact that the United States spends $300 billion a year on welfare and also the fact that the number of children in poverty has increased 40% since 1970 (paragraph 24). He also tells the audience that a new child born this year will "pay $187,000 in taxes in their lifetimes" (paragraph 32). A few other uses of statistics are found in the speech.

Statistics are most powerful when they show us the size of the problem and provide new information that we didn't know about previously. In this case, Gingrich's use of statistics fits the first criteria, but probably not the second. For example, the $187,000 figure shows the magnitude of Federal taxation over the life of an average person. On the other hand, it is hardly late-breaking news to say that Americans pay a lot of taxes. Since Gingrich does not include new statistical material that would be unfamiliar to an audience, he is unlikely to be able to persuade viewers who have different views than he does. This means that Gingrich's statistics are likely to work best for reinforcing the perspective of that portion of the audience that already agrees with him.

On the other hand, it is important to note that Gingrich largely avoids the main pitfalls associated with use of statistics. He does not use so many that he makes the material dull. He also uses information that is generally easy to follow and, as I will demonstrate in a moment, does a good job of combining different forms of evidence to achieve maximum effect.

Authority ◆ Gingrich does not cite authorities to any significant degree. On the other hand, for some members of his audience, Gingrich himself may function as an authority. As the leader of the "Contract With America," Congressional campaign and the new Speaker of the House, Gingrich undoubtedly has a great deal of credibility with fellow conservatives and Republicans. However, Gingrich clearly lacks authority with liberals and Democrats. Thus, Gingrich's use of himself as an authority may be effective for reinforcing the views of that portion of the audience that already agrees with what he has to say, but it will have little effect on the remainder of his audience. In fact, for those who are undecided or disagree with him, Gingrich's failure to cite authorities other than himself may be perceived as a significant failing or even as a sign of arrogance.

Comparisons ◆ Gingrich relies heavily on both literal and figurative comparisons. For example, he says that "By 1997, we will pay more for interest on the debt than for the national defense" (paragraph 32). In this statement, Gingrich draws a literal comparison between the amount of money that the United States spends on defense and on interest payments on the national debt. With this comparison, Gingrich is making the point that the debt is too high.

While Gingrich uses a few literal comparisons, he relies more heavily on figurative analogies. In some cases, these comparisons are undeveloped. For example, in paragraph 35 he says, "We don't want our children to drown in debt." Here, he compares the size of the debt with water so deep that a person could drown in it. In other cases, he develops the figurative comparison in more depth. For example, Gingrich develops a two-part comparison between the current out-dated Federal Government and a new innovative Federal Government that will be brought into being by Republican leadership:

> New ideas, new ways and old-fashioned common sense can improve government while reducing its costs. Let me give you an example. The United States Government is the largest purchaser of vacuum tubes in the Western world. This is a Federal Aviation Administration vacuum tube. [He holds up a vacuum tube]. Good solid 1930s technology. This is the updated mid-1950s version. When you fly in America, vacuum tubes in the air traffic control system keep you safe. Our purchasing rules are so complicated and so wasteful that our government has not been able in seven years to figure out how to replace vacuum tubes with this. This is a microchip that has the computing power of 3 million vacuum tubes. [He holds up a microchip]. So today's government operates this way [like a vacuum tube]; after we remake it, the government of the future will operate this way [like a microchip]. (paragraph 20)

With this complicated comparison, Gingrich argues that Republicans can remake government to transform an antiquated Federal "vacuum tube" into an efficient Federal "microchip." Part of the appeal of the comparison was that Gingrich held up a vacuum tube and a microchip as he explained his point.

Gingrich clearly relies on comparisons to add interest to his speech. The vacuum tube/microchip analogy is obviously designed to achieve that aim. He also hopes that the comparisons can make unfamiliar material seem familiar. At the same time, there are significant weaknesses in his use of comparisons. For example, the vacuum tube/microchip comparison works best for that portion of his audience which knows something about high tech products. It will not resonate very well for others. And many in his audience may react that the Federal Government is not very similar to either a microchip or a vacuum tube. If Gingrich has a way to dramatically improve the functioning of the Federal Government some might ask, why doesn't he tell us about it?

Summary of Gingrich's Use of Evidence ◆ Gingrich cites a variety of examples, statistics and comparisons. He also sets himself up as an authority on government. In general, his evidence usage, along with his use of enthymemes and refutation, was well designed to reinforce the views of those who already agreed with his perspective. On the other hand, the evidence he cited was not well designed to persuade his opponents or the undecided. Part of the problem is that he provides very little evidence that would have been truly new to the audience. In order to persuade people to change their minds, the rhetor must provide substantial new material. Gingrich did not do that.

Another weakness of Gingrich's evidence usage is that he did not present adequate examples to personalize the various issues with which he was concerned. Nor did he use experts to add to his credibility and simplify complex issues. In relying so heavily on his own expertise, he all but guaranteed that the speech would be effective only with those who already were "true believers" in the Republican revolution.

Strengths and Weaknesses of Rational Argument as a Rhetorical Strategy

Is rational argument a powerful strategy for producing persuasion? There is inconsistent evidence on this point. On the one hand, there is a large amount of research indicating that rational argument is rarely an effective strategy for producing persuasion. A great deal of research in political science indicates that the public in general is not very well informed and rarely makes decisions based on the issues.[2] Certainly, advertisers (in politics and elsewhere) apparently do not believe that most people are heavily influenced by rational argument. If they believed that, they would orient their advertising towards rational argumentative strategies and take a kind of *Consumer Reports* approach to selling products and services. Clearly, few commercials use this kind of argumentative approach. Instead, they tend to rely on humor, sexuality, and mini-narratives that tie to basic needs and values.

There is also social scientific research indicating that rational argument has relatively little impact on the perceived persuasiveness of a given work.[3] Research in this tradition has focused on whether citing evidence adds to the persuasiveness of the message. Several researchers have found no significant effect, a conclusion that would seem to deny that rational argument is a powerful persuasive strategy.

On the other hand, there is a great deal of evidence indicating that people are heavily influenced by rational means of persuasion. A research tradition has developed in political science indicating that the issues make a great deal of difference in politics.[4] In this view, beginning in the 1960s a large percentage of the public began to pay attention to the issues and make decisions based on them. Proponents of the issue-oriented perspective argue that while the public may not know the details about specific issues, they are informed about the big picture.

There is also research from what is known as "persuasive argument theory" which indicates that people are moved by the weight of available evidence. This research, which has been conducted on "problem-solving" groups, suggests that people in the group are likely to choose the particular alternative that is supported by the largest number of valued arguments and that new information is particularly important in this process.[5] Persuasive argument theory seems to suggest that people are highly rational and that, therefore, rational argument is a very powerful strategy.

How can the two research traditions concerning the power of rational argument be reconciled? One possibility is that both sides are partially right. Rational argument is an extremely powerful means of persuasion, but only in limited circumstances.

What are those limitations? First, rational argument does not work very well on issues that are tied to basic values. The reason is that rational argument applies to the world of facts. Value claims, by contrast, are not fundamentally about facts. In the debate about abortion, for example, the fundamental conflict is between the values of freedom and life. Pro-choice advocates say that the woman's right to choose is the pre-eminent value. Anti-abortion advocates say that life is the preeminent value. There is no argumentative means of resolving this conflict.

Second, rational argument also fails, especially in the short-term, if the audience already possesses a strongly-held position on the subject. This is why rational argument works better in the problem-solving group context than in politics. No matter how good the argument, no Democrat is going to persuade Newt Gingrich to change his mind on a major point. Nor is Gingrich going to persuade Ted Kennedy to change his views and become a Reagan Republican. The same point could be said of any issue on which people already have a fixed point of view.

However, when people either have not decided what they think or are not fixed in their viewpoint, rational argument can be very persuasive. In the problem-solving group context the aim is to solve some problem (finding the cheapest pizza for a large party, for instance). In such a situation, rational argument can be quite persuasive, because everyone wants the same goal, good pizza at a cheap price.

Third, rational argument does not work very well if the issue is highly complicated. On highly complex issues, the audience may not be able to understand the details of the argument being presented. That was the point that I made in relation to nuclear power earlier in this section. The complexity of the issue makes it almost impossible to effectively use rational argument as a primary strategy.[6]

Fourth, rational argument is unlikely to be effective, if the audience is not at least somewhat concerned with the issue. If the audience lacks interest, they are likely to turn off the argumentative discussion. This point is illustrated in relation to issues such as the ozone layer. Few people find a discussion of the ozone layer to be extremely exciting. This means that it is difficult to get the attention of the public in relation to that issue. If there were some dramatic incident involving ozone depletion, however, then it might be possible to influence public attitudes via rational argument.

Finally, rational argument is unlikely to be effective if the issue is a familiar one and there is no new data to be presented. On an issue like capital punishment, for example, the basic positions of the two sides are quite familiar. The pro side says that capital punishment is justified by horrible crimes and deters criminal behavior. The anti side denies that capital punishment is effective, labels it as barbarous, and says that innocent people sometimes are executed. We all have heard these arguments many times. Therefore, rhetoric presenting one of these positions is unlikely to change anyone's minds, unless some new material is added. This principle is directly supported by persuasive argument theory, which finds that new information is especially important in influencing group attitudes. If there were new information, even on a tired issue like capital punishment, it might be possible to alter public opinion.

Of course, the above principles can be turned around to define when rational argument is likely to be effective. It will work best on factual (non-value) issues which are not too complicated, on which the audience has some interest, but does not yet have a firm position, and where there is new material to be considered.

One other point is relevant. Rational argument is especially powerful over time. When Tiger Woods turned pro, some doubted that he would be one of the dominant golfers on the PGA tour. Others said he would be good, but it would take time. After he won the Masters in his first try, these critics of Woods said, "Never mind!" In the long-term, on any dispute, being right is a powerful thing indeed.

Conclusion

In this chapter, I defined the characteristics of argumentative form, identified the three primary ways that argument can function as a persuasive device, discussed the strengths and weaknesses of the four types of evidence as persuasive devices, and outlined the situations in which rational argument is likely to be persuasive.

Notes

1. The speech was presented to a national television audience on April 7, 1995.
2. A classic work in this area is Angus Campbell, Philip E. Converse, Warren E. Miller and Donald E. Stokes, *The American Voter* (New York: Wiley, 1960). Also see Gerald Pomper, *Voter's Choice* (New York: Harper & Row, 1975).
3. Most of this research was conducted in the 1950s and 1960s. For a review see James C. McCroskey, "A Summary of Experimental Research on the Effects of Evidence in Persuasive Communication," *Quarterly Journal of Speech* 55 (1969): 169–176.
4. The classic work on this theme is Norman H. Nie, Sidney Verba, and John R. Petrocik, *The Changing American Voter* (Cambridge: Harvard University Press, 1976).
5. See for instance Eugene Burnstein and Amiram Vinokur, "What a Person Thinks Upon Learning He Has Chosen Differently From Others: Nice Evidence for the Persuasive-Arguments Explanation of Choice Shifts," *Journal of Experimental Social Psychology* 11 (1975): 412–426.

6. In "A Reanalysis of the Argumentation at Three Mile Island," I considered public debate and discussion about the Three Mile Island nuclear disaster. I discovered that the accident had been misunderstood by the public through no fault of their own. In fact, rather than a catastrophe, the accident at Three Mile Island indicated that the nuclear safety systems at the reactor site worked well. The essay can be found in *Argument in Controversy: Proeceedings of the 7th SCA-AFA Conference on Argumentation*, Donn Parson ed., (Annandale, Virginia: SCA, 1991): 277–283.

CHAPTER FIVE

Narrative Forms of Rhetoric

Narrative rhetoric tells a story and is one of the most effective forms of persuasion.[1] Some of the most powerful rhetoricians in human history have been storytellers. For example, Jesus told stories in the form of parables to his disciples. The result of these stories was the creation of one of the world's great religions. This example is not unique. In fact, much of our most powerful religious rhetoric in Christianity and other religions has been narrative. The same is true all across human society. Narrative has been and is a powerful rhetorical form in politics, business, mass movements, and elsewhere.

The power of narrative rhetoric to bring a point home to an audience is illustrated by the success of one of the most powerful contemporary rhetoricians, Steven Spielberg. Thousands of books have been written about the Holocaust and World War II, some of them by distinguished scholars and academics. Yet, it is two movies that have made these subjects come alive for most Americans: *Schindler's List* and *Saving Private Ryan*. Spielberg is not our greatest historian or theoretician of the Holocaust or D-day. But he is unquestionably our greatest contemporary rhetorician. What Spielberg understands is the power of a well-told narrative to bring a subject alive for an audience. While Spielberg is an accomplished storyteller and a powerful rhetorician, he is not unique. Throughout human history, there have been many storytellers who used the power of narration to influence a group, a tribe, a city, or a nation.

The power of narrative rhetoric makes it important to understand the components of narrative and the way that narrative functions. It is also important to recognize that narrative is not always a force for good, as it has been in Spielberg's wonderful films about the Holocaust and World War II. Sometimes, narrative can be used for evil ends. It must be remembered that Hitler was an accomplished storyteller. He created a story in which Germany was a victim of terrible mistreatment from the Allies at the end of the First World War and from one group of her own citizens, the Jews. In this story, a revitalized Aryan people would cleanse Germany of those who had weakened her and bring the nation to dominance in the world. Hitler's story was not remotely accurate, but it certainly was effective in creating a mass movement that ultimately took control of Germany and caused World War II and the Holocaust. Stories can be powerful forces for good *and* evil.

In this chapter, I sketch the characteristics of narrative rhetoric, beginning with a discussion of narrative form. I then identify the functions fulfilled by narrative and apply the formal/functional components of narrative to the testimony of John Anjain before a United States Senate Committee.

Formal Components of Narrative Rhetoric

In narrative rhetoric a story is told in order to make some point. In some cases, the entire work of rhetoric is a story and the main point is implied. For example, Harriet Beecher Stowe's novel, *Uncle Tom's Cabin* was a biting attack on slavery. In other instances, the rhetor may use a number of small stories to make a point. Ronald Reagan often used these micro-narratives[2] to back up his conservative perspective. In still other instances, the rhetor may refer to, but not tell in any detail, a widely known story. This type of narrative is somewhat similar to enthymematic argument and is used most often in reference to the dominant stories in any organization or society. For the United States as a whole, for instance, this approach might be used with stories of the pioneers or the founding of the nation, because these narratives are familiar to everyone.

What makes up a narrative? Narrative rhetoric is defined by four components: plot, setting, characters, and theme.

Plot ◆ The plot is the story-line. It is what happens in the tale. While there are many possible types of plots, it is important to recognize that principles of plot development demand that a story be introduced by some sort of scene that sets the stage for the plot that follows. The plot then builds gradually to greater and greater conflict. Ultimately, a point of greatest conflict or tension is reached (the climax), and the conflict or tension is then resolved. This is followed by a return to normalcy.

The basic plot pattern I have described can take many specific forms, but the overall design is found in most narrative rhetoric. The pattern typifies adventure stories (the *Star Wars* films for instance), serious drama, and even comedy (from Shakespeare to Tim Allen). This general plot pattern is tied to the logic of storytelling. Clearly, the story would not be very exciting if the biggest battle occurred in the first scene. In that case, there would be no conflict to resolve, no interesting character development, and so on. The logic of telling a good story requires that the point of greatest conflict must come at the end. Similarly, the pattern of rising action, which I have described, is generally present, not because life always works that way, but because that pattern works best to gradually increase tension and excitement in the audience over time.

It is important to note at this point that what makes a good plot is not necessarily what makes a true story. Real life rarely develops in the set pattern of plot development I have described. In real life, the point of greatest conflict may be in the beginning, the end, or anywhere in between.

Scene ◆ The second component of narrative rhetoric is a scene. This is the place/time where the story occurs. The scene can be literally anywhere. For example, Robert A.

Heinlein's acclaimed science fiction novel, *Job: A Comedy of Justice* appears to be set in the United States in the near future. In fact, as becomes clear in the middle of the book, the story is set in an alternative universe. As this example makes clear, a story can be set in any place that can be imagined by the human mind. Many stories have been set, for example, in heaven or hell.

One of the reasons that narrative rhetoric is so important is that it can transport the reader/viewer/listener to a very different place and time. It can take us out of the contemporary United States and transport us mentally to witness ethnic cleansing in Kosovo or Rwanda, or to see what life was like in the death camps or in Elizabethan England.

Characters ◆ The third component of any narrative consists of the characters. Narratives generally revolve around the conflict between the protagonist (also known as the hero) and the antagonist or villain. Other characters may serve a variety of functions including as helpers of the hero/villain, innocent victims of some act of the villain, people to represent a given viewpoint and so forth.

One point concerning characterization is particularly important from a persuasive point of view. As a rule, the protagonist will be either a hero who is greater than average people or he/she will be a representative of the people. The first type of protagonist serves as a model to be followed or emulated. In the language of a recent popular television commercial, we all want to "be like Mike." Mike (Michael Jordan) is a hero to be imitated. The second type of protagonist is used in a rhetoric of identification. In that case, the protagonist is not greater than all of us, but he/she is one of us and serves as an example of what an average person can accomplish. We don't so much admire this second type of protagonist as identify with them. We see the similarity between their life and our own.

Thus, characters both act in and are acted upon in the plot and serve as models to be imitated or as average folk with whom to identify.

Theme ◆ The final component of narrative rhetoric is the theme. The theme is the message; it is the point of the story. The theme is built by the combination of the actions of the characters in a given setting. It is constructed out of the previous three elements. Some stories have powerful persuasive messages. For example, the theme of the 1980s TV movie, *The Day After,* was that nuclear war would be a very bad thing and the United States should work harder to avoid any risk of it. As this case illustrates, in some works of rhetoric the theme may be immediately obvious. In others, the theme may be less obvious, but still present. Tim Allen's television show, *Home Improvement,* gets laughs by telling stories about how Allen's character gets into trouble by trying to be macho. On the surface, the show glories in everything that is male. Below the surface, it has almost a feminist message in the way it makes fun of male stereotypes.

It is in relation to theme that narrative rhetoric and narrative literature differ. Narrative rhetoric of necessity has a persuasive theme. In contrast, some narrative literature has such a theme, but it is not required. Of course, a work of narrative may fall into the classification of both literature and rhetoric. Mark Twain's novel *Huckleberry Finn,* which has been called the greatest American novel, is both a work of fiction and a work of rhetoric. As rhetoric, Twain is among other things, attacking racism.

Functions of Narrative Rhetoric

Narrative rhetoric can function in six different ways to produce persuasion. First, narratives add interest to material that otherwise might bore an audience. Rhetorical theorist and critic Walter Fisher argues that humans are inherently story-telling animals.[3] He means that one of the defining characteristics of being human is telling stories. Fisher is clearly onto something. In all cultures and throughout history, human beings have told stories to amuse, inform, and persuade.

One sign of the human affection for stories is the dominance of the form in the media. When was the last time that a hit TV show or a big summer movie concerned a topic like "Statistics on a Major Issue," or "Harvard Experts Talk for Three Hours"? This point could have been made at any point in human history. One hundred years ago, there was no television or radio, but other forms of stories played a crucial role in U.S. culture. People like stories because they add interest to our lives.

Second, narrative rhetoric can create identification between the characters and the members of the audience. In so doing, it can break down barriers to understanding. By identification I do not mean the ability to identify different objects. Identification in a rhetorical sense is an understanding of shared commonalty among people. The rhetorical theorist Kenneth Burke argues that creating a sense of shared identity, which he sometimes calls consubstantiality, is essential to persuasion.[4]

Identification is important in two ways. First, identification is essential to breaking down barriers between people who come from different backgrounds. Two people may be very different in terms of birthplace, race, gender, age, and so forth, but through a rhetoric of identification discover that in other ways they are quite similar. These two people may discover that they have had similar life experiences or love the same books or have the same values or support the same causes and so forth. In so doing, the barriers between them may be eliminated. At that point, these two very different people may become friends.

Second, identification is linked to identity. We all need an identity, a sense of who we are. People define themselves as Republicans, or feminists, or Cowboys fans, or labor union member, or of Italian ancestry, and so forth. These definitions of the self often have both a literal and a symbolic dimension. A person may literally be the son or daughter of an Italian immigrant. But that person also may symbolically define him/herself as an Italian-American. The symbolic definition of self provides the person with an identity. It tells the person who he/she is. In the last line of his First Inaugural Address, which is included in the readings volume that goes with this book, Ronald Reagan first asks and then answers a question. "And after all, why shouldn't we believe that [we can do great things]? We are Americans." Clearly, Reagan understood the power of identification.

He believed that by revitalizing a sense of shared national identity as Americans that he also could revitalize the nation. His many political successes over his two terms demonstrate that he was right.

It should be obvious that the symbolic sense of identity is more important than the literal one. I may not ever have been closer to Italy than a dinner at the local pizza joint, but still define myself as an Italian-American.

Narrative rhetoric is one of the most powerful means of creating a sense of shared identity. A good story can show people of different races or cultures that they really are in some ways the same. The award wining movie, *Philadelphia,* illustrates this point. The film told the story of a young lawyer with AIDS, who was fired by his law firm when they found out that he was gay and had the terrible disease. The lawyer, played by Tom Hanks, sues and eventually wins a judgment, but the tragedy remains, for he is dying. One primary message of the film was that anti-gay discrimination is wrong. In order to get that point across, the film narrative created a sense of identification between Hank's character and other characters in the film and those of us in the audience. The film showed us that the young lawyer had a loving family and partner. It showed us that he was a hard-working lawyer and a good person. It showed us that he had the same kinds of hopes and dreams that all of us have. The attorney for Hanks's character, played by Denzel Washington, started out as homophobic. Over the course of the film, however, he gradually identified with his client, leading to a change in his ideas about gay people. As the *Philadelphia* example indicates narratives are a powerful way of creating identification.

Third, stories are important forms of persuasion in part because they sometimes possess aesthetic qualities that make a message far more appealing than it otherwise would be. The message in a story may be powerful, not only because of what it is, but also because of how it is told.

The movie, *The China Syndrome,* illustrates this point. The film drew a chilling picture of the danger of a nuclear meltdown. In the film, the fine acting of Jane Fonda and Jack Lemmon made the threat of a nuclear accident come alive. For many people, the film, which opened at roughly the same time as the accident at Three Mile Island, came to symbolize what a nuclear accident would be like. The aesthetic quality of the film, including the acting, camera angles, the way the plot developed, and so forth, made the threat of nuclear power accident seem very real to many Americans.

In actuality, the accident at Three Mile Island produced very little radioactivity and almost no harm.[5] There is even an argument that the greatest negative effect of the accident was unnecessary stress among the residents around the plant. Despite the reality that no significant harm was produced, most Americans saw the accident as a major disaster. This message was reinforced by the film's treatment of a nuclear accident. In that way, the aesthetic qualities of *The China Syndrome* played a role in influencing public opinion in a direction not supported by the actual experience with a real nuclear power accident.

Fourth, narratives persuade not with proof, but by encapsulating a point. The story functions as a rhetorical whole, rather than as a supporting example. For many years,

Ronald Reagan and other conservative politicians told stories about welfare cheaters as part of an attack on "big government." Their stories of people using welfare or food stamps to buy liquor or otherwise waste the government money struck a nerve with the American people. No one wants his/her hard-earned money to go to a welfare cheat, who is about to go off on a drunken spree. In this case, the stories encapsulated the point and made it very difficult to answer. The fact that statistical evidence suggested that there were relatively few welfare cheaters, did not make much difference. Many people had seen an example similar to one told by Reagan or others and so that example encapsulated the point for them. The capacity of narrative to encapsulate a point makes it very difficult to refute the claims in a narrative.

Fifth, narrative rhetoric provides a powerful vehicle for creating an emotional response, especially through the creation of pity and guilt. For example, a narrative can show us a wholly innocent victim being hurt by monstrous evil. Or it can create guilt by showing us the terrible results on innocent people of some action that we may have taken.

Think for a moment about the works in contemporary popular culture that produce the strongest emotional response. For kids, the all time greatest may be the Disney film, *"Bambi."* More recently, movies like *"Titanic,"* and *"Schindler's List,"* have created very powerful emotional reactions. The key point is that every one of the artifacts I have cited is a story. If you want to move people emotionally, one powerful means of doing so is to tell a story.

Finally, narrative has the power to break down barriers to understanding. It does this by taking us out of our here and now and placing us in someone else's life in a different place/time. Narrative can lift us out of our lives and place us in the midst of the Holocaust or in the depression or even on a different world. In so doing, narrative can make real the evils of slavery, the Nazi system, or Stalin's Soviet Union in a way that argumentative rhetoric cannot.

One sign of the power of narrative to transport us to a different place or time is the way that people respond to characters in fictional narratives. For millions of people, Captain James T. Kirk of the Starship Enterprise is a real person that they care about. So is Captain Picard. Everyone knows that Kirk and Picard are just characters, but over time they have become trusted friends. The narratives have made these two people quite real to us. If narrative can make us feel close to two invented characters who "live" in a time that is still hundreds of years away from the present day, then think about how narrative can bring home to us actual events and/or people in the real world.

John Anjain and Narrative Form

The four components of narrative form and the six functions served by narrative are readily apparent in John Anjain's testimony to a Congressional Committee in June of 1977. Anjain and his family were victims of fallout from a 1954 hydrogen bomb blast in the South Pacific. He appeared before the Senate Committee on Energy and

---

Summary of Narrative Functions

1. Narratives add interest;
2. Narratives create identification;
3. Narratives function aesthetically to persuade;
4. Narratives encapsulate claims;
5. Narratives can be used to create an emotional response;
6. Narratives transport us to another place/time.

Natural Research on June 15, 1977 to ask for compensation. A close reading of his testimony reveals the plot pattern I have described, along with how Anjain depicts the scene in his story, and his use of characterization. These components are combined to produce Anjain's themes, which are to place the blame for sickness among his people on the United States, emphasize the innocence of the islanders and ask for compensation.

◆◆◆

Statement by John Anjain before the Senate Committee on Energy and Natural Resources

Mr. Chairman and members of this committee: 1
  My name is John Anjain. I am a citizen of the Marshall Islands District of the Trust   2
Territory. I am here today to speak to you in support of a bill which will provide compensation
for the people of Rongelap and Utirik Atolls in my district. I welcome this opportunity to appear before you. I ask for your support of this bill. My only regret is that English is a second
language for me, I cannot speak directly to you in your own language.

  I am here today to tell you of my experiences as one of the Marshallese who was exposed   3
to radiation because of the bomb in 1954.

  In 1954, I was the Chief Magistrate of Rongelap Island, in Rongelap Atoll. At that time your   4
country was making tests of atomic bombs at Bikini and Enewetak. Our people did not fully
understand about these tests, or about the bombs. But we had learned to trust the Americans
after the Japanese had gone. We believed they would do nothing to harm us. We believed
that they were on our islands to help us.

  In March of 1954, I was on Rongelap with my wife and family, including one year old son,   5
Lekoj. Lekoj was just learning to walk.

Testimony presented June 19, 1977

We were very happy with Lekoj. He was a happy child. But as a father, a husband and provider, and as a magistrate I was worried. I was worried because of what one Hawaiian had said to me when the field trip ship came to our island. He said that "Your life is about that long." He said this and placed his thumb half way down his first finger. I asked him why. He said because of the tests. He did not explain. He just made a statement. 6

On March 1, 1954, there were 64 people on Rongelap. There were another 18 of our people on nearby Ailihghae. They were cutting copra, and catching fish. 7

In the morning, the sun rose in the east. And then something very strange happened. It looked like a second sun was rising in the west. We heard noise like thunder. We saw some strange clouds over the horizon. But the sun in the west, which we know now was the bomb, faded away. We heard no more noise. But we did see the cloud. 8

In the afternoon, something began falling from the sky upon our island. It looked like ash from a fire. It fell on me, it fell on my wife, it fell on our infant son. It fell on the trees, and the roofs of our houses. It fell on the reefs, and into the lagoon. 9

We were very curious about this ash falling from the sky. Some people put it in their mouths and tasted it. One man rubbed it into his eye to see if it would cure an old ailment. People walked in it, and children played with it. 10

An airplane passed by our island. Some people thought that the plane was spraying for mosquitoes. The Americans had done that after the war. We thought maybe the ash came from the plane. But we did not really know. We did not understand. No one told us what to expect. We were not prepared. 11

Later on, in the early evening it rained. The rain fell on the roofs of our houses. It washed away the ash. The water mixed with the ash which fell into our water catchments. Men, women, and children drank that water. It did not taste like rainwater, but some people drank it anyway. 12

Then the next day, I think it was the next day, some Americans came to our island in a boat. They had a machine with them. They went around the island. They looked very worried, and talked rapidly to each other. They told us we must not drink the water in our catchment tanks. They left. They did not explain anything. 13

On the second day, some ships came. Americans again came on our island. They explained that we were in great danger because of the ash. They said if we did not leave, we would die. They told us to leave everything and to only take our clothes. Some people were very afraid and fell into the water trying to get into the landing boat. Some people were taken away to Kawjaleih by airplane. The rest of us went by boat. 14

We looked at our island as we left. We did not know that we would never see our island again for three years. We did not know that the people of Utirik 100 miles to the east, had the same experience. 15

We still did not understand what had happened, but now we were afraid. 16

Some people were feeling sick. Some people had an itching on their skin where the ash was. Later, some people got very sick. They threw up. They felt weak. Later, the hair of men, women and children began to fall out. A lot of people had burns on their skin. There were doctors at Kwajaleih and they examined us. Now we were very afraid. 17

We thought we were going to die. But we did not die. We got better and we were sent to an island in the Hajuro Atoll. We were told that we could not go back for a long time. The people of Utirik also could not go back soon. 18

We waited. We were given some new clothing. Houses were built. We were also given 19
some money every month. This money was to take the place of the copra we could not make.
It was not much money and the people were unhappy. We were given some food, but we
were still not happy. We were not living on our island. We had left our ancestral lands. We left
behind our houses, and possessions. We left our pigs and chickens. We did not know when
we would return.

Three years passed very slowly. The American doctors came to examine us from time to 20
time. Many people complained that they did not feel well. Many women said that they had
miscarriages, and that the babies did not look like human babies. Some babies were born
dead. The doctors said that they did not know why. They did not see the dead babies, so they
said they could not tell why.

In 1957, we returned to Rongelap. The Utirikese were returned after only three months. 21
We were happy to return. The Americans were very kind. They built us new homes, a school, a
dispensary. They built new water catchments. But they told us not to eat certain foods, especially coconut crabs. Coconut crabs are one of our favorite foods. But we could not eat any, until a couple of years ago. We still cannot eat coconut crabs from the north part of our lagoon.
We can eat other coconut crabs, but only one crab for one person, in one day. They say that
they still have some poison in them from the bomb. We were home and we were still afraid.

But even though the Americans were kind, we were still not happy. Some people still did 22
not feel good. We could not eat the food we wanted to eat. The American doctors came every
year to examine us. Every year they came, and they told us that we were not sick, and then
they would return the next year. But they did find something wrong. They found one boy did
not grow as fast as boys his age. They gave him medicine. Then they began finding the thyroid sickness.

My son, Lekoj was 13 when they found his thyroid was sick. They took him away to a hos- 23
pital in America. They cut out his thyroid. They gave him some medicine and told him to take
it every day for the rest of his life. The same thing happened to other people. The doctors kept
returning and examining us. Several years ago, they took me to a hospital in America and they
cut out my thyroid. They gave me medicine, and told me to take it every day for the rest of my
life.

A few years after the bomb, Senator Ahata Kabua tried to get some compensation for the 24
people of Rongelap. He got a lawyer and the lawyer made a case in court. The court turned
our case down. The court said it could not consider our case because we were not part of the
United States. Dwight Heine went to the United Nations to tell them about us. People from
the United Nations came to see us and we told them how we felt. Finally, in 1964, the U.S.
Congress passed a bill. The bill gave us money as a payment for our experience. Some of the
people spent all their money, some of them still have money in the bank. After we got the
money, they began finding the thyroid sickness.

In 1972, they took Lekoj away again. They said they wanted to examine him. They took 25
him to America, to a big hospital near Washington. Later, they took me to this hospital near
Washington because they said he was very sick. My son Lekoj died after I arrived. He never
saw his island again. He returned to our home in a box. He is buried on our island. The doctors say he had a sickness called Leukemia. They are quite sure it was from the bomb.

And I am positive. 26

I saw the ash fall on him. I know it was the bomb. I saw him die. 27

Now, it is 22 years after the bomb, and I am here to ask for your help. I know that money   28
cannot bring back my thyroid. It cannot bring back my son. It cannot give me back three years
of my life. It cannot take the poison from the coconut crabs. It cannot make us stop being
afraid.

But it can help us. It will tell us that the Americans are sorry, and that they want to help.   29
It can help our islands, our people, and our children. We can build things. We can send our
children to school. We can do many things. We ask for your help.

The doctors still come every year, sometimes two times a year. But the people are not   30
happy. They are still afraid. The doctors tell us that we are not sick. Then they take someone
away and cut out a thyroid. Then they return. The people ask, if we are not sick, why do you
come? If we are sick, why don't you tell us? The doctors say they just want to check on us.

It is 22 years after the bomb. They are still finding thyroid sickness. Now they are finding   31
it on Utirik, too. We are still afraid. They said it was an accident that the ash fell on us. They say
that we are not being used for an experiment.

We like the Americans. They have been kind to us. We are not angry, only afraid. When we   32
get sick, we think of the bomb. When people die, we think of the bomb. May God forgive
America for what it has done to our people.

I have lost my health, I have lost three years of my life, and I have lost my son.   33

Please help us.   34

Thank you.   35

Narrative Form in Anjain's Testimony

Plot ◆ The first three paragraphs of Anjain's testimony introduce the story to follow. He tells the committee who he is and why he is testifying before the committee.
In paragraph 4 he begins the story itself, by setting the scene for the action to follow.
He describes his family and their life on the island of Rongelap. In paragraph 6 he fore-
casts the crisis to come by telling of how an Hawaiian man warned him that his life was
threatened.

In paragraph 8, the first crisis of the story—the bomb itself—begins. He tells of
how the islanders saw "a second sun" in the west and then of how they played in the
atomic ash that fell on their island (paragraph 10). They drank water that had been
contaminated with the ash because no one had told them "what to expect" (paragraph
11). It is at this point, that the Americans come to the island. "They went around the
island. They looked very worried, and talked rapidly to each other." Following that
visit, Anjain and the other islanders were taken away into a kind of exile. The first crisis ends in paragraph 18 after the islanders begin to get sick. "We thought we were going to die. But we did not die."

The second main aspect of the plot, which might be labeled "Exile," is discussed in
paragraphs 19–21. Here the plot plateaus. The islanders do not face the bomb, but they
do face continuing illness, miscarriages, and unhappiness at being away from their home.

In paragraph 21, Anjain describes the return of the islanders to Rongelap. This paragraph stands as a point of transition to the last great crisis in the story—the thyroid sickness. In paragraphs 22–27, Anjain tells us about how his child Lekoj got sick with the "thyroid sickenss." Later, Anjain himself has to have his thyroid removed. In paragraph 24, Anjain tells of how the islanders received compensation from the government, before people started getting the thyroid sickness. His obvious point is that past compensation was not adequate because it did not take into account the thyroid problem.

The final portion of the main body is found in paragraphs 25–27, which tell the story of how Lekoj became ill again, was taken to the United States, and eventually died. In paragraphs 26 and 27, Anjain states his certainty that it was the bomb which made Lekoj sick. "And I am positive. I saw the ash fall on him. I know it was the bomb. I saw him die."

Paragraphs 28 through 35 constitute the conclusion, the epilogue to the story. In them, Anjain pulls together the themes from the story and ask for compensation.

Anjain's narrative develops in precisely the pattern noted earlier. Initially, he sets the stage for the story. He then begins with the second greatest crisis in the narrative, the explosion of the bomb and the aftermath of the explosion. The plot then plateaus with the exile stage, before it moves to a climax with the death of Lekoj. The conclusion pulls together the themes that drive the narrative.

Scene ◆ The primary scene for the story is obviously the island of Rongelap. In relation to scene, Anjain's primary goal is to make the place seem real. In the first few paragraphs of the story itself, he gives us a picture of an idyllic place where people are one with nature. They live and work in this beautiful island environment. With this description, Anjain breaks down barriers to understanding the terrible thing that we did to the people of Rongelap. He also is setting up the appeal to guilt that I will discuss in relation to the functions of narrative.

Characters ◆ The protagonist of Anjain's narrative is obviously Anjain himself. He is an ordinary person caught in an impossible situation. Anjain describes himself as a family man, who loved his wife and child, and as village magistrate trying to take care of his people. Anjain is not a heroic protagonist. Rather, he is someone with whom the audience can identify.

The antagonist is not a person, but the bomb and the American government. Anjain describes the government of the United States as largely unconcerned about the welfare of the island people. After the fact, the government tries to take care of them, but beforehand the government did not consider the danger that the ash might float over the island.

The other main character is Anjain's son Lekoj, whose function in the story is to create sympathy for Anjain and all of the islanders and guilt about the failure of the United States to protect these innocent people. Other characters in the story primarily serve plot functions. For example, Anjain tells us about a man who "rubbed it [the atomic ash] into his eye to see if it would cure an old ailment." In narrative terms, this man demonstrates the innocence of the island people. They knew so little about the bomb that they played in nuclear ash.

Theme ◆ The dominant theme of the story is that the United States harmed the people of Rongelap and should compensate them for that harm. Obviously, this theme is divided into two sub-themes: the people of Rongelap were harmed and the United States was responsible for harming them. Along with these themes and sub-themes, Anjain aims at creating guilt in the audience. Very early in the story, Anjain says, "But we had learned to trust the Americans after the Japanese had gone. We believed they would do nothing to harm us. We believed that they were on our islands to help us." With this statement, Anjain distinguishes Americans from Japanese in order to create guilt about how badly we behaved. He is saying: we trusted you, but you let us down.

The Functions of Narrative in Anjain's Testimony

Anjain's testimony to the Senate committee fulfills all six of the functions of narrative rhetoric. First, the story is much more interesting than a similar argument would have been. Building an interesting argument about the failures of U.S. policy at Rongelap some twenty-five years after the bomb blast, would have been nearly impossible. But Anjain's narrative adds interest to his point.

Second, Anjain breaks down barriers to understanding and creates identification with his narrative. One problem that Anjain faces in his testimony is stereotyping about "primitive" people on a South Pacific island. By describing himself as a family man who loved his son and worked for his people, Anjain demonstrates to the Senators that he is a person just like them.

Third, the aesthetic character of Anjain's testimony gives him great credibility. In the first third of his testimony in particular, Anjain is quite choppy. He uses a number of very short sentences and a simple vocabulary that fits his role as village magistrates. This style fits who Anjain is. It adds to his credibilty.

Fourth, Anjain uses the story to encapsulate his point. In the story, he can state with great certainty that "I saw the ash fall on him. I know it was the bomb." In medical terms this makes no sense. Seeing the ash fall on his son does not prove that the bomb caused him to get cancer. Do some kids get cancer without being exposed to the bomb? Of course they do. In a purely logical way, there is no certainty that the bomb caused Lekoj's death, although it does seem highly likely that the bomb was the cause.

The key point is that in a narrative, Anjain can encapsulate the point and make it impossible to refute. In the story, Anjain saw the ash fall and he does know with absolute certainty in his heart that it killed Lekoj.

Fifth, Anjain skillfully creates both pity and guilt. Both emotions are produced when Anjain describes the simple innocence of the people on the island and contrasts them with the United States, which did not even warn the islanders of the risk they faced. He also creates guilt by comparing the actions of the United States to those of Japan. On a couple occasions, he tells the Senators that the people on the island had come to trust the United States forces, because they weren't like the Japanese. Of course, his real point is that the United States should have done better.

Finally, Anjain uses the power of setting to take us out of the contemporary United States to his island home on that fateful day when the hydrogen bomb test took place. He is using close description to break down barriers to acceptance of his views. He also humanizes the people of the island with this description. After Anjain describes them and their life they are no longer part of an event that happened twenty-five years ago and many thousand miles away; they are instead real people whose lives were destroyed by our thoughtlessness.

Summary of Anjain's Use of Narrative Dramatic Form

Anjain faced a difficult situation in his testimony before the Senate committee. Anajain was asking for compensation for an event that had happened roughly twenty-five years before. It is hard to get people to care about something that happened so long ago. To make matters worse, the people harmed were not American citizens (as Anjain himself notes), although they were under the protection of the United States. And there weren't very many who were harmed. Anjain told the committee that there were 82 total people on the two islands and not all of these people were harmed. Thus, Anjain faced a major barrier in relation to getting the attention of the committee and also an attitudinal barrier in that the committee members could have concluded that the issue was no longer very important, if it ever was. He may also have faced an attitudinal barrier relating to American stereotypes of island people. And since the islanders are not Americans, there was no electoral interest in helping them.

Anjain also faced the problem that the United States already had compensated the islanders previously. Thus, it would be quite easy for a Senator to respond to his plea by shrugging and saying, "we already paid you."

Finally, Anjain had to deal with a problem of proof. It isn't possible to identify the specific cause of a given cancer in the same way that you can prove that bad potato salad caused food poisoning. Some people just get cancer for no apparent reason. Thus, Anjain could not prove in a scientific sense that Lekoj got cancer from the bomb.

While Anjain faced significant barriers, he had no rhetorical advantages. He had to deal with a very difficult rhetorical situation.

Anjain could have confronted these barriers by building a strong rational argument. He could have laid out the statistical data on the cancer rates among islanders, cited experts on the effects of the ash, and so forth. But if he had taken this tact, he would have magnified the attention problem. Rational argument is not a good way to get the attention of a group that believes your problem to be insignificant. And rational argument provided no way around the problem of proof.

With narrative, in contrast, Anjain had a good strategy for persuading the committee. Anjain responds to the problem of attention by telling the story of real people who were harmed by the United States. He shows us those people and their lives. In so doing, he makes the numbers issues less important. Yes, there were less than 100 of the islanders, but they still were real people. He also creates both pity for the islanders and guilt about our inaction.

In relation to the barrier that the islanders already had been compensated, Anjain carefully notes that they began finding the thyroid disease after the compensation had been received. This means that the compensation couldn't have been adequate.

Finally, Anjain uses the story to prove in an absolute sense that Lekoj was killed by the bomb. While nothing can be proved absolutely in science, in the context of the story, he clearly proves that the bomb caused the terrible disease. Who could respond to his statement—"I saw the ash fall on him. I know it was the bomb. I saw him die."—by challenging causation?

In summary, Anjain does a masterful job of using narrative to respond to the rhetorical barriers that he faced. In so doing, he also successfully fulfills all six of the functions of narrative rhetoric.

Conclusion

Narrative is a very powerful form of rhetoric. A person who could control the stories told in any culture, would have a great deal of influence over the culture. At the same time, the influence of narrative should not be overstated. Walter Fisher, who was cited earlier, goes so far as to argue that all forms of rhetoric are really types of narrative, a conclusion that obviously goes against the way that stories are used in the real world.[6] The *News Hour with Jim Lehrer* is obviously not a narrative in the same sense as *ER*.

The major weakness of narrative rhetoric is that it may be perceived as just a story, not something that typically happens in the real world. This means that narrative will be most powerful when it is understood as either a "true" story or as telling a fictional story about a real situation. In other situations, narrative will need to be combined with rational argument in order to achieve all of the six functions that I have described.

Notes

1. On the importance of narrative see Alisdair MacIntyre, *After Virtue: A Study in Moral Theory* (Notre Dame: University of Notre Dame Press, 1981); Wallace Martin, *Recent Theories of Narrative* (Ithaca, New York: Cornell University Press, 1986).

2. See William F. Lewis, "Telling America's Story: Narrative Form and the Reagan Presidency," *Quarterly Journal of Speech* 73 (1987): 280–302.

3. Walter R. Fisher, "Narration as a Human Communication Paradigm: The Case of Public Moral Argument," *Communication Mongraphs* 51 (1984): 1–22.

4. For a discussion of identification and consubstantiality see Kenneth Burke, *A Rhetoric of Motives* (Berkeley: University of California Press, 1969, pp. 20–29, 45–46, 55–59. For an analysis of Burke's views on identification see Sonja K. Foss, Karen A. Foss, and Robert Trapp, *Contemporary Perspectives on Rhetoric,* 2nd ed. (Prospect Heights, Illinois: Waveland, 1991), pp. 174–178.

5. See *Report of the President's Commission on the Accident at Three Mile Island: The Need For Change: The Legacy of TMI* (Washington: Government Printing Office, 1979).

6. For an analysis of Fisher's views see Robert C. Rowland, "Narrative: Mode of Discourse or Paradigm," *Communication Monographs* 54 (1987): 264–275.

Credibility Strategies

The third main rhetorical strategy is credibility. Since the Greeks invented the study of rhetoric more than two thousand years ago, we have known that the credibility of the rhetor plays a crucial role in the effectiveness of any work of rhetoric. In fact, Aristotle labeled ethos, which today we would define as credibility, as one of the three modes of persuasion.[1]

Two examples make the importance of credibility clear. Colin Powell has been a national hero since the end of the Gulf War. People clamor to hear him speak or read things he has written. He perennially is mentioned as a possible Republican candidate for President or Vice President. And the Democrats would love it if he switched parties. Where does this popularity come from? The obvious answer is that he has enormous credibility with the American people because of his leadership role, during the Gulf War and at other times in his military career. Powell has so much credibility, especially on military issues, that many people believe him, simply because of who he is. They don't demand strong arguments or powerful narratives. It is enough for them that he is Colin Powell.

On the other hand, there is the example of Gary Hart, who was the front runner for the Democratic presidential nomination in 1988, until his credibility was tarnished in a sex scandal. After that scandal occurred, Hart's popularity dropped and he failed to mount a serious campaign for the nomination.[2] In that instance, it wasn't Hart's arguments or narratives or any other rhetorical strategy that failed him. He widely was believed to have been one of the brightest members of the United States Senate. Hart failed because he lost credibility.

As these two examples indicate, in some cases, rhetoric persuades not because of the power of the argument or a compelling narrative, but via the credibility of the rhetor. That is people are persuaded by the expertise or good character which is presented in the rhetoric. The remainder of this chapter explores the way that credibility functions in persuasion. In the first section, I explore the influence of credibility, draw a distinction between internal and external credibility, and identify the dimensions that make up credibility. I then analyze two speeches to illustrate how credibility functions as a persuasive strategy: anti-Vietnam war testimony to Congress by John Kerry, then a leader of the Vietnam Veterans Against the War and now a United States Senator from Massachusetts, and Barbara Jordan's acclaimed keynote address at the 1976 Democratic National Convention.

The Influence of Credibility on Persuasion

Credibility is rarely the dominant strategy found in a work of rhetoric. It is only in exceptional cases (such as Colin Powell) that a person has so much credibility that we accept their comments immediately. If it is Michael Jordan talking about basketball or Ken Griffey on baseball, we might accept their words without comment. With those rare exceptions in mind, credibility is best understood as both a supporting strategy and, at some minimum level, a necessary requirement for persuasion to occur.

If a rhetor lacks this minimum level of credibility the audience simply will ignore him or her. Occasionally, someone will lose their credibility in some sort of scandal. When that happens, the person also loses their audience. When the Watergate tapes finally were released, many people who previously had supported Richard Nixon were confronted with clear evidence of a cover-up. The result was that Nixon lost all credibility and was forced to resign. A similar result has occurred often in U.S. politics, such as with Gary Hart.

Thus, credibility can be understood as always necessary for persuasion and only in very rare cases sufficient to produce that persuasive effect.

Credibility is also a supporting strategy. Thus, a rhetor may back up a claim with language strategies, strong arguments, and so forth, and also by demonstrating that he/she has high credibility on a given subject. A great deal of research has been conducted to back up this claim. This research has measured the importance of credibility by keeping constant the content of a speech or essay, but varying the characteristics of the rhetor. While there are many complexities to this research, the general conclusion is that credibility makes a difference. One survey of this literature concluded:

> For most persuasive communication situations, however, sources who are perceived as having either high-positive or high-negative source credibility *can* make a difference in the attitude change of a receiver or group of receivers.[3]

Many researchers have drawn similar conclusions. One summary of experimental findings concluded some years ago that "The finding is almost universal that the ethos of the source is related in some way to the impact of the message."[4]

At this point, it is important not to overstate the importance of credibility. Only in rare cases is credibility the decisive factor, either in a positive or negative sense. In most instances, credibility is one among several important persuasive strategies.

Finally, one additional limitation on credibility as a strategy should be recognized. Credibility is in a sense derivative of rational argument. We tend to trust someone if we perceive that person as both honest and expert on a subject. In this way credibility is at the core of authoritative proof. But it is important to recognize that credibility is, therefore, built on the storehouse of examples, statistics and metaphors at the disposal of the authority. And that storehouse can be overwhelmed by stronger data. An example may make this point clear. Imagine that the world's greatest expert on UFOs is arguing that there are in fact no aliens visiting the earth. This person might have enormous credibility based upon their experience and training. But all that credibility could be overwhelmed immediately if another researcher said, "Yes that nice, but here is my friend ET the Alien."

Credibility is a crucial strategy, but it is not as basic a strategy as rational argument.

Internal and External Credibility

Credibility may be brought to a work of rhetoric or created in it. Extrinsic (external) credibility exists when the rhetor has credentials that are well-known to the audience. Michael Jordan is the world's most famous athlete; he brings that credibility with him whenever he speaks.

Intrinsic or internal credibility is created in a work of rhetoric, when the rhetor demonstrates his/her competence, honesty and so forth. Any time a rhetor mentions his or her credentials or relevant work on the topic, or past actions, he or she is building intrinsic credibility.

Of the two forms of credibility, extrinsic is probably more powerful, but intrinsic credibility more important. It is when someone possesses enormous extrinsic credibility, as in the cases of Colin Powell and Michael Jordan, that credibility becomes sufficient for persuasion. Obviously, such occurrences are more the exception than the rule. Thus, the primary focus of rhetorical analysis is on internal credibility and more specifically, how the speaker/writer/director convinces the audience that he/she is a highly credible source.

Types of Credibility

There are four sub-types of credibility, three of which have been recognized at least since Aristotle.[5] The four types of credibility are: expertise/experience, good character, good will, and charisma.

Expertise/Experience ◆ The first sub-type is expertise/experience. I discussed these concepts earlier in the consideration of the types of authoritative evidence. To recapitulate, an expert is someone with training in an area. Thus, we give more credibility to a person who has studied an issue for decades than to someone who spent thirty minutes on the internet looking up a subject. Similarly, we treat a person who has had experience working in an area as more credible than someone who is new to the topic.

In relation to expertise and experience, it is important to remember that expertise is the more important sub-dimension when the issue under consideration is a generalization about a topic. On the other hand, if the issue is a specific incident or fact, then experience is more important than expertise. This only makes sense. An expert on handguns can tell an audience in general about how guns are used. But only an eyewitness can tell the audience about how a particular gun was used in a particular incident

Good Character ◆ The second sub-type of credibility is good character. A person with good character is known for his/her trustworthiness, sincerity, honesty and so forth. We all value people whom we can trust. This is just as true in relation to persuasive communication as it is in our interpersonal lives. There are some people who we perceive as honest and moral and, consequently, we tend to believe what we have to say. For example, despite his conservative views, many moderates and even liberals admire Arizona Republican Senator John McCain.[6] They find him trustworthy because he seems to speak his mind, regardless of the political implications. McCain was, for example, one of the two sponsors of a campaign finance bill (along with Wisconsin Democrat Russell Feingold), that was opposed by nearly every other Republican in the Senate. McCain's willingness to take a position, regardless of what others think, is seen by many as a sign of his fundamental honesty. That is why many liberals and moderates admire McCain, even though they disagree with him on many issues.

Good Will ◆ The third sub-type of credibility is usually referred to as "good will." Good will includes attractiveness, similarity, and an ability to identify with the audience. Why do advertisers pick beautiful actresses or handsome actors for their commercials? The obvious answer is that humans like attractive people. It is not late breaking news to say that attractiveness counts for a lot in appealing to an audience. For example, any political candidate would love to have Gwynneth Paltrow or Matt Damon accompany them on a speaking tour, even if Paltrow or Damon knew nothing about the issues.

While attractiveness is an important sub-dimension of good will, it is less important that similarity and identification. We like people who are beautiful/handsome, but even more than that, we like people who are similar to us. In the last chapter, I cited the rhetorical theorist and critic Kenneth Burke, who argues that the ability to establish a connection with an audience is essential to persuasion. Burke understood that humans tend to be put off by people who seem to be different than they are. But if you can establish similarity between yourself and the audience, then that barrier evaporates. It is the need to establish similarity or identification with an audience that leads skilled speakers to talk about their background and experience. When a speaker says to a rural audience, "I was once a country boy/girl myself," he or she is trying to create identification with the audience.

Charisma ◆ The fourth form of credibility is power or charisma. It is an ability to project an energetic and active image and, at the same time, adapt to the audience perspectives. Unlike the other three forms of credibility, charisma cannot be created. The ability to produce a charismatic reaction seems to be closely tied to personality characteristics of the rhetor. Some people have charisma and others don't. Ronald Reagan had it; George Bush didn't. Bill Clinton has it; Al Gore doesn't.

What is charisma? The answer to that is somewhat uncertain. Charisma is not merely physical power or attractiveness. Nor is it verbal ability, although it may be related to all of these factors. More than anything else charisma seems to be tied to an empathic understanding of the audience. Some rhetors seem to have an ability to sense how an audience is reacting and adapt to those feelings. It is that ability, more than anything else, that creates charisma.

Charisma is of course a powerful persuasive factor. Rhetors with charisma may be able to persuade an audience to support their views. But that also makes charisma dangerous. American Presidents like Ronald Reagan and Franklin Roosevelt used their charisma to energize the country behind their agendas. Hitler did the same thing in Germany.

Summary of the Dimensions of Credibility

Which of the dimensions of credibility is most important? The answer is that it depends upon the context. If a person is an eyewitness in a trial, then good character is the most important dimension of credibility. The key for the jury to believe him/her is their trust in his/her character. If the person is an expert witness in that trial, then both good character and expertise/experience will be critical. In these first two circumstances, good will and charisma are important, but not as crucial as the other dimensions of credibility. On the other hand, if the circumstance were a neighborhood outing than good will would be the most important dimension of credibility. And if the focus were on motivating a group, charisma might be the most important dimension. The key point is that the relative importance of the four dimensions of credibility will depend upon the context in which the rhetoric is presented and the purpose of the rhetor.

Creating Credibility

Earlier in this chapter, I explained the difference between intrinsic and extrinsic credibility. From the perspective of rhetorical analysis, intrinsic (or internal) credibility is clearly the more important concept. Extrinsic credibility is an important persuasive factor only in rare cases. There are not that many people in our society who bring massive amounts of credibility to a speech or essay presented to an average audience of Americans.

It is because intrinsic credibility is far more common than extrinsic credibility, that it is important to focus on the ways that people increase credibility in a speech or essay. One clue that credibility is an important strategy in a work of rhetoric is if the rhetor focuses on his/her personal characteristics or experiences, either as they relate to the subject or as they relate to the audience. If this happens, the rhetor probably is trying to show himself or herself as a bright-capable-honest person whom the audience can trust.

In order to illustrate the ways that credibility may be created in a work of rhetoric, testimony before the Senate Foreign Relations Committee by John Kerry, then a leader of a veterans organizations against the war in Vietnam and now a United States Senator from Massachusetts, has been included. The speech testimony was presented in April 1971 when the United States still was deeply involved in the Vietnam War. Kerry uses a number of strategies to develop his credibility, especially in relation to the common perception at the time that opponents of the war were in some way unpatriotic.

Vietnam Veterans against the War

Statement of John Kerry

Mr. Kerry. Thank you very much. Senator Fulbright, Senator Javits, Senator Symington, Senator Pell. I would like to say for the record, and also for the men behind me who are also wearing the uniforms and their medals, that my sitting here is really symbolic. I am not here as John Kerry, I am here as one member of the group of 1,000, which is a small representation of a very much larger group of veterans in this country, and were it possible for all of them to sit at this table they would be here and have the same kind of testimony.   1

I would simply like to speak in very general terms. I apologize if my statement is general because I received notification yesterday you would hear me and I am afraid because of the injunction I was up most of the night and haven't had a great deal of chance to prepare.   2

Winter Soldier Investigation

I would like to talk, representing all those veterans, and say that several months ago in Detroit, we had an investigation at which over 150 honorably discharged and many very highly decorated veterans testified to war crimes committed in Southeast Asia, not isolated incidents but crimes committed on a day-to-day basis with the full awareness of officers at all levels of command.   3

It is impossible to describe to you exactly what did happen in Detroit, the emotions in the room, the feelings of the men who were reliving their experiences in Vietnam, but they did. They relived the absolute horror of what this country, in a sense, made them do.   4

They told the stories at times they had personally raped, cut off ears, cut off heads, taped wires from portable telephones to human genitals and turned up the power, cut off limbs, blown up bodies, randomly shot at civilians, razed villages in fashion reminiscent of Genghis Kahn, shot cattle and dogs for fun, poisoned food stocks, and generally ravaged the countryside of South Vietnam in addition to the normal ravage of war, and the normal and very particular ravaging which is done by the applied bombing power of this country.   5

We call this investigation the "Winter Soldier Investigation." The term "Winter soldier" is a play on words of Thomas Paine in 1776 when he spoke of the Sunshine Patriot and summertime soldiers who deserted at Valley Forge because the going was rough. 6

We who have come here to Washington have come here because we feel we have to be winter soldiers now. We could come back to this country; we could be quiet; we could hold our silence; we could not tell what went on in Vietnam, but we feel because of what threatens this country, the fact that the crimes threaten it, not reds, and not redcoats but the crimes which we are committing that threaten it, that we have to speak out. 7

Feelings of Men Coming Back from Vietnam

I would like to talk to you a little bit about what the result is of the feelings these men carry with them after coming back from Vietnam. The country doesn't know it yet, but it has created a monster, a monster in the form of millions of men who have been taught to deal and to trade in violence, and who are given the chance to die for the biggest nothing in history; men who have returned with a sense of anger and a sense of betrayal which no one has yet grasped. 8

As a veteran and one who feels this anger, I would like to talk about it. We are angry because we feel we have been used in the worst fashion by the administration of this country. 9

In 1970 at West Point, Vice President Agnew said "some glamorize the criminal misfits of society while our best men die in Asian rice paddies to preserve the freedom which most of those misfits abuse," and this was used as a rallying point for our effort in Vietnam. 10

But for us, as boys in Asia whom the country was supposed to support, his statement is a terrible distortion from which we can only draw a very deep sense of revulsion. Hence the anger of some of the men who are here in Washington today. It is a distortion because we in no way consider ourselves the best men of this country, because those he calls misfits were standing up for us in a way that nobody else in this country dared to, because so many who have died would have returned to this country to join the misfits in their efforts to ask for an immediate withdrawal from South Vietnam, because so many of those best men have returned as quadriplegics and amputees, and they lie forgotten in Veterans' Administration hospitals in this country which fly the flag which so many have chosen as their own personal symbol. And we cannot consider ourselves America's best men when we are ashamed of and hated what we were called on to do in Southeast Asia. 11

In our opinion, and from our experience, there is nothing in South Vietnam, nothing which could happen that realistically threatens the United States of America. And to attempt to justify the loss of one American life in Vietnam, Cambodia, or Laos by linking such loss to the preservation of freedom, which those misfits supposedly abuse, is to us the height of criminal hypocrisy, and it is that kind of hypocrisy which we feel has torn this country apart. 12

We are probably much more angry than that and I don't want to go into the foreign policy aspects because I am outclassed here. I know that all of you talk about every possible alternative of getting out of Vietnam. We understand that. We know you have considered the seriousness of the aspects to the utmost level and I am not going to try to dwell on that, but I want to relate to you the feeling that many of the men who have returned to this country express because we are probably angriest about all that we were told about Vietnam and about the mystical war against communism. 13

What Was Found and Learned in Vietnam

We found that not only was it a civil war, an effort by a people who had for years been   14
seeking their liberation from any colonial influence whatsoever, but also we found that the
Vietnamese whom we had enthusiastically molded after our own image were hard put to
take up the fight against the threat we were supposedly saving them from.

We found most people didn't even know the difference between communism and   15
democracy. They only wanted to work in rice paddies without helicopters strafing them and
bombs with napalm burning their villages and tearing their country apart. They wanted
everything to do with the war, particularly with this foreign presence of the United States of
America, to leave them alone in peace, and they practiced the art of survival by siding with
whichever military force was present at a particular time, be it Vietcong, North Vietnamese,
or American.

We found also that all too often American men were dying in those rice paddies for want   16
of support from their allies. We saw first hand how money from American taxes was used for
a corrupt dictatorial regime. We saw that many people in this country had a one-sided idea
of who was kept free by our flag, as blacks provided the highest percentage of casualties. We
saw Vietnam ravaged equally by American bombs as well as by search and destroy missions,
as well as by Vietcong terrorism, and yet we listened while this country tried to blame all of
the havoc on the Vietcong.

We rationalized destroying villages in order to save them. We saw America lose her sense   17
of morality as she accepted very coolly a My Lai and refused to give up the image of American soldiers who hand out chocolate bars and chewing gum.

We learned the meaning of free fire zones, shooting anything that moves, and we   18
watched while America placed a cheapness on the lives of orientals.

We watched the U.S. falsification of body counts, in fact the glorification of body counts.   19
We listened while month after month we were told the back of the enemy was about to
break. We fought using weapons against "oriental human beings," with quotation marks
around that. We fought using weapons against those people which I do not believe this country would dream of using were we fighting in the European theater or let us say a non-third-
world people theater, and so we watched while men charged up hills because a general said
that hill has to be taken, and after losing one platoon or two platoons they marched away to
leave the hill for the reoccupation by the North Vietnamese because we watched pride allow
the most unimportant of battles to be blown into extravaganzas, because we couldn't lose,
and we couldn't retreat, and because it didn't matter how many American bodies were lost to
prove that point. And so there were Hamburger Hills and Khe Sanhs and Hill 881's and Fire
Base 6's and so many others.

Vietnamization

No we are told that the men who fought there must watch quietly while American lives   20
are lost so that we can exercise the incredible arrogance of Vietnamizing the Vietnamese.
Each day—
[Applause.]

The Chairman. I hope you won't interrupt. He is making a very significant statement. Let him proceed.

Mr. Kerry. Each day to facilitate the process by which the United States washes her hands   21
of Vietnam someone has to give up his life so that the United States doesn't have to admit something that the entire world already knows, so that we can't say that we have made a mistake. Someone has to die so that President Nixon won't be, and these are his words, "the first President to lose a war."

We are asking Americans to think about that because how do you ask a man to be the   22
last man to die in Vietnam? How do you ask a man to be the last man to die for a mistake? But we are trying to do that, and we are doing it with thousands of rationalizations, and if you read carefully the President's last speech to the people of this country, you can see that he says, and says clearly:

> But the issue, gentlemen, the issue is communism, and the question is whether or not we will leave that country to the Communists or whether or not we will try to give it hope to be a free people.

But the point is they are not a free people now under us. They are not a free people, and   23
we cannot fight communism all over the world, and I think we should have learned that lesson by now.

Returning Veterans Are Not Really Wanted

But the problem of veterans goes beyond this personal problem, because you think   24
about a poster in this country with a picture of Uncle Sam and the picture says "I want you." And a young man comes out of high school and says, "That is fine. I am going to serve my country." And he goes to Vietnam and he shoots and he kills and he does his job or maybe he doesn't kill, maybe he just goes and he comes back, and when he gets back to this country he finds that he isn't really wanted, because the largest unemployment figure in the country—it varies depending on who you get it from, the VA Administration 15 percent, various other sources 22 percent. But the largest corps of unemployed in this country are veterans of this war, and of those veterans 33 percent of the unemployed are black. That means 1 out of every 10 of the Nation's unemployed is a veteran of Vietnam.

The hospitals across the country won't, or can't meet their demands. It is not a question   25
of not trying. They don't have the appropriations. A man recently died after he had a tracheotomy in California, not because of the operation but because there weren't enough personnel to clean the mucous out of his tube and he suffocated to death.

Another young man just died in a New York VA hospital the other day. A friend of mine   26
was lying in a bed two beds away and tried to help him, but he couldn't. He rang a bell and there was nobody there to service that man and so he died of convulsions.

I understand 57 percent of all those entering the VA hospitals talk about suicide. Some 27   27
percent have tried, and they try because they come back to this country and they have to face what they did in Vietnam, and then they come back and find the indifference of a country that doesn't really care, that doesn't really care.

Lack of Moral Indignation in United States

Suddenly we are faced with a very sickening situation in this country, because there is no   28
moral indignation and, if there is, it comes from people who are almost exhausted by their
past indignations, and I know that many of them are sitting in front of me. The country seems
to have lain down and shrugged off something as serious as Laos, just as we calmly shrugged
off the loss of 700,000 lives in Pakistan, the so-called greatest disaster of all times.

But we are here as veterans to say we think we are in the midst of the greatest disaster of   29
all times now because they are still dying over there, and not just Americans, Vietnamese, and
we are rationalizing leaving that country so that those people can go on killing each other for
years to come.

Americans seem to have accepted the idea that the war is winding down, at least for   30
Americans, and they have also allowed the bodies which were once used by a President for
statistics to prove that we were winning the war, to be used as evidence against a man who
followed orders and who interpreted those orders no differently than hundreds of other men
in Vietnam.

We veterans can only look with amazement on the fact that this country has been unable   31
to see there is absolutely no difference between ground troops and a helicopter crew, and yet
people have accepted a differentiation fed them by the administration.

No ground troops are in Laos, so it is all right to kill Laotians by remote control. But be-   32
lieve me the helicopter crews fill the same body bags and they wreak the same kind of damage on the Vietnamese and Laotian countryside as anybody else, and the President is talking
about allowing that to go on for many years to come. One can only ask if we will really be sat-
isfied when the troops march into Hanoi.

Request for Action by Congress

We are asking here is Washington for some action, action from the Congress of the   33
United States of America which has the power to raise and maintain armies, and which by the
Constitution also has the power to declare war.

We have come here, not to the President, because we believe that this body can be re-   34
sponsive to the will of the people, and we believe that the will of the people says that we
should be out of Vietnam now.

Extent of Problem of Vietnam War

We are here in Washington also to say that the problem of this war is not just a question   35
of war and diplomacy. It is part and parcel of everything that we are trying as human beings
to communicate to people in this country, the question of racism, which is rampant in the military, and so many other questions also, the use of weapons, the hypocrisy in our taking um-
brage in the Geneva Conventions and using that as justification for a continuation of this war,
when we are more guilty than any other body of violations of those Geneva Conventions, in
the use of free fire zones, harassment interdiction fire, search and destroy missions, the

bombings, the torture of prisoners, the killing of prisoners, accepted policy by many units in South Vietnam. That is what we are trying to say. It is part and parcel of everything.

An American Indian friend of mine who lives in the Indian Nation of Alcatraz put it to me   36 very succinctly. He told me how as a boy on an Indian reservation he had watched television and he used to cheer the cowboys when they came in and shot the Indians, and then suddenly one day he stopped in Vietnam and he said "My God, I am doing to these people the very same thing that was done to my people." And he stopped. And that is what we are trying to say, that we think this thing has to end.

Where Is the Leadership?

We are also here to ask, and we are here to ask vehemently, where are the leaders of our   37 country? Where is the leadership? We are here to ask where are McNamara, Rostow, Bundy, Gilpatric and so many others. Where are they now that we, the men whom they sent off to war, have returned? These are commanders who have deserted their troops, and there is no more serious crime in the law of war. The Army says they never leave their wounded.

The Marines say they never leave even their dead. These men have left all the casualties   38 and retreated behind a pious shield of public rectitude. They have left the real stuff of their reputations bleaching behind them in the sun in this country.

Administration's Attempt to Disown Veterans

Finally, this administration has done us the ultimate dishonor. They have attempted to   39 disown us and the sacrifice we made for this country. In their blindness and fear they have tried to deny that we are veterans or that we served in Nam. We do not need their testimony. Our own scars and stumps of limbs are witnesses enough for others and for ourselves.

We wish that a merciful God could wipe away our own memories of that service as eas-   40 ily as this administration has wiped their memories of us. But all that they have done and all that they can do by this denial is to make more clear than ever our own determination to undertake one last mission, to search out and destroy the last vestige of this barbaric war, to pacify our own hearts, to conquer the hate and the fear that have driven this country these last 10 years and more, and so when, in 30 years from now, our brothers go down the street without a leg, without an arm, or a face, and small boys ask why, we will be able to say "Vietnam" and not mean a desert, not a filthy obscene memory but mean instead the place where America finally turned and where soldiers like us helped it in the turning.

Thank you. [Applause.]

The Chairman. Mr. Kerry, it is quite evident from that demonstration that you are speak-   41 ing not only for yourself but for all your associates, as you properly said in the beginning.

◆◆◆

Analysis of the Kerry Speech

Kerry's goal in this statement to the Senate Foreign Relations Committee is to persuade the committee and via press reporting the country to support a policy to end the war in Vietnam as quickly as possible. He makes this clear throughout the speech, but especially in the concluding paragraphs. In paragraph 40, he labels the mission of his anti-war veterans group as "to search out and destroy the last vestige of this barbaric war. . ." Kerry also advocates increased support for Vietnam veterans returning to the United States. In paragraphs 24 through 27 he describes problems facing returning veterans including unemployment, lack of medical care, suicide and so forth. While he does not detail a solution, he clearly implies the need for increased governmental support.

In developing these positions, Kerry faces severe rhetorical barriers and lacks significant rhetorical advantages. One problem is that the Vietnam War has been the most important issue facing the nation since the middle 1960s. By 1971, people have heard every possible position on the war. Therefore, it will be difficult to come up with new material to influence the audience. A second barrier is Kerry's lack of expertise. Kerry was not a foreign policy specialist. Nor was he a high officer in Vietnam. He actually was not an officer at all. This leaves Kerry in the difficult position of speaking to a committee that over the years has heard testimony from the most qualified experts in the nation. Kerry seems to recognize this problem when he notes in paragraph 13 that "I don't want to go into the foreign policy aspects because I am outclassed here."

Finally, Kerry faces the public perception that war protesters are unpatriotic. Throughout American history, those who opposed a given war have been labeled as unpatriotic. Kerry is clearly aware that this problem exists in regard to opposition to the war in Vietnam. In paragraph 10, he cites a statement attacking protesters by then Vice President Spiro Agnew.

It is important to recognize that pro-war attitudes are not a primary barrier facing Kerry because he is not aiming his rhetoric at those strongly on the other side of the Vietnam issue. Kerry would have little chance of persuading a strong supporter of the war to change his/her mind. Thus, he focuses on those whose views are not totally fixed, as well as on reinforcing the positions of those who already oppose the war.

In confronting the barriers I have described, Kerry clearly relies on internal credibility as a primary strategy. He also utilizes a strategy closely related to credibility—rhetorical re-definition. Of course, Kerry relies on other strategies as well. He uses the language strategy of detailed depiction to make the conflict come alive for the audience. He also uses a powerful metaphor/allusion, which I will discuss in a moment, to support the redefinition strategy. And Kerry also appeals to the values of the audience. However, the dominant strategies are the attempt to increase credibility and the redefinition of the nature of the conflict.

Kerry's Use of Internal Credibility

Kerry builds his internal credibility in several ways. First, he emphasizes that he is testifying as a member of a much larger group of veterans. In the 1st paragraph of his testimony, he states "I am here as one member of the group of 1,000, which is a small representation of a very much larger group of veterans in this country, and were it possible for all of them to sit at this table they would be here and have the same kind of testimony." With this statement, Kerry emphasizes that there are many more veterans who support the same position that he does on the issue.

Second, Kerry argues that the anti-war veterans did their duty and now have returned to this nation to do their duty again, by fighting to end the war. In the first paragraph, he refers to "the men behind me who are also wearing the uniforms and their medals." A picture of Kerry at the table in the Senate hearing room shows that he too was wearing a uniform with medals. Thus, Kerry is representing a group of veterans who were willing to sacrifice for the nation. In paragraph 7, he emphasizes that the sacrifice continues with his testimony. First, he notes that "we could be quiet; we could hold our silence." Later he adds that the veterans see the problem as so large that "we have to speak out."

Third, Kerry picks inclusive pronouns to consistently remind the committee that he is speaking for a host of other veterans. For example, in paragraph 7 alone, he uses "we" 9 times to refer to the actions of his organization.

Fourth, Kerry emphasizes the importance of experience over expertise in relation to understanding the Vietnam war. I already have noted that Kerry admitted to the committee that he was "outclassed" on foreign policy issues. But on the events in Vietnam, Kerry implicitly argues that those who have been there know more than those who haven't. He begins to emphasize this theme very early in the statement in the 3rd paragraph, where he describes how his group "had an investigation at which over 150 honorably discharged and many very highly decorated veterans testified to war crimes committed in Southeast Asia." Then throughout the testimony, Kerry emphasizes that his experience and that of his fellow veterans does not match with what the "experts" or the Nixon administration was saying. For example, in paragraph 12, he explains, "In our opinion, and from our experience, there is nothing in South Vietnam, nothing which could happen that realistically threatens the United States of America." Later, in paragraphs 17 through 19, he describes the experience of veterans with destroying villages, free fire zones in which innocent people were killed, and falsified body counts. Implicitly, throughout the speech, Kerry emphasizes the fact that the veterans had been there and seen the war with their own eyes.

Fifth, Kerry uses reluctant testimony to add to the credibility of his group. Reluctant testimony is a special type of internal credibility strategy in which the rhetor states some sort of claim that goes against his/her interest to demonstrate the honesty of the position. It would be reluctant testimony if one of the members of the Coors family went to Congress to testify in favor of restrictions on beer sales. In this instance, Kerry uses reluctant testimony (as well as emphasizing the importance of experience over expertise), in paragraph 5, where he cites horrible actions committed by members of his group.

> They told the stories at times they had personally raped, cut off ears, cut off heads, taped wires from portable telephones to human genitals and turned up the power, cut off limbs, blown up bodies, randomly shot at civilians, razed villages in fashion reminiscent of Genghis Khan, shot cattle and dogs for fun, poisoned food stocks, and generally ravaged th countryside of South Vietnam . . .

It might at first seem that Kerry would damage his credibility by admitting that members of his group had committed these terrible acts. However, his very willingness to admit to the acts is a sign of his fundamental honesty. In addition, Kerry makes it very clear, as I will explain in a moment, that the primary cause of these actions was the war itself. In paragraph 4, immediately prior to the statement I just cited, Kerry refers to the "horror" experience by the veterans, a "horror of what this country, in a sense, made them do."

In summary, Kerry utilizes internal credibility as a primary strategy in his testimony. He emphasizes that he is a representative of a large group of honorably discharged veterans who did their duty in Vietnam and who are doing it again. He emphasizes that priority should be given to experience over expertise. And he uses reluctant testimony, to demonstrate that the veterans must be telling the truth.

Kerry's use of credibility strategies, especially his emphasis on the power of eyewitness testimony of people who were there, skillfully responded to the rhetorical barriers that he confronted. He used this strategy to provide new information to the Senators and also to devalue any testimony that they might hear from "experts."

Kerry's Use of Redefinition

Redefinition occurs when a rhetor literally redefines a situation to give the audience a better way of understanding an issue. The redefinition is used to change the way the audience thinks about the claim. Kerry relies on three related instances of redefinition. He redefines what it means to be an American soldier. He redefines what it means to be a war protester. And he redefines what it means to be a military leader in the Vietnam War.

The first level of redefinition occurs in relation to American soldiers. For many, probably most Americans, the dominant image of an American soldier had been established by World War II and the depictions of that war in the media. From that vantage point, an American soldier was brave, honorable, competent, and essentially moral. American soldiers did not commit atrocities; they helped kids. Many Hollywood movies reinforced this image. Kerry radically rejects the stereotype of who American soldiers are and what they do.

I already cited Kerry's discussion of the terrible atrocities committed in Vietnam. Crucially, Kerry does not argue that American soldiers are themselves evil. Rather, he argues that the war has "created a monster, a monster in the form of millions of men who have been taught to deal and to trade in violence, and who are given the chance to die for the biggest nothing in history" (paragraph 8). Kerry is arguing that the war is evil, not just because of what it is doing to the people of South Vietnam, but also because of what it is doing to us. In this way, he gives the Senators a strong reason to oppose the war based on self-interest.

Kerry uses a similar strategy in relation to the image of war protesters. In my discussion of barriers, I noted the common perception that war protesters are unpatriotic. Kerry turns around this view and redefines protesters as the true patriots. He cites an attack on protesters by Vice President Agnew, who labelled protesters as "criminal misfits" (paragraph 10), and then states that "those he calls misfits were standing up for us [soldiers in Vietnam] in a way that nobody else in this country dared to, because so many who have died would have returned to this country to join the misfits in their efforts to ask for an immediate withdrawal from South Vietnam. . ." (paragraph 11).

Kerry also uses the redefinition strategy in relation to his own group, Vietnam Veterans Against the War. In paragraph 6, he explains to the committee that:

We call this investigation the 'Winter Soldier Investigation.' The term 'Winter soldier' is a play on words of Thomas Paine in 1776 when he spoke of the Sunshine Patriot and the summertime soldiers who deserted at Valley Forge because the going was rough. (paragraph 6)

In the next paragraph, he adds that "We who have come here to Washington have come here because we feel we have to be winter soldiers now." It is as "winter soldiers," that they oppose the war.

The "winter soldier" section combines an allusion, a metaphor and redefinition. The allusion is to the work of Thomas Paine, who was one of the most important writers during the American Revolution. Kerry draws on Paine to create the metaphor of the "winter soldier." A "winter soldier" was there at Valley Forge in the snow. The "sunshine patriot" marched in April and May, but was gone by December. But the "winter soldier" stayed and did his job. Kerry is arguing that like the soldiers at Valley Forge, his group of Veterans is composed of "winter soldiers." They are not anti-American protesters, but the true patriots, who know the importance of telling the truth to the American people.

The third level of redefinition relates to the country's military leaders in the war. Throughout our history, from Washington to Colin Powell, Americans have tended to idolize our most successful military leaders. In contrast to the view of military leaders as heroes, Kerry redefines their role in Vietnam as decidedly unheroic. In fact he says that the leaders in Vietnam are deserters. In paragraphs 37 and 38, he makes this redefinition quite clear:

We are also here to ask, and we are here to ask vehemently, where are the leaders of our country? Where is the leadership? We are here to ask where are Mc-Namara, Rostow, Bundy, Gilpatric and so many others. Where are they now that we, the men whom they sent off to war, have returned? These are commanders who have deserted their troops, and there is no more serious crime in the law of war. The army says they never leave their wounded.

The Marines say they never leave even their dead. These men have left all the casualties and retreated behind a pious shield of public rectitude.

Here, Kerry attacks four of the main leaders who got the United States involved in the war. Robert McNamara was Secretary of Defense. Walt Rostow was Lyndon Johnson's chief of staff. McGeorge Bundy worked for the National Security Council and Roswell Gilpatric was Deputy Secretary of Defense.

At this point, the redefinition is complete. The leaders who sent the soldiers to Vietnam are not heroes, but deserters. The soldiers in Vietnam are not moral and heroic, but monsters in the making. And those who protest the war are not unpatriotic, but the true patriots.

Evaluation of Kerry's Testimony

Kerry's use of redefinition, internal ethos, and other supporting strategies was well-designed to overcome the barriers that he faced in his testimony before the Senate committee. With the credibility and redefinition strategies, Kerry tried to give the committee a new way to think about the war. By privileging personal experience over other forms of evidence, he also gave the committee new information. In addition, Kerry's use of redefinition was well-designed to confront negative attitudes toward protesters.

Overall, Kerry's testimony was carefully crafted to overcome the barriers that he faced. This does not mean that Kerry actually changed a single mind, although he may well have done so. There is no external evidence that bears on this question. But it is fair to conclude that Kerry did a superior job of adapting to a difficult rhetorical situation. The rhetorical skill shown by Kerry in his testimony may well be one reason that a few years later he was successful in winning election to the Senate himself.

Barbara Jordan and Enactment

In 1976 Barbara Jordan, then a Member of the House of Representatives from Texas, presented one of the most famous convention keynote addresses of the 20th century. According to Wayne Thompson, both press and public reaction was overwhelmingly positive. He cites a Harris poll that found 54% of those responding were positive about the speech against only 9% negative, along with strong praise from media commentators.[7] Thompson concludes that the address "held unusually high attention" and produced a "most resoundingly heartfelt ovation."[8] The address is still remembered. It made such an impact that Democrats invited her back at later conventions as one among several keynote speakers.

◆◆◆

Barbara Jordan's Keynote Address to the Democratic National Convention July 14, 1976

Thank you ladies and gentlemen for a very warm reception.   1

It was one hundred and forty-four years ago that members of the Democratic Party first   2
met in convention to select a Presidential candidate. Since that time, Democrats have continued to convene once every four years and draft a party platform and nominate a presidential
candidate. And our meeting this week is a continuation of that tradition.

But there is something different about tonight. There is something special about tonight.   3
What is different? What is special? I, Barbara Jordan, am a keynote speaker.

A lot of years have passed since 1832, and during that time it would have been most un-   4
usual for any national political party to ask a Barbara Jordan to deliver a keynote address . . .
but tonight here I am. And I feel that notwithstanding the past that my presence here is one
additional piece of evidence that the American dream need not forever be deferred.

Now . . . now that I have this grand distinction, what in the world am I supposed to say?   5

I could easily spend this time praising the accomplishments of this party and attacking   6
the Republicans but I don't choose to do that.

I could list the many problems which Americans have. I could list the problems which   7
cause people to feel cynical, angry, frustrated: problems which include lack of integrity in
government; the feeling that the individual no longer counts; the reality of material and spir-
itual poverty; the feeling that the grand American experiment is failing or has failed. I could
recite these problems and then I could sit down and offer no solutions. But I don't choose to
do that either.

The citizens of America expect more. They deserve and they want more than a recital of   8
problems.

We are a people in a quandary about the present. We are a people in search of our future.   9
We are a people in search of a national community.

We are a people trying not only to solve the problems of the present: unemployment, in-   10
flation . . . but we are attempting on a larger scale to fulfill the promise of America. We are attempting to fulfill our national purpose; to create and sustain a society in which all of us are
equal.

Throughout . . . throughout our history, when people have looked for new ways to solve   11
their problems, and to uphold the principles of this nation, many times they have turned to
political parties. They have often turned to the Democratic Party.

What is it . . . what is it about the Democratic Party that makes it the instrument the people use when they search for ways to shape their future? Well, I believe the answer to that question lies in our concept of governing. Our concept of governing is derived from our view of people. It is a concept deeply rooted in a set of beliefs firmly etched in the national conscience of all of us.   12

Now what are these beliefs?   13

First, we believe in equality for all and privileges for none. This a belief, this is a belief that each American regardless of background has equal standing in the public forum, all of us. Because . . . because we believe this idea so firmly, we are an inclusive rather than an exclusive party. Let everybody come.   14

I think it no accident that most of those immigrating to America in the nineteenth century identified with the Democratic Party. We are a heterogenous party made up of Americans of diverse backgrounds.   15

We believe that the people are the source of governmental power; that the authority of the people is to be extended, not restricted. This, this can be accomplished only by providing each citizen with every opportunity to participate in the management of the government. They must have that, we believe.   16

We believe that the government which represents the authority of all the people, not just one interest group, but all the people, has an obligation to actively, underscore actively, seek to remove those obstacles which would block individual achievement . . . obstacles emanating from race, sex, economic condition. The government must remove them, seek to remove them.   17

We, we are a party of innovation. We do not reject our traditions, but we are willing to adapt to changing circumstances, when change we must. We are willing to suffer the discomfort of change in order to achieve a better future.   18

We have a positive vision of the future founded on the belief that the gap between the promise and reality of America can one day be finally closed. We believe that.   19

This, my friends, is the bedrock of our concept of governing. This is a part of the reason why Americans have turned to the Democratic Party. These are the foundations upon which a national community can be built.   20

Let all understand that these guiding principles cannot be discarded for short-term political gains. They represent what this country is all about. They are indigenous to the American idea. And these are principles which are not negotiable.   21

In other times, in other times, I could stand here and give this kind of exposition on the beliefs of the Democratic Party and that would be enough. But today this is not enough. People want more. That is not sufficient reason for the majority of the people of this country to decide to vote Democratic. We have made mistakes. We realize that. We admit our mistakes. In our haste to do all things for all people, we did not foresee the full consequences of our actions. And when the people raised their voices, we didn't hear. But our deafness was only a temporary condition, and not an irreversible condition.   22

Even as I stand here and admit that we have made mistakes, I still believe that as the people of America sit in judgment on each party, they will recognize that our mistakes were mistakes of the heart. They'll recognize that.   23

And now, now we must look to the future. Let us heed the voice of the people and recognize their common sense. If we do not, we not only blaspheme our political heritage, we ignore the common ties that bind all Americans.   24

Many fear the future. Many are distrustful of their leaders, and believe that their voices aren't ever heard. Many seek only to satisfy their private work . . . wants, to satisfy their private interests.   25

But this is the great danger America faces. That we will cease to be one nation and become instead a collection of interest groups: city against suburb, region against region, individual against individual. Each seeking to satisfy private wants.   26

If that happens, who then will speak for America?   27

Who then will speak for the common good?   28

This is the question which must be answered in 1976.   29

Are we to be one people bound together by common spirit sharing in a common endeavor or will we become a divided nation?   30

For all of its uncertainty, we cannot flee the future. We must not become the new puritans and reject our society. We must address and master the future together. It can be done if we restore the belief that we share a sense of national endeavor. It can be done.   31

There is no executive order; there is no law that can require the American people to form a national community. This we must do as individuals, and if we do it as individuals, there is no President of the United States who can veto that decision.   32

As a first step, as a first step, we must restore our belief in ourselves. We are a generous people so why can't we be generous with each other? We need to take to heart the words spoken by Thomas Jefferson: 33

> "Let us restore the social intercourse, let us restore to social intercourse that harmony and that affection without which liberty and even life are but dreary things."

A nation is formed by the willingness of each of us to share in the responsibility for upholding the common good.   34

A government is invigorated when each one of us is willing to participate in shaping the future of this nation.   35

In this election year we must define the common good and begin again to shape a common future. Let each person do his or her part. If one citizen is unwilling to participate, all of us are going to suffer. For the American idea, though it is shared by all of us, is realized in each one of us.   36

And now, what are those of us who are elected public officials supposed to do? We call ourselves public servants, but I'll tell you this: we as public servants must set an example for the rest of the nation. It is hypocritical for the public official to admonish and exhort the people to uphold the common good if we are derelict in upholding the common good. More is required, more is required of public officials than slogans and handshakes and press releases. More is required. We must hold ourselves strictly accountable. We must provide the people with the vision of the future.   37

If we promise as public officials, we must deliver. If . . . if we as public officials propose, we must produce. If we say to the American people, it is time for you to be sacrificial, sacrifice, if the public official says that, we (public officials) must be the first to give. We must be. And again, if we make mistakes, we must be willing to admit them. We have to do that. What we have to do is strike a balance between the idea that government should do everything and the idea, the belief, that government ought to do nothing. Strike a balance.   38

Let there be no illusions about the difficulty of forming this type of national community.   39
It's tough, difficult, not easy. But a spirit of harmony will survive in America only if each of us
remembers that we share a common destiny. If each of us remembers, when self-interest and
bitterness seem to prevail, that we share a common destiny.

I have confidence that we can form this kind of national community.   40

I have confidence that the Democratic Party can lead the way. I have that confidence. We   41
cannot improve on the system of government handed down to us by the founders of the Republic, there is no way to improve upon that. But what we can do is to find new ways to implement that system and realize our destiny.

Now, I began this speech by commenting to you on the uniqueness of a Barbara Jordan   42
making a keynote address. Well, I am going to close my speech by quoting a Republican president, and I ask that as you listen to these words of Abraham Lincoln, relate to them to the
concept of a national community in which every last one of us participates: "As I would not
be a slave, so I would not be a master. This . . . this, this expresses my idea of Democracy. Whatever differs from this, to the extent of the difference is no Democracy." Thank you.

Why did the speech produce such a strong reaction? One partial explanation undoubtedly relates to Jordan's powerful delivery. Jordan had a rich, deep resonant voice
that in reporting on one of her speeches Peter Jennings once compared to "the voice of
God." While delivery is rarely a major factor in the success of a speech, in this case it
undoubtedly played a role.

Professor Thompson suggests that an additional reason for her success was a "skillful use of appeal to values."[9] There is no doubt that Jordan used value appeals throughout her address. In paragraphs 7 & 8 she rejects a focus on problems alone and instead
calls for a "search" for "a national community" (paragraph 9). Later, she endorses
equality (paragraphs 10, 14), diversity (paragraphs 15–17), innovation (paragraph 18),
a positive vision (paragraph 19), common sense (paragraph 24), unity and the common
good (paragraphs 28–35), accountability for public officials (paragraphs 37–38), and
confidence in the future (paragraphs 40–41).

Despite her reliance on value appeals, it seems unlikely that this strategy explains
the success of her address. The problem is that everyone agrees with the values she endorses. A conservative Republican could have used virtually the same speech, from the
beginning of the focus on values to the conclusion. In fact, in the conclusion she mem-
orably quotes a Republican President, Abraham Lincoln:

As I would not be a slave, so I would not be a master. This . . . this, this expresses my idea of Democracy. Whatever differs from this, to the extent of the
difference is no Democracy. (paragraph 42)

Lincoln's definition of democracy is eloquent, but hardly controversial. Given the absolutely standard character of her value appeals it is hard to see why they would energize her audience.

If the explanation of the success for Jordan's address cannot be found in the main body, which was dominated by the value appeals, it must lie in what she said in the introduction. In paragraphs two, three, and four of her address Jordan uses the rhetorical strategy of enactment to create one of the most memorable moments in any American political speech of the last half-century. Enactment is a strategy in which the speaker uses himself/herself as proof of the point he/she is making. In this case, Jordan's very presence on the podium as a keynoter is used to demonstrate the fact that the Democratic party stands for equality, freedom, diversity and the other values she identifies. Jordan uses the fact that she is a Black woman from the South to prove her point.

> It was one hundred and forty-four years ago that members of the Democratic Party first met in convention to select a presidential candidate. Since that time, Democrats have continued once every four years and draft a party platform and nominate a presidential candidate. And our meeting this week is a continuation of that tradition.
>
> But there is something different about tonight. There is something special about tonight. What is different? What is special? I, Barbara Jordan, am a keynote speaker.
>
> A lot of years have passed since 1832, and during that time it would have been most unusual for any national political party to ask a Barbara Jordan to deliver a keynote address . . . but tonight here I am. And I feel that notwithstanding the past that my presence here is one additional piece of evidence that the American dream need not forever be deferred. (paragraphs 2–4)

With these words, Jordan enacts her message. She is the proof that the Democratic party has broken with a past in which minorities and women were not allowed representation. It was her presence and the wonderful introduction, especially her reference to the American dream, that made the speech so memorable.

And Jordan herself seemed to recognize that it was her presence that was most important in sending a message about what it meant to be a Democrat. Immediately after the wonderful introduction, Jordan asks, "now that I have this grand distinction, what in the world am I supposed to say?" (paragraph 5). In actuality, it made little difference what she had to say from that point on in the speech. Her utterly conventional recital of basic values was perfectly appropriate, although hardly memorable. But the introduction where she enacted the basic message of the party was a very memorable use of enactment as a special type of credibility.

Conclusion

One of the most important principles in understanding rhetoric is that it isn't just the words (and other symbols) that speak to an audience, but the person behind those words. In some cases, especially those in which a person possesses a great deal of external credibility, the mere fact that a given individual favors a position may be enough for an audience. The flip side of this principle is that once credibility has been lost, it matters very little what you have to say. The audience isn't going to listen to you. Thus, credibility is occasionally a decisive strategy, always necessary for persuasion, and in many cases a dominant strategy for producing persuasion.

Notes

1. See Aristotle, *The Rhetoric* in *The Basic Works of Aristotle,* ed. Richard McKeon (New York: Random House, 1941), Book I, Ch. 2, p. 1329.
2. I discuss the Hart scandal in "The Fall and Fall of Gary Hart," Speech Communication Association National Convention, New Orleans, November 1988.
3. See Edwin P. Bettinighaus and Michael J. Cody, *Persuasive Communication,* 4th ed. (New York: Holt, Rinehart and Winston, 1987), p. 103.
4. See Kenneth Andersen and Theodore Clevenger Jr., "A Summary of Experimental Research in Ethos," in *The Process of Social Influence: Readings in Persuasion,* Thomas D. Beisecker and Donn W. Parson, eds. (Englewood Cliffs: Prentice Hall, 1972), p. 246.
5. Aristotle, *The Rhetoric,* Book I, ch. 2, pp. 1329–1330.
6. See for instance Kirk Victor, "The Lone Ranger," *National Journal* 12 April 1997, pp. 694–697; Jack W. Germond and Jules Witcover, *National Journal* 2 & 9 January 1999, p. 68.
7. See Wayne N. Thompson, "Barbara Jordan's Keynote Address: The Juxtaposition of Contradictory Values," *Southern Speech Communication Journal* 44 (1979), pp. 223–224.
8. Thompson, p. 223.
9. Thompson, p. 232.

CHAPTER SEVEN

Aesthetic Strategies

Aesthetics is the study of beauty. How does aesthetics relate to rhetoric? The answer is that there is an aesthetic dimension to rhetoric. A short example may make this point clear. Former President Reagan often emphasized the greatness of America by saying that this nation had a "rendezvous with destiny," a phrase he borrowed from Franklin Roosevelt. Reagan used those words to highlight the history of the nation and to argue that we have a special role to play in the world.

Reagan's idea was important, but of equal importance was the way that he expressed the idea. One of our less articulate presidents might have expressed the same idea by saying that "America always has been on the way to an important meeting." While the content is the same, the meaning is radically different because the second phrase lacks the aesthetic power of Reagan's usage.

The key point is that rhetoric persuades not merely with content, but also with the style of the presentation. The dominant means of expressing the aesthetic dimension of rhetoric is through language, but there are other possible devices as well. Film rhetoric might use particular camera angles or the picture itself to present a point. In his famous painting, "Guernica," Picasso used his artistic style to expose the horrors of the Spanish Civil War. There is also obviously an aesthetic dimension to works of persuasive music.

Types of Aesthetic Strategies

There are five main types of aesthetic strategies: language, graphic, objects, pictures, and sound.

Language ◆ Language strategies are the most important type of aesthetic strategy and the bulk of the remainder of this chapter discusses types and functions of them.

Graphic ◆ Graphic aesthetic strategies includes drawings, bullet points, charts, subheads, underlining, and other devices that are designed to make written rhetoric more persuasive. The primary functions of graphic strategies are to emphasize points and make the material easier to understand. While graphic strategies are important, they are more a supporting than a dominant form of persuasion. No one ever finished reading a report by exclaiming: "Wow what bullet points. I'm persuaded!"

Objects ◆ Objects can be used as an aesthetic strategy in a speech or other presentation. Chapter four includes a speech by Newt Gingrich, in which he held up a microchip and a vacuum tube in order to make a point about inefficiency in the Federal government. Gingrich was using the microchip and the vacuum tube as part of a developed comparison, but he also was using them as objects to add interest to his speech. Objects can be used for other purposes as well. A speaker may hold up an object to get the attention of the audience, to clarify the point, or to tap into values or needs. A grisly example of the last strategy occurs when a terrorist shows the media a body part such as a severed finger of a kidnap victim. The terrorist is using the severed finger to make the point that he/she is willing to kill the hostages.

Pictures ◆ The fourth type of aesthetic strategy is a picture. Still pictures may be used to visually demonstrate a point. Alternatively, film or video may be used to reveal a situation, support an argument, or tell a story.

Pictures, whether still or moving, are used to fulfill a variety of aesthetic functions. A picture may be cited as support for an argument. Since the Gulf War, we have gotten used to seeing footage of bombing raids. Those pictures demonstrate the success or failure of the raid. Alternatively, pictures may be used to tap into values or needs. Both pro-choice and pro-life advocates use pictures to create an emotional response. The pro-life activist uses a picture of a dead fetus to link to the value of life. In contrast, the pro-choice activist uses a picture of a woman in chains to support freedom of choice.

Pictures also can be used to emphasize a point or clarify a position. The adage that a "picture is worth a thousand words," is often correct.

Paintings and other artwork also can function rhetorically. Much of the great art of the Western World, from the Middle Ages until at least the beginning of the 19th century, was focused on supporting Christianity. This art was both beautiful and highly rhetorical in that it used the power of aesthetics to support Christian doctrine.

What should a critic look for in regard to the rhetorical use of pictures? This is a difficult question to answer because so much has been written about art, photography, film, and video. For example, entire books have been written discussing the use of different camera techniques in film and video. An example may make clear how complex film rhetoric can be. At the beginning of *Saving Private Ryan*, Steven Spielberg tries to make us feel as if we were there on Omaha beach on June 6, 1944. He uses a handheld camera and jumps back and forth among different images to give us the feel for the battle. This is only one example of how different camera techniques can influence the way that visual rhetoric functions. And of course, there are many other film and video strategies for producing persuasion.

From the perspective of rhetorical analysis, however, the important point is to describe how the visual strategy functions persuasively. The critic need not know every detail of film theory to make such a judgment. Instead, the key is simply to explain how the image relates to the other strategies in the rhetoric.

Sound ◆ The final category of aesthetic strategy is sound, primarily music. Sound can be used to add interest to a work of rhetoric in the same way that a sound track adds interest to a film or television. Sound also can be used to tap into values, needs or symbols. If you want to get a crowd of alumni from a particular school excited, just play the fight song for their school. In some cases, sound also can be used to support an argument.

Summary of Types of Aesthetic Strategies

The four non-language aesthetic strategies primarily are used to add interest to and clarify the meaning of a persuasive claim. In some instances, these aesthetic strategies also may be used to tap into one of the other main categories of persuasion. In particular, visual images are a powerful way of building supporting arguments, telling narratives, and tapping into values and needs.

All five types of aesthetic strategies are important. There are cases in which each of these types of aesthetic strategy is the dominant form of persuasion in a given work of rhetoric. However, of the five types, language is far and away the most important. Language is the most important aesthetic strategy for two reasons. First, language is the dominant symbol system which humans use to communicate. Second, each of the other aesthetic strategies must be translated into language in the mind of the audience before it can function to produce persuasion. Take Spielberg's use of camera techniques in *Saving Private Ryan* as an example. Those film techniques give the viewer a sense of the horror of war and the great heroism of the men who landed in Normandy in June 1944. That visual sense of what they went through could be translated into support for a claim such as "we must never again have to fight such a war" or "we don't do enough for our veterans" or "we should not go to war unless the very security of the nation is at risk." The visual aesthetic strategy is very important, but to reach the level of a persuasive claim, it must be translated into language in the mind of the audience.

Functions of Language Strategies

Language strategies serve several important persuasive functions. First, language strategies may be used to make a point more vivid. A speaker might build an argument concerning recent genocide in Rwanda. Alternatively, he/she might combine that argument with a detailed description of one instance of murder. That detailed description might make the argument much more effective because it would hit home with the audience.

Second, language strategies can be used to make a conclusion more understandable and memorable. In this way, the language strategy both can clarify the claim being made and also make it more likely to be remembered. So, for example, a comparison might be used to clarify a complicated policy argument. That comparison could help the audience remember the argument at a later time.

Finally, language strategies can be used to add emphasis to any point. Politicians (and advertisers) use repetition to make their conclusion clear and to emphasize its importance. Think about how many times you have heard a given advertising slogan. Politicians do the same thing. For example, the familiar chant "No New Taxes," is used by Republicans to distinguish themselves from the Democrats and to emphasize their commitment to cutting taxes.

Types of Language Strategies

Language strategies can be grouped into the following sub-categories:

1. Metaphor and other Forms of Comparison
2. Antithesis
3. Parallel Structure and Repetition
4. Rhetorical Questions
5. Depiction or Description
6. Personification
7. Rhythm and Rhyme
8. Definition
9. Alliteration and Assonance
10. Allusion
11. Labeling
12. Irony

Metaphor ◆ The most important language strategy is clearly metaphorical usage, including metaphor itself and other forms of comparison such as analogies and similes. A somewhat more complex type of metaphor is a synechdoche in which a part of an object is used to refer to the entire object. In a statement referring to a fleet of ships as "fifty smokestacks on the horizon," the word smokestack is a synechdoche referring to the ships.

Reduced to its simplest form a comparison says that two object/ideas/people are similar in some way. When Martin Luther King, Jr. wanted to describe a harmonious future society, he called it a "dream." Both Republicans and Democrats often compare America to a family. In a speech considered in the next chapter, Jesse Jackson compares America to both a "rainbow" and a "quilt." In all of these examples, the speaker is relying on the power of metaphor to identify the inherent similarity between two things or people.

There are two important dimensions to metaphor: degree of development and a literal-figurative distinction. Some metaphors (or analogies or similes) are developed in more detail, while others are left as a single phrase. A politician might spend an entire speech developing an analogy between the economic problems facing the United States in the 1990s and those that faced the nation on the eve of the Great Depression. On the other hand, a metaphor might simply be thrown out as I did the word "eve" in the previous sentence.

A distinction also can be drawn between figurative and literal forms of comparison. A literal comparison is drawn when the two objects being compared fall into the same category. Comparisons of two presidents, two football players, two film stars and so forth all would fall into the literal category because in each case the comparison is between two people from the same category of life. On the other hand, a comparison of Harrison Ford to President Clinton would be a figurative comparison because the jobs of movie star and President of the United States are obviously different.

It should be clear that a continuum exists from the purely literal to the purely figurative. For example, a comparison of Meryl Streep to Katherine Hepburn would fall on the literal side of the continuum because both Streep and Hepburn are film stars. But it would not be a purely literal comparison since the two acted in different eras.

What are the functions of the various forms of metaphor? Metaphor usage serves two main functions. First, metaphors are often added to works of rhetoric very much as seasoning is added to a dish of food. In this way, the metaphor adds interest to the rhetoric. A speaker or writer might sprinkle a variety of metaphors in a work on pollution in order to make that rhetoric more interesting. Air pollution could be called "an invisible cloud of death." Pollution controls might be labeled "a sure-thing investment," rather than a business expense. In these examples, the comparison functions to make a topic more interesting and vivid.

Second, in some instances metaphor is used, not merely to make a work more interesting, but becomes the underlying core of the work. In these instances, metaphor functions as a worldview for understanding social conditions. For example, a number of United States Supreme Court cases have used a metaphor originally created by Thomas Jefferson to interpret the proper relationship between church and state in this nation. These cases have said that there should be a "wall" separating government from religion. The wall metaphor has functioned as more than a mere comparison.[1] To some extent it has shaped discussion at the court. For example, some have argued that the wall should be high and wide. Others have argued that wall should not provide absolute separation, but that there should be gates in it. In this example, the metaphor is functioning as a model for understanding the world.

Another example illustrates this same point. In the 1960s some African American activists compared poor and mainly Black sections of some cities to a colony.[2] With this comparison, they argued that America treated people of color the same way that colonial powers treated natives. The colony metaphor provided a framework for understanding racial conflict; it functioned as a "paradigm" for approaching the world.

In most instances, metaphors and other comparisons are used merely as spice, to liven up a work of rhetoric. But it is important to recognize that in some cases comparisons are used as a model or paradigm to reveal the world. Used in this second sense, metaphors are powerful devices that shape human understanding. If you can change someone's metaphors, you can change how that person understands the world.[3]

Antithesis ◆ Antithesis occurs when two opposing thoughts are juxtaposed in the same sentence or paragraph. Earlier I cited John Kennedy's famous statement "ask not what your country can do for you. Ask what you can do for your country." In this comment, JFK relies on the "not this, but that" form which is common to antithesis to emphasize his point. Antithesis is also often used to draw distinctions between opposing ideas.

Parallel Structure and Repetition ◆ Parallel structure and repetition are closely related strategies that are used to emphasize the importance of a point and make it more memorable. Repetition occurs when a sentence, phrase, or even a single word is repeated. Advertisers do this with slogans. A Democrat might repeat the phrase "protect the elderly, no more cuts," to emphasize his/her commitment to programs like Social Security and Medicare.

Parallel structure is a special form of repetition. It occurs when a speaker/writer begins several paragraphs or sentences in a row with the same sentence structure. Imagine a Democrat defending a variety of social programs. He/she might begin a number of paragraphs by saying: "They say that we cannot afford adequate funding for Medicare, but I say we cannot afford not to fully fund that program." Succeeding paragraphs would begin with the same sentence, but a different program inserted in place of Medicare. In such an instance (which is also an example of antithesis), the speaker would be using parallel structure to defend current social programs. The parallel structure would both add interest and make the speech more memorable.

Rhetorical Question ◆ A rhetorical question is a question asked by a speaker/writer which implies an answer. The point of the question is not to elicit information, but to get the audience involved in the presentation. At the end of the "New South" speech, which is included in the readings volume that goes with this book, Henry Grady uses a number of rhetorical questions to gain support from the audience. He asks "Now, what answer has New England to this message? Will she permit the prejudices of war to remain in the hearts of the conquerors, when it has died in the hearts of the conquered?" Grady uses these questions and others to pull the audience to his side. He obviously expects the audience to think or say "NO!" in response to the second rhetorical question. And that is exactly what they did. The questions both drew participation from the audience and also added interest to the speech. Rhetorical questions also often are used as transition devices.

It should be recognized, however, that rhetorical questions are most effective when the rhetor knows how the audience will react. If a speaker asks a rhetorical question expecting the audience to respond, "Yes, Yes, Yes," and instead they shout out NO, that would be a major problem.

Depiction or Description ◆ Depiction or description is used when the speaker/writer creates a vivid picture of some situation. Depiction is the equivalent of a verbal snapshot or a passage setting the scene in a story. It is used to add interest and make a conclusion more vivid. In a courtroom, for example, a prosecutor might use a portion of his/her opening statement to describe a murder in detail. There is no legal requirement to provide this detailed description. Under the law, the prosecutor would need to do no more than prove that the accused criminal had committed the murder. But the prosecutor might describe the crime in great detail in order to get the sympathy of the jury for the victim's family and make them hate the defendant.

Personification ◆ Personification is a strategy in which an inanimate object or concept is given human form. The "Jolly Green Giant is not a real vegetable, but a personification of all vegetables transformed into a giant person. Personification is a kind of metaphor, which usually takes the form of a reference to some part of human anatomy. Thus, rhetors often refer to the "heart" or "backbone" of a nation. It is primarily a strategy of emphasis, although it is sometimes used to change the connotative meaning associated with a term. A conservative Republican might say, for instance that "where once labor unions were America's muscle, they now are our beer belly."

Rhythm and Rhyme. ◆ Rhythm and rhyme work both to make rhetoric more interesting and also to aid the audience in remembering the point. Since the Greeks, humans have known that rhyme functions as a memory aid. In the era before writing, the power of rhyme was used to help people memorize epic poems and other literature and rhetoric. To some extent this function is still being fulfilled. Today, people find it much easier to remember song lyrics than passages from public speeches, largely because of the rhyme.

Rhyme or rhythm (when used in moderation) also can make a work of rhetoric more interesting. Johnny Cochran used a brief rhyme in his closing statement in the O.J. Simpson trial to bring home a point to the jury, "If the gloves don't fit, you must acquit." There is, however, a danger that use of rhyme may seem hokey; that is why this language strategy should be used in moderation.

Definition and Redefinition ◆ Definition works as a language strategy to define the terms under consideration. If you can control the subject of discussion, you often can control the discussion itself. For example, a definitional strategy might be used in a discussion of sexual harassment, either to magnify or minimize the problem. Using a very restrictive definition would reduce the amount of sexual harassment occurring in this nation. (Or more accurately it would reduce the amount of behavior included in the category). On the other hand, use of a broad definition (any remark or action making any woman feel uncomfortable) dramatically would expand the size of the problem.

As I explained in relation to the Kerry address considered in the previous chapter, redefinition is used literally to re-define a problem. It is a language strategy designed to get people to see a different reality than they previously had understood.

Alliteration and Assonance ◆ Alliteration is a strategy in which the speaker uses several words in a row all beginning with the same consonant. A liberal Democrat (assuming that one could be found) might refer to "callous, cruel, contemporary conservatism." Assonance is a similar strategy in which several words in a row contain the same vowel sound. In his Inaugural Address, which is included in the readings volume, John F. Kennedy refers to the "steady spread of the deadly atom," a phrase in which steady, spread, and deadly contain the same vowel sound.

Assonance is rarely used in contemporary rhetoric and when it is used might not even be noticed by the audience. Alliteration is somewhat more important. Both assonance and alliteration are strategies designed to make rhetoric more interesting. Obviously, no one will be persuaded merely through the use of alliteration or assonance.

Allusion ◆ An allusion is an indirect reference to a work of rhetoric, literature, or history. In a speech following the assassination of John F. Kennedy, President Lyndon Johnson alluded to the Gettysburg Address when he said, "So let us here highly resolve that John Fitzgerald Kennedy did not live—or die—in vain."[4] Johnson was referring to a passage in the Gettysburg Address where Lincoln said, "that we here highly resolve that these dead shall not have died in vain. . ."[5] Allusions also may be made to works of literature, history, or even figures in current events. In the 1950s and 1960s, some referred to the danger of aggressive communism in Asia as threatening to create a "bamboo curtain." This phrase combined metaphor with an allusion to the phrase, which Winston Churchill used to describe Soviet tyranny in Eastern Europe, an "iron curtain."

Allusion works by tapping into the knowledge of the audience. The audience then fills in the reference. Again, it is a strategy to add interest to the rhetoric. In some instances, allusion also may function as an enthymeme. In that case, the allusion is used to support an implied argumentative judgment. Note, that not all allusions are also enthymemes. Some allusions are simply references to other material and make no argument.

Labeling ◆ A label or slogan is used to characterize a person, object, idea, or position. A liberal might refer, for example, to "Neanderthal Conservatism," as part of an attack on a budget proposal. The liberal would be using the word "Neanderthal," not as a reference to an earlier species in human evolution, but to label the particular conservative agenda as cruel or uncaring. Note, that in this example a metaphor is used as part of the label. Such combination of language strategies in a sort of mix and match approach is common.

Labels are used to reduce a point to a phrase that encapsulates the concept. The label (or slogan) then can be used again and again to hammer the point home.

Irony ◆ Irony is a language strategy in which the speaker explicitly says one thing, but means another altogether. A conservative might use irony in referring to a liberal Senator as "that well known budget slasher." He/she would be implying that the Senator was anything but a budget slasher.

An example of unintentional irony was published several years ago at the University of Kansas when a conservative student group included a "cultural literacy" quiz as part of an attack the quality of education being received by students. The quiz was designed to make the point that students are unaware of essential facts relating to our history. Question four asked "What document is the following quote from? 'We hold these truths to be self-evident: that all men are created equal. . .'"[6] The answer listed was the Constitution of the United States. Of course, the passage cited is the introduction to The Declaration of Independence. In this case, the conservative student group unintentionally and ironically supported their point about lack of cultural knowledge by mislabeling the most famous passage in the most famous document in American history.

Irony is closely related to allusion and enthymematic argument since it relies on audience knowledge. But irony is somewhat different from these other strategies. Irony undercuts a position by poking fun at it. It is a strategy used primarily to add interest and depends upon audience knowledge in order to be successful.

Irony is a risky strategy both because it depends upon audience knowledge and also because it can produce backlash in the audience.

Analysis of Mario Cuomo's 1984 "Keynote Address"

To illustrate the various language strategies discussed in this section, a speech by former Governor Mario Cuomo of New York is included. The speech was presented at the 1984 Democratic National Convention in San Francisco. Cuomo used a variety of language strategies to defend the Democratic ticket and attack the Reagan administration.

Keynote Address
1984 Democratic National Convention
Mario Cuomo

On behalf of the Empire State and the family of New York, I thank you for the great privilege of being allowed to address this convention.   1

Please allow me to skip the stories and the poetry and the temptation to deal in nice but vague rhetoric.   2

Let me instead use this valuable opportunity to deal with the questions that should determine this election and that are vital to the American people.   3

Delivered in San Francisco, CA on July 17, 1984.

Ten days ago, President Reagan admitted that although some people in this country   4
seemed to be doing well nowadays, others were unhappy, and even worried, about themselves, their families and their futures.

The President said he didn't understand that fear. He said, "Why, this country is a shining   5
city on a hill."

The President is right. In many ways we are "a shining city on a hill."   6

But the hard truth is that not everyone is sharing in this city's splendor and glory.   7

A shining city is perhaps all the President sees from the portico of the White House and   8
the veranda of his ranch, where everyone seems to be doing well.

But there's another part of the city, the part where some people can't pay their mort-   9
gages and most young people can't afford one, where students can't afford the education
they need and middle-class parents watch the dreams they hold for their children evaporate.

In this part of the city there are more poor than ever, more families in trouble. More and   10
more people who need help but can't find it.

Even worse: There are elderly people who tremble in the basements of the houses there.   11

There are people who sleep in the city's streets, in the gutter, where the glitter doesn't   12
show.

There are ghettos where thousands of young people, without an education or a job, give   13
their lives away to drug dealers every day.

There is despair, Mr. President, in faces you never see, in the places you never visit in your   14
shining city.

In fact, Mr. President, this nation is more a "Tale of Two Cities" than it is a "Shining City on   15
a Hill."

Maybe if you visited more places, Mr. President, you'd understand.   16

Maybe if you went to Appalachia where some people still live in sheds and to Lack-   17
awanna where thousands of unemployed steel workers wonder why we subsidized foreign
steel while we surrender their dignity to unemployment and to welfare checks; maybe if you
stepped into a shelter in Chicago and talked with some of the homeless there; maybe, Mr.
President if you asked a woman who'd been denied the help she needs to feed her children
because you say we need the money to give a tax break to a millionaire or to build a missile
we can't even afford to use—maybe then you'd understand.

Maybe, Mr. President.   18

But I'm afraid not.   19

Because, the truth is, this is how we were warned it would be.   20

President Reagan told us from the beginning that he believes in a kind of social Darwin-   21
ism. Survival of the fittest. "Government can't do everything," we were told. "So it should settle for taking care of the strong and hope that economic ambition and charity will do the rest.
Make the rich richer and what falls from their table will be enough for the middle class and
those trying to make it into the middle class."

The Republicans called it trickle-down when Hoover tried it. Now they call it supply side.   22
It is the same shining city for those relative few who are lucky enough to live in its good
neighborhoods.

But for the people who are excluded—locked out—all they can do is to stare from a dis-   23
tance at the city's glimmering towers.

It's an old story. as old as our history.   24

The difference between Democrats and Republicans has always been measured in   25
courage and confidence. The Republicans believe the wagon train will not make it to the
frontier unless some of our old, some of our young and some of our weak are left behind by
the side of the trail.

The strong will inherit the land!   26

We Democrats believe that we can make it all the way with the whole family intact.   27

We have. More than once.   28

Ever since Franklin Roosevelt lifted himself from his wheelchair to lift the nation from its   29
knees. Wagon train after wagon train. To new frontier of education, housing, peace. The whole
family aboard. Constantly reaching out to extend and enlarge that family. Lifting them up into
the wagon on the way. Blacks and Hispanics, people of every ethnic group, and Native Americans—all those struggling to build their families claim some small share of America.

For nearly 50 years we carried them to new levels of comfort, security, dignity, even   30
affluence.

Some of us are in this room today only because this nation had that confidence.   31

It would be wrong to forget that.   32

So, we are at this convention to remind ourselves where we come from and to claim the   33
future for ourselves and for our children.

Today, our great Democratic Party, which has saved this nation from depression, from fas-   34
cism, from racism, from corruption, is called upon to do it again—this time to save the nation
from confusion and division, most of all from a fear of a nuclear holocaust.

In order to succeed, we must answer our opponent's polished and appealing rhetoric   35
with a more telling reasonableness and rationality.

We must win this case on the merits.   36

We must get the American public to look past the glitter, beyond the showmanship—to   37
reality, to the hard substance of things. And we will do that not so much with speeches that
sound good as with speeches that are good and sound.

Not so much with speeches that bring people to their feet as with speeches that bring   38
people to their senses.

We must make the American people hear our "tale of two cities."   39

We must convince them that we don't have to settle for two cities, that we can have one   40
city, indivisible, shining for all its people.

We will have no chance to do that if what comes out of the convention, what is heard   41
throughout the campaign, is a babel of arguing voices.

To succeed we will have to surrender small parts of our individual interests, to build a   42
platform we can all stand on, at once, comfortably, proudly singing out the truth for the nation to hear, in chorus, its logic so clear and commanding that no slick commercial, no
amount of geniality, no martial music will be able to muffle it.

We Democrats must unite so that the entire nation can. Surely the Republicans won't   43
bring the convention together. Their policies divide the nation: into the lucky and the left-out,
the royalty and the rabble.

The Republicans are willing to treat that division as victory. They would cut this nation in   44
half, into those temporarily better off and those worse off than before, and call it recovery.

We should not be embarrassed or dismayed if the process of unifying is difficult, even at   45
times wrenching.

Unlike any other party, we embrace men and women of every color, every creed, every orientation, every economic class. In our family are gathered everyone from the abject poor of Essex County in New York to the enlightened affluent of the gold coasts of both ends of our nation. And in between is the heart of our constituency. The middle class, the people not rich enough to be worry-free but not poor enough to be on welfare, those who work for a living because they have to. White collar and blue collar. Young professionals. Men and women in small business desperate for the capital and contracts they need to prove their worth. 46

We speak for the minorities who have not yet entered the mainstream. 47

For ethnics who want to add their culture to the mosaic that is America. 48

For women indignant that we refuse to etch into our governmental commandments the simple rule "thou shalt not sin against equality," a commandment so obvious it can be spelled in three letters: E.R.A.! 49

For young people demanding an education and a future. 50

For senior citizens terrorized by the idea that their only security, their Social Security, is being threatened. 51

For millions of reasoning people fighting to preserve our environment from greed and stupidity. And fighting to preserve our very existence from a macho intransigence that refuses to make intelligent attempts to discuss the possibility of nuclear holocaust with our enemy. Refusing because they believe we can pile missiles so high that they will pierce the clouds and the sight of them will frighten our enemies into submission. 52

We're proud of this diversity. Grateful we don't have to manufacture its appearance the way the Republicans will next month in Dallas, by propping up mannequin delegates on the convention floor. 53

But we pay a price for it. 54

The different people we represent have many points of view. Sometimes they compete and then we have debates, even arguments. That's what our primaries were. 55

But now the primaries are over, and it is time to lock arms and move into this campaign together. 56

If we need any inspiration to make the effort to put aside our small differences, all we need to do is to reflect on the Republican policy of divide and cajole and how it has injured our land since 1980. 57

The President has asked us to judge him on whether or not he's fulfilled the promises he made four years ago. I accept that. Just consider what he said and what he's done. 58

Inflation is down since 1980. But not because of the supply-side miracle promoted by the President. Inflation was reduced the old-fashioned way, with a recession, the worst since 1932. More then 55,000 bankruptcies. Two years of massive unemployment. Two-hundred-thousand farmers and ranchers forced off the land. More homeless than at any time since the Great Depression. More hungry, more poor—mostly women—and a nearly $200 billion deficit threatening our future. 59

The President's deficit is a direct and dramatic repudiation of his promise to balance our budget by 1983. 60

That deficit is the largest in the history of this universe; more than three times larger than the deficit in President Carter's last year. 61

It is a deficit that, according to the President's own fiscal advisor, could grow as high as $300 billion a year, stretching "as far as the eye can see." 62

It is a debt so large that as much as one-half of our revenue from the income tax goes to   63
pay the interest on it each year.

It is a mortgage on our children's futures that can only be paid in pain and that could   64
eventually bring this nation to its knees.

Don't take my word for it—I'm a Democrat   65

Ask the Republican investment bankers on Wall Street what they think the chances are   66
this recovery will be permanent. If they're not too embarrassed to tell you the truth, they'll say
they are appalled and frightened by the President's deficit. Ask them what they think of our
economy, now that it has been driven by the distorted value of the dollar back to its colonial
condition, exporting agricultural products and importing manufactured ones.

Ask those Republican investment bankers what they expect the interest rate to be a year   67
from now. And ask them what they predict for the inflation rate then.

How important is this question of the deficit?   68

Think about it: What chance would the Republican candidate have had in 1980 if he had   69
told the American people that he intended to pay for his so-called economic recovery with
bankruptcies, unemployment and the largest Government debt known to humankind?
Would American voters have signed the loan certificate for him on Election Day? Of course
not! It was an election won with smoke and mirrors, with illusions. It is a recovery made of the
same stuff.

And what about foreign policy?   70

They said they would make us and the whole world safer. They say they have.   71

By creating the largest defense budget in history, one even they now admit is excessive,   72
failed to discuss peace with our enemies. By the loss of 279 young Americans in Lebanon in
pursuit of a plan and a policy no one can find or describe.

We give monies to Latin American governments that murder nuns, and then lie about it.   73

We have been less than zealous in our support of the only real friend we have in the Mid-   74
dle East, the one democracy there, our flesh and blood ally, the state of Israel.

Our policy drifts with no real direction, other than an hysterical commitment to an arms   75
race that leads nowhere, if we're lucky. If we're not—it could lead us to bankruptcy or war.

Of course we must have a strong defense!   76

Of course Democrats believe that there are times when we must stand and fight. And we   77
have. Thousands of us have paid for freedom with our lives. But always, when we've been at
our best, our purposes were clear.

Now they're not. Now our allies are as confused as our enemies.   78

Now we have no real commitment to our friends or our ideals to human rights, to the   79
refusenicks, to Sakharov, to Bishop Tutu and the others struggling for freedom in South Africa.

We have spent more than we can afford. We have pounded our chest and made bold   80
speeches. But we lost 279 young Americans in Lebanon and we are forced to live behind sand
bags in Washington.

How can anyone believe that we are stronger, safer or better?   81

That's the Republican record.   82

That its disastrous quality is not more fully understood by the American people is attrib-   83
utable, I think, to the President's amiability and the failure by some to separate the salesman
from the product.

It's now up to us to make the case to America.   84

And to remind Americans that if they are not happy with all the President has done so   85
far, they should consider how much worse it will be if he is left to his radical proclivities for another four years unrestrained by the need once again to come before the American people.

If July brings back Anne Gorsuch Burford, what can we expect of December?   86

Where would another four years take us?   87

How much larger will the deficit be?   88

How much deeper the cuts in programs for the struggling middle class and the poor to   89
limit that deficit? How high the interest rates? How much more acid rain killing our forests and fouling our lakes?

What kind of Supreme Court? What kind of court and country will be fashioned by the   90
man who believes in having government mandate people's religion and morality?

The man who believes that trees pollute the environment, that the laws against discrim-   91
ination go too far. The man who threatens Social Security and Medicaid and help for the disabled.

How high will we pile the missiles?   92

How much deeper will be the gulf between us and our enemies?   93

Will we make meaner the spirit of our people?   94

This election will measure the record of the past four years. But more than that, it will an-   95
swer the question of what kind of people we want to be.

We Democrats still have a dream. We still believe in this nation's future.   96

And this is our answer—our credo: 97

We believe in only the government we need, but we insist on all the government we need.   98

We believe in a government characterized by fairness and reasonableness, a reasonable-   99
ness that goes beyond labels, that doesn't distort or promise to do what it knows it can't do.

A government strong enough to use the words "love" and "compassion" and smart   100
enough to convert our noblest aspirations.

We believe in encouraging the talented, but we believe that while survival of the fittest   101
may be a good working description of the process of evolution, a government of humans should elevate itself to a higher order, one which fills the gaps left by chance or a wisdom we don't understand.

We would rather have laws written by the patron of this great city, the man called the   102
"world's most sincere Democrat," St. Francis of Assisi, than laws written by Darwin.

We believe, as Democrats, that a society as blessed as ours, the most affluent democracy   103
in the world's history, that can spend trillions on instruments of destruction, ought to be able to help the middle class in its struggle, ought to be able to find work for all who can do it, room at the table, shelter for the homeless, care for the elderly and infirm, hope for the destitute.

We proclaim as loudly as we can the utter insanity of nuclear proliferation and the need   104
for a nuclear freeze, if only to affirm the simple truth that peace is better than war because life is better than death.

We believe in firm but fair law and order, in the union movement, in privacy for people,   105
openness by government, civil rights, and human rights.

We believe in a single fundamental idea that describes better than most textbooks and   106
any speech what a proper government should be. The idea of family. Mutuality. The sharing

of benefits and burdens for the good of all. Feeling one another's pain. Sharing one another's blessings. Reasonably, honestly, fairly, without respect to race, or sex, or geography or political affiliation.

We believe we must be the family of America, recognizing that at the heart of the matter   107
we are bound one to another, that the problems of a retired school teacher in Duluth are our problems. That the future of the child in Buffalo is our future. The struggle of a disabled man in Boston to survive, to live decently is our struggle. The hunger of a woman in Little Rock is our hunger. The failure anywhere to provide what reasonably we might, to avoid pain, is our failure.

For 50 years we Democrats created a better future for our children, using traditional dem-   108
ocratic principles as a fixed beacon, giving us direction and purpose, but constantly innovating, adapting to new realities; Roosevelt's alphabet programs; Truman's NATO and the GI Bill of rights; Kennedy's intelligent tax incentives and the Alliance For Progress; Johnson's civil rights; Carter's human rights and the nearly miraculous Camp David peace accord.

Democrats did it—and Democrats can do it again.   109
We can build a future that deals with our deficit.   110
Remember, 50 years of progress never cost us what the last four years of stagnation have.   111
We can deal with that deficit intelligently, by shared sacrifice, with all parts of the nation's family contributing, building partnerships with the private sector, providing a sound defense without depriving ourselves of what we need to feed our children and care for our people.

We can have a future that provides for all the young of the present by marrying common   112
sense and compassion.

We know we can, because we did it for nearly 50 years before 1980.   113
We can do it again. If we do not forget. Forget that this entire nation has profited by these   114
progressive principles. That they helped lift up generations to the middle class and higher: gave us a chance to work, to go to college, to raise a family, to own a house, to be secure in our old age and, before that, to reach heights that our own parents would not have dared dream of.

That struggle to live with dignity is the real story of the shining city. It's a story I   115
didn't read in a book, or learn in a classroom. I saw it, and lived it. Like many of you.

I watched a small man with thick calluses on both hands work 15 and 16 hours a day. I   116
saw him once literally bleed from the bottoms of his feet, a man who came here uneducated, alone, unable to speak the language, who taught me all I needed to know about faith and hard work by the simple eloquence of his example. I learned about our kind of democracy from my father. I learned about our obligation to each other from him and from my mother. They asked only for a chance to work and to make the world better for their children and to be protected in those moments when they would not be able to protect themselves. This nation and its government did that for them.

And that they were able to build a family and live in dignity and see one of their children   117
go from behind their little grocery store on the other side of the tracks in south Jamaica where he was born, to occupy the highest seat in the greatest state of the greatest nation in the only world we know, is an ineffably beautiful tribute to the democratic process.

And on Jan. 20, 1985, it will happen again. Only on a much grander scale. We will have a   118
new President of the United States, a Democrat born not to the blood of kings but to the blood of immigrants and pioneers.

We will have America's first woman Vice President, the child of immigrants, a New Yorker,   119
opening with one magnificent stroke a whole new frontier for the United States.

It will happen, if we make it happen.   120

I ask you, ladies and gentlemen, brothers and sisters—for the good of all of us, for the   121
love of this great nation, for the family of America, for the love of God. Please make this nation remember how futures are built.

◆◆◆

Mario Cuomo's 1984 speech was a "keynote" address to the 1984 Democratic convention. A "keynote" address is designed to do exactly what its name implies—hit the
key note for the convention. A convention keynote address is aimed at two audiences:
the faithful and to a lesser degree undecided voters. In this case, Cuomo's primary task
was to unify and energize the Democratic party behind the presidential ticket of Walter Mondale and Geraldine Ferraro.

It is important to recognize that Cuomo definitely was not aiming at Republicans.
From the second paragraph on, he sharply attacked the Reagan administration in general and President Reagan in particular.

What kind of barriers did Cuomo confront in his keynote address? One set of barriers facing Cuomo came from the nature of the occasion.[7] Traditionally, a convention
keynote is designed to unify and energize the faithful supporters of a particular party.
Therefore, these addresses generally have focused upon the history of the party, the basic values and other principles that unify supporters of the party, and points of com-
monality among all the groups that make up the party. In contrast, keynote addresses
generally have not focused on public policy in any detail. Given the situation in which
keynotes are presented, it is understandable that the style of most such addresses has
been relatively formal. In a formal setting we expect a formal style. The defining characteristics of previous keynote addresses are important, because in order to succeed in
his particular address, Cuomo had to adapt to the expectations of the audience about
keynote addresses in general.[8]

The second set of barriers facing Cuomo came from the nature of the political situation in 1984. By the summer of 1984 when the Democratic convention occurred, it
was obvious that the Democrats were facing a serious political problem. The economy
had come out of recession and was beginning to pick up steam. And Ronald Reagan remained personally quite popular with the American people. Nor was there any foreign
or domestic crisis that might aid the Democrats. A situation defined by a strong economy, a popular president, and a nation at peace gave an enormous political advantage
to the incumbent president. It was this situation that Cuomo faced in 1984.

Cuomo's 1984 address to the Democratic convention is justly famous as one of the
great speeches of the last quarter century. For example, David Henry concludes that
Cuomo's address "received wide praise from the press and general public. . ."[9] Even

Republicans agreed that it was a great speech. Henry quotes Senator Barry Goldwater as rating it "'one of the best speeches I've ever heard.'" [10]

In the address, Cuomo adapts to the demands of the keynote situation and brilliantly uses narrative, value-laden appeals, and language strategies to unify and energize the audience. Cuomo relies on three primary strategies in the speech. Given the length of the address and the many attacks on the Reagan administration contained within it, one might expect that the speech would be heavily argumentative. However, that is not the case. Cuomo does claim that Reagan's policies have been extremist, that his positions threaten the health of the economy, that they risk war, and so forth. But he does not so much build arguments as draw on ones that his primary audience of Democrats already accepts. For example, in a long introductory section, he mentions "elderly people who tremble in the basements" of their homes (paragraph 11). Here, he refers to the fear that many elderly had over potential cuts in Social Security. Note that Cuomo simply asserts that the elderly are "trembling" in their homes. He references no evidence on this point. Clearly, statements like the one I cited are designed to appeal to an audience that already believes that Reagan's policies have gone too far. While Cuomo does build arguments, rational argument is not one of the primary strategies defining the speech.

Rather than argument, Cuomo uses appeals to values and needs, narrative, and language strategies. Throughout the address, he emphasizes the need for security and values such as equality and opportunity. In the opening section of the speech, Cuomo alludes to Charles Dickens' novel, *A Tale of Two Cities*. He claims that like the novel, Reagan's America is also "a tale of two cities." He then focuses on the part of the city where "there are more poor than ever, more families in trouble," where there "are people who sleep in the city's streets," and where there is "despair" (paragraphs 10, 12, 14). Clearly, Cuomo is drawing upon the basic human need for security and the necessities of life. He does this throughout the speech.

Cuomo also uses appeals to basic values in all sections of the speech. For example, in paragraph 46, he links the Democrats to equality, opportunity, family, and diversity. Cuomo says:

> Unlike any other party, we embrace men and women of every color, every creed, every orientation, every economic class. In our family are gathered everyone from the abject poor of Essex County in New York to the enlightened affluent of the gold coasts of both ends of our nation. And in between is the heart of our constituency. The middle class, the pepole not rich enough to be worry-free but not poor enough to be on welfare, those who work for a living because they have to. White collar and blue collar.

In the following paragraphs, he claims that Democrats speak for minorities, for ethnics, for women, for the young and for senior citizens (paragraphs 47–51).

Cuomo skillfully uses both basic needs and basic values to unify and energize his audience. By saying that basic needs are threatened, he hopes to motivate Democrats to act. By appealing to shared values, he pulls the party together.

Cuomo's second major strategy is narrative. He uses narrative in several different ways. First, he uses short anecdotes to support his larger theme that the Reagan administration had failed the nation. For example, in paragraph 86, he refers to Anne Gorsuch Burford. Burford had been forced out as head of the Environmental Protection Agency when allegations were made that the EPA was not adequately regulating polluters and in fact had maintained inappropriate contacts with some companies.[11] Cuomo does not tell this story in detail. He merely refers to Gorsuch, confident that his audience will recall the incident.

Second and much more importantly, Cuomo tells a story of what might be called the "Democratic History of the United States." In that story, it is Democrats who have saved the country time and time again.

Early in the speech, he uses a metaphor of the wagon train to lay out the theme of the Democratic history. He says that "Republicans believe the wagon train will not make it to the frontier unless some of our old, some of our young and some of our weak are left behind by the side of the trail" (paragraph 25). In contrast, "We Democrats believe that we can make it all the way with the whole family intact" (paragraph 27). He then turns to a great hero in this Democratic history, Franklin Roosevelt, who, according to Cuomo, "lifted himself from his wheelchair to lift the nation from its knees" (paragraph 29). Roosevelt led this nation "To new frontiers of education, housing, peace" (paragraph 29).

And since FDR, the Democrats have continued to save the nation. It was Democrats who "saved this nation from depression, from fascism, from racism, from corruption" and, consequently, they are "called up to do it again—this time to save the nation from confusion and division, most of all from fear of a nuclear holocaust" (paragraph 34). He returns to the Democratic history near the conclusion of his address when he talks about great Democratic leaders including Truman, Kennedy, and Carter (paragraph 108).

In the conclusion, Cuomo shifts the focus of his Democratic History from the heroes of the Demcratic party to the people they helped. He uses the story of his own father to reaffirm the importance of the values undergirding the party:

> I watched a small man with thick calluses on both hands work 15 and 16 hours a day. I saw him once literally bleed from the bottoms of his feet, a man who came here uneducated, alone, unable to speak the language, who taught me all I needed to know about faith and hard work by the simple eloquence of his example. I learned about our kind of democracy from my father. I learned about our obligation to each other from him and from my mother. They asked only for a chance to work and to make the world better for their children and to be protected in those moments when they would not be able to protect themselves. This nation and its government did that for them. (paragraph 116)

With the story of his father, Cuomo links together his appeals to values and needs with the Democratic history. The Democrats, in Cuomo's story, always have been the party that took care of people like his own father. The final story powerfully unifies the narrative and value appeals.

While Cuomo's strategic appeals to values, needs, and his use of narrative were skillful, it was his language strategies that made the speech memorable. The content of the address can be summarized quite simply: Reagan and the Republicans are bad; Democrats are good. Cuomo is effective in the way he uses appeals to values and needs, narrative, and to a lesser degree argument to develop this simple dichotomy. But these strategies do not explain the reaction to the address.

Cuomo's 1984 convention speech is justly famous primarily because of the way he uses language strategies to add interest, clarify his position, and excite his audience.

Language Strategies in Cuomo's Address

Cuomo uses each of the main language strategies discussed earlier in his address.

Metaphor ◆ Given the importance of metaphor and other forms of comparison, it is unsurprising that Cuomo's address is filled with examples of this language strategy. For example, in paragraph 53 he refers to "mannequin delegates" at the Republican convention as a way of attacking the Republican party for representing only the rich and not the diverse nature of our entire society. In the next paragraph, he says that Democrats need to "lock arms and move into this campaign." The metaphor of "locking arms" is his way of calling for Democratic unity. In the following paragraph, he refers to the Republican policy of "divide and cajole" as a way of attacking Reagan. I picked these examples of metaphor from the middle of Cuomo's address at random to illustrate the point that nearly every paragraph has one or more metaphors or other comparisons. Clearly, Cuomo is quite skillful at using metaphor to add interest to his speech.

There is one metaphor, however, that potentially functions as a paradigm for distinguishing between Democrats and Republicans. With the "wagon train" comparison that I cited earlier, Cuomo claims that the basic difference between Republicans and Democrats is that Democrats care about all the people, while Republicans only care about the rich. This metaphor has the potential to inform his entire attack on Reaganism. However, Cuomo essentially drops the metaphor after using it in the first third of the address.

Antithesis ◆ Cuomo uses antithesis throughout the speech to juxtapose caring and compassionate Democrats with uncaring and extreme Republicans. Early in the address, he uses antithesis as a structural strategy to organize a series of distinctions between Republicans and Democrats. After noting that Reagan often refers to the United States as a "shining city on a hill," he says that "this nation is more a "Tale of Two Cities" than it is a "Shining City on a Hill" (paragraph 15). He then talks about the two cities, which reflect the Republican rich who are doing well and the rest of us, who are facing a variety of problems.

Cuomo also uses antithesis in individual sentences to contrast Democrats and Republicans. For example, in paragraph 35, he says that "In order to succeed, we must answer our opponent's polished and appealing rhetoric with a more telling reasonableness and rationality." Here, he combines metaphor with antithesis, as he does three paragraphs later when he calls for the people "to look past the glitter . . . to reality." He continues this theme, saying "And we will do that not so much with speeches that sound good as with speeches that are good and sound. Not so much with speeches that bring people to their feet as with speeches that bring people to their senses" (paragraphs 37, 38). With this extended series of antithesis, Cuomo casts Democrats as reasonable and Republicans as fundamentally unreasonable. Democrats are concerned with issues, while Republicans are concerned with style. Of course, the irony is that Cuomo is skillfully using the persuasive power of rhetoric to attack Reagan for doing exactly the same thing.

Parallel Structure and Repetition ◆ Cuomo relies on parallel structure in a long passage toward the conclusion of his address. Beginning with paragraph 98 and continuing through paragraph 107, he emphasizes the commitment of the Democratic party to a certain set of values and policies by beginning nearly every paragraph with "We believe." He calls this entire section the Demcratic "credo" (paragraph 97). He varies this pattern slightly in paragraphs 102 and 104, where he uses a verb other than "believe" that better fits his message. For example, in paragraph 104, he uses "proclaim" rather than "believe" in order to state opposition to nuclear proliferation as strongly as possible. With this long "credo," Cuomo uses parallel structure to emphasize the basic Democratic message.

Rhetorical Questions ◆ Cuomo uses rhetorical questions both as transition devices and to emphasize his conclusion that Republicans are extreme and represent special interests. In paragraph 68, he asks "How important is this question of the deficit?" as a transition device to an attack on the budget policies of the Reagan administration. In contrast, beginning with paragraph 86 and continuing through paragraph 94, he asks a series of questions to emphasize failures in the Reagan administration. Paragraph 93 is typical, "How much deeper will be the gulf between us and our enemies?" This question emphasizes Cuomo's claim that Reagan's defense policies risk war.

Depiction and Description ◆ Cuomo focuses on the life of the poor throughout the address. In several of these passages, he uses one or two words to give the audience a feel for the problems the poor face. For example, as I noted earlier in paragraph 11 he refers to the "elderly people who tremble in the basements" to help us understand the problems facing older Americans. His use of the verb "tremble" makes this statement quite vivid.

The only extended use of depiction in Cuomo's address comes at the end when he describes his father. I cited this passage earlier, but a portion of it bears repeating. Cuomo says of his father, "I watched a small man with thick calluses on both hands work 15 and 16 hours a day. I saw him once literally bleed from the bottoms of his feet. . ." (paragraph 116). With this description, Cuomo helps us picture his father as a hard-working immigrant who came to this nation to provide a better life for his family. Cuomo's vivid description of his father is a very important strategy in the address.

Personification ◆ Cuomo does not rely on personification to any great extent, although he does refer to Roosevelt lifting "the nation from its knees" (paragraph 29).

Rhythm and Rhyme ◆ As with personification, Cuomo does not rely heavily on rhythm or rhyme. There are, however, places in the address where there is a natural rhythm to the language that helps makes the speech flow. For example, very early in the speech he says "There is despair, Mr. President, in faces you never see, in the places you never visit in your shining city" (paragraph 14). The phrases "in faces you never see, in the places you never visit," have a natural rhythm that adds to the power of the passage.

Another example of rhythm is in the conclusion when he refers to the "highest seat in the greatest state of the greatest nation in the only world we know" (paragraph 117). The natural progression of "highest" to "greatest" to "highest" again is set off with the words "only world we know." In this statement, it isn't the content that matters, but the way the sentence works rhythmically.

In both of the statements I have cited (and others), there is a natural rhythm to the phrasing that helps make Cuomo more interesting.

Definition and Redefinition ◆ The most obvious use of redefinition in Cuomo's address is his statement that America is not "a shining city," but actually "A Tale of Two Cities." In this extended section, Cuomo redefines the social situation in America as one in which the vast majority of Americans are not doing well.

Alliteration and Assonance ◆ Cuomo uses alliteration at several points in the address. For example, he says that the "President's deficit is a direct and dramatic repudiation of his promise to balance our budget by 1983" (paragraph 60). In paragraph 43 he says that Republican policies "divide the nation: into the lucky and the left-out, the royalty and the rabble." In this statement, Cuomo combines alliteration, metaphor, antithesis, and labeling to emphasize his characterization of the Reagan administration as fundamentally uncaring.

Allusion ◆ Cuomo relies on allusion at a couple points in the address, most notably in the introduction with the reference to Dickens. He also alludes to a statement Reagan made that trees are a major source of pollution (paragraph 91) and to the scandal that led Anne Gorsuch Burford to be fired from the EPA (paragraph 86). Still, allusion is not a major aesthetic strategy in Cuomo's address.

Labeling ◆ Cuomo uses labeling when he says that the poor have been "locked out" (paragraph 23). This statement functions as Cuomo's way of defining the essence of Reagan's social policy. He also labels support for an Equal Rights Amendment (ERA) for women as a "commandment" "thou shalt not sin against equality" (paragraph 49). It is somewhat surprising that Cuomo does not rely more heavily on labeling.

Irony ◆ Cuomo relies primarily on direct attacks on the Reagan administration. This approach means that there is little room for irony. The rhetorical question concerning Anne Gorsuch Burford is the only important example of irony in the speech (paragraph 86).

Summary of Cuomo's Use of Language Strategies

As I noted in the discussion of antithesis, Cuomo sharply distinguishes the "reasonableness" of Democratic rhetoric, from what he labels the show and substance of Reagan. It is ironic, therefore, that the key element in the persuasiveness of Cuomo's address is his use of a wide variety of language strategies. Cuomo is every bit as showy as he accuses Reagan of being.

Cuomo uses language strategies as a way of making his narrative, value-laden, and argumentative strategies more interesting and memorable. With the exception of the "wagon train" metaphor and the "two cities" redefinition, the language strategies do not add to the content of his position. But the language strategies make that position quite memorable.

Was Cuomo successful? The 1984 elections were a disaster for Democrats. Mondale-Ferraro were crushed by Reagan-Bush at the polls. Judged from the perspective of ultimate political effect, the speech must be labeled a failure. However, judged as a work of rhetoric designed to unify and energize Democrats, the speech must be graded as near perfect. Cuomo did little if anything in the speech to broaden the base of the Democratic party. But the combination of narrative, appeals to values/needs, and language strategies was very well designed to do what he accused Reagan of doing, bringing "people to their feet" (paragraph 38).

Strengths and Weaknesses of Aesthetic Strategies

There is no question that aesthetic strategies play a major role in successful rhetoric, whether in the form of a public speech, an essay, a film, or a music video. On the other hand, it is also easy to overestimate the importance of aesthetic strategies in general and language strategies in particular. How you say it is important, but you also have to have something to say. With this limitation in mind, the following generalizations can be made about aesthetic strategies.

First, aesthetic strategies do not, in general, work by themselves. Rather, their role is to make content more exciting, more memorable, and to provide emphasis. Second, the exception to this rule relates to metaphor. Unlike other language and aesthetic strategies, metaphor may form the very substance of a work of rhetoric. In most cases metaphor functions as a rhetorical spice, but in some instances, metaphor works as a model for understanding the world. If a rhetor can change the metaphor through which an audience understands the world, the result may be to change their thinking and behavior.

Third, there is no single style that works for all people in all occasions. In fact, only very broad generalizations can be drawn about appropriate aesthetic strategies. As a rule the language or other aesthetic strategies used should be appropriate to the subject, the context, the speaker, and the audience. The rhetor should use language strategies to add interest to his/her rhetoric and to clarify complex or ambiguous information. These sensible generalizations help identify inappropriate use of language strategies, but they are not helpful in distinguishing between powerful style and the merely adequate.

Fourth, aesthetic strategies should be combined with other rhetorical strategies to produce the maximum effect. This is especially important when the dominant strategy is some form of rational argument. To be maximally effective, rational argument should be supported with a variety of aesthetic strategies that add interest or provide emphasis.

Conclusion

Aesthetic strategies in general and language strategies in particular play an important part in persuasion. The skillful use of aesthetic strategies can be used to enliven a presentation or make any work of rhetoric more understandable. But it is also important to recognize that with the exception of metaphor and perhaps some visual strategies in film and video, aesthetic strategies mainly play a supporting role. They make the argument or value appeal more understandable and more powerful, but they don't function to produce persuasion by themselves.

An anecdote may make this point clear. There is a story that when a movie executive was told that Ronald Reagan was going to run for Governor of California, the executive exclaimed, "No, Jimmy Stewart for Governor; Ronald Reagan for best friend." The executive meant that Stewart was a far better actor than Reagan. The executive was wrong, however, because the essence of politics is not acting, but building a persuasive message. Reagan may not have been a great actor, but he was a great politician who was able to combine narrative and argument with strong appeals to values and needs. Reagan was skilled at using language and other aesthetic strategies, but in his rhetoric, as in the case of almost all successful persuaders, they played a supporting role.

Notes

1. A discussion of how the "wall" metaphor has shaped Supreme Court analysis can be found in Benjamin Voth, "The Wall Separating Church and State," Doctoral Dissertation, University of Kansas, 1994.

2. See for instance "Stokely Carmichael Explains Black Power to a White Audience in Whitewater, Wisconsin," in Robert L. Scott and Wayne Brockriede, *The Rhetoric of Black Power* (New York: Harper and Row, 1969): 96–111. This article is a speech by Carmichael.

3. See George Lakoff and Mark Johnson, *Metaphors We Live By* (Chicago: University of Chicago Press, 1980).

4. Lyndon Baines Johnson, "Address Before a Joint Session of the Congress, November 27, 1963," *Public Papers of the Presidents of the United States: Lyndon Johnson, Book I* (Washington: Government Printing Office, 1965): 9.

5. Abraham Lincoln, "The Gettysburg Address," in *Three Centuries of American Rhetorical Discourse: An Anthology and Review*, ed. Ronald F. Reid (Prospect Heights: IL: Waveland, 1988): 463.

6. "Cultural Literacy at KU," *The Oread Review* 1 (March 1992): 1.

7. See David Henry, "The Rhetorical Dynamics of Mario Cuomo's 1984 Keynote Address: Situation, Speaker, Metaphor," *Southern Speech Communication Journal* 53 (1988), pp, 107–109.

8. Keynote addresses are one type of a rhetorical genre. In chapter ten, I discuss the way that genres influence rhetorical action.

9. Henry, p. 105.

10. Henry, p. 105.

11. For a description of the crisis see Robert C. Rowland and Thea Rademacher, "The Passive Style of Rhetorical Crisis Management: A Case Study of the Superfund Controversy," *Communication Studies* 41 (1990), pp. 328–330.

CHAPTER EIGHT

Generating an Emotional Response: Tapping into Values, Needs and Symbols

It is common to hear the press speak of an emotional appeal in a politician's speech in negative terms. The comment, "Senator X gave an emotional speech last night," nearly always contains an implied criticism of the address as not rational, but over emotional. In some cases, this criticism may be well taken. There certainly are many speeches, essays, films, and other works of rhetoric that are designed to provoke emotions, not thought. It is for that reason, among others, that the focus of chapter eleven is on developing a system to identify deceptive and irrational rhetoric. On the other hand, rhetoric that fails to produce an emotional response often fails to produce any response at all.

The main emphasis of this chapter is on identifying the characteristics of rhetoric that produces a strong emotional reaction. In the first section, I define the characteristics of emotion-producing rhetoric. I then consider dangers associated with such rhetoric and also the need for emotion-producing rhetoric as a means of generating action. In the next section, I outline nine sub-strategies for producing an emotional response and illustrate how they work by discussing an address by Jesse Jackson's at the 1988 Democratic National Convention.

A Definition of Emotion-Producing Rhetoric

It has been traditional, since Aristotle wrote his classic rhetorical handbook, *The Rhetoric,* to distinguish among three modes of persuasion: logos, ethos, and pathos,[1] which correspond with argument, credibility, and emotional appeals, respectively. In earlier chapters, I have discussed credibility and argument as ways of persuading an audience. However, in relation to pathos or appeals to the emotions, the traditional label is not adequate.

While rhetoric producing an emotional response is quite important, it is not useful to talk about appeals to the emotions. The emotions are not an organ in the human body that one somehow addresses. Rather than *appealing* to the emotions, certain types of rhetoric *produce* a strong emotional response. For example, it is common for rhetoricians in the United States and around the world to use a nation's flag as a patriotic symbol representing the nation. The rhetor refers to the flag in order to tap into the strong societal association between the flag and the particular nation. It is by tapping that association that the rhetor produces the emotional response in the audience. As this example indicates, rhetoric is not itself emotional or non-emotional. Rather, some forms of rhetoric tap into values, needs, or symbols that have strong emotional associations and the result is an emotional response. The sub-types of rhetoric that produce a strong emotional response will be discussed later in this chapter.

Dangers Associated with Emotion-Producing Rhetoric

There are two major dangers associated with rhetoric that produces a strong emotional reaction. First, that rhetoric may lead people to make irrational decisions. We all know that strong emotion can cloud our thinking. The research that I summarized in chapter four on when rational argument fails certainly supports this judgment.

Second, strong emotional reactions may lead to the creation of hate and societal conflict. Hitler used rhetoric to persuade the German people that the Jews had harmed Germany and must be destroyed. Over the last few years, Slobodan Milosevic, the leader of Serbia, has used rhetoric to persuade soldiers, police, and others to commit horrible acts, first in Bosnia and more recently in Kosovo. He has tapped into Serbian history and nationalism to produce these strong reactions. Clearly, rhetoric that produces such strong reactions can be quite dangerous.

Given these dangers one might think that the best solution would be to avoid rhetoric that produces a strong emotional response altogether. The judgment that emotion-producing rhetoric is always dangerous is, however, incorrect. Rhetoric may produce a strong emotional reaction and be quite rational. Two examples make this point clear. I have a friend whose father was a death camp survivor. My friend passionately hates the Nazis and bitterly criticizes so-called Holocaust Revisionists, who deny that the Holocaust happened. His reaction to the Holocaust Revisionists is both strongly emotional *and* highly rational. It makes sense that he hates the Nazis and those who defend them.

Similarly, it is not irrational for a gunshot victim to be a passionate supporter of gun control. Some years ago, I had a student who strongly defended restrictions on gun ownership, largely based on a personal experience in which he was shot in a robbery of a convenience store. The student described in detail what it was like to have a gun pointed at you and then see the muzzle flash and feel the bullet hit your chest. This student's support for gun control was based on emotion and equally on reason. In both the cases I have described, the beliefs of the individual were both strongly emotional and perfectly reasonable. The point is that oftentimes emotional reactions are completely rational. Aristotle himself made this exact point almost 2500 years ago.[2] Of course, not all emotional reactions are rational. Some are quite irrational and extremely dangerous. But in other cases, an emotional reaction and a rational evaluation of the situation may be quite consistent.

Moreover, humans are by their very nature emotional beings. It is unreasonable to think that an emotionless "Spock-like" rhetoric ever could be effective. Very few, if any, people are motivated by pure reason. It is for this reason that politicians who cannot use rhetoric to produce strong emotional responses are often referred to as wooden.[3] The politician is not an oak. But the media is onto something, even if the metaphor is misleading. It is not the stiffness of the politician that is the problem, but his/her inability to utilize strategies that produce strong human emotions.

Finally, if one is to combat immoral emotional rhetoric, one has no choice but to rely on rhetoric that can produce a strong countervailing emotional response. It is very common for historians to argue that Franklin Roosevelt saved the United States from demagogues such as former Louisiana Senator Huey Long.[4] In this view, Roosevelt was all that stood in the way of a turn toward extremism during the Great Depression. Of course, not everyone agrees that U.S. democracy was threatened or even that Long was a demagogue. But they do agree that Roosevelt was successful because he used all of the available rhetorical strategies, not just rational argument. His First Inaugural Address in which he reassured the country that "the only thing we have to fear is fear itself"[5] is a magnificent example of how a politician can use strategies that tap into human emotion in order to calm an audience.

For all of these reasons, rhetoric that produces a strong emotional content plays a crucial role in public persuasion and any skilled rhetorician must be able to utilize it effectively.

Strategies for Producing a Strong Emotional Response

There are nine main sub-strategies for producing a strong emotional response in an audience, and one important notation concerning language usage. In regard to language, the rule of thumb is that concrete descriptive language is more adapted to producing a strong emotional reaction than other forms of language. Here, it is important to distinguish between graphic and abstract language. Abstract language is used to deal with complex issues in a purely rational framework. It also allows humans to talk about ideas that have no direct real world referent, including scientific theories. Abstract language plays an essential role in human civilization; it is one key to the ability of people to use conceptual thought.

On the other hand, graphic, specific language is better adapted to producing a strong emotional reaction than is the use of abstract language. A detailed graphic description of what happened to a victim of genocide in Rwanda might produce a very powerful emotional reaction in an audience. Through describing the life and then murder of this person in detail, the speaker would bring home the horror of his/her death. Graphic or concrete language is used to tap into the emotional content of an issue, while ambiguous or abstract language avoids that content.

It is important to recognize, however, that use of graphic descriptive language is not itself a sub-strategy for producing a strong emotional reaction. A detailed description of a wiring diagram will not produce a strong emotional reaction in any one. Thus, the graphic language will produce a strong emotional reaction only if it links to one of the sub-strategies discussed in the following section.

In relation to emotional reaction, the sub-types of strategies for producing that effect are:

1. Appeals to Basic Needs
2. Appeals to Basic Values
3. Appeals to Self-interest
4. Appeals to Guilt
5. Appeals to History
6. Appeals to Religion
7. Appeals to Myth
8. Appeals to Elemental Symbols
9. Appeals to Societal Symbols.

Appeals to Basic Needs ◆ An appeal to basic needs is aimed at a "need" that is inherent in human psychology. Basic needs include life itself, security, the resources of life (food, water, housing, and so forth), sex, social support and so forth. Maslow's hierarchy of needs is one common analysis of basic needs shared by humans.

A rhetor appeals to needs by pointing to a need that is not being met or that could be threatened in the future. He/she then either draws on audience fear of the need not being fulfilled or promises a better means of fulfilling it in the future.

In political rhetoric, for instance, it is common for politicians to focus on the need for security in relation to crime, the death penalty, gun control, and social support programs. The power of an appeal to basic needs is most easily illustrated in relation to Social Security, which has been called the "third rail" of American politics. The "third rail" metaphor is a reference to the "third rail" in a subway, which is electrified. A person who touches the third rail in a subway is electrocuted. Similarly, according to the metaphor, a politician who threatens Social Security, will be defeated. Why is Social Security the "third rail" of American politics? The answer is that people fear being old and unable to take care of themselves. Social Security has guaranteed at least a minimum level of income and people don't want to lose that guarantee.

In appealing to needs, it is important to keep in mind the following rules of thumb. First, it doesn't make sense to appeal to the needs of the audience if those needs are both being met currently and do not seem threatened in the future. If people feel secure in relation to crime, then a scare rhetoric will not have much impact. Thus, the "need" being appealed to must be one that credibly could be threatened in the world of the audience. Second, an appeal to needs should be strong enough to elicit a response, but not so strong that it loses credibility. Persuasion research in the area of fear appeals indicates that if a fear appeal seems excessive, the result will be to produce audience backlash instead of persuasion.[6] Too high a fear appeal may seem incredible to the audience. But a low fear appeal will not generate action. The same point applies when the rhetor is promising a better future. That better future must be a significant improvement or no one will care. But when someone promises us a perfect future, we are likely to be skeptical.

Third, fear appeals and other messages tapping basic needs work most effectively when there is some direct action that the audience can take to reduce whatever risk is at issue or otherwise achieve the basic need. This makes perfect sense. If you tell a group that there is a problem facing them that threatens their existence, but that there is nothing that can be done about it, the likely reaction of the audience will be to throw up their hands and ignore the issue.

In summary, appeals to needs, either positive or negative, are most powerful when three conditions are present: 1) basic needs are not being met or are threatened; 2) the rhetor can show the existence of a significant problem or potential benefit, but not one so large that it lacks credibility; 3) it is possible to take relatively simple steps either to protect the individual or to fulfill the need in the future.

Appeals to Basic Values ◆ An appeal to basic values taps into the value structure of a given society. The contrast between values and needs can be thought of as similar to the distinction between hardware and software in the context of computers. Needs are the equivalent of hardware; they apparently are inherent in human psychology. We all need food, water, shelter, love and so forth. Values, by contrast, are like software; they differ across culture. For example, Americans tend to value "progress" very highly. Consequently, there is a great deal of focus on creating a better country, improving the quality of our infrastructure, and so forth. By contrast, in many societies progress is valued less and stability is more highly valued.

Values, therefore, are basic statements of good and bad in a society or a sub-set of that society. The most basic values in the United States include freedom, peace, equality, justice, opportunity, and progress. In sub-sets of the society, other values are important. For example, in the culture of an American research university, values such as diversity, knowledge, and intellectual rigor are important, along with the basic values of American society as a whole.

The essential point is that a skilled rhetorician can tap into the dominant values that undergird any society (or part of a society). The rhetorician either cites the values in support or opposition to an idea or says that the values are threatened in order to motivate action. For example, conservatives often use the values of freedom and opportunity in opposing affirmative action programs. In contrast, Democrats cite the values of diversity and equality in defending those programs. As this example indicates, the values that define a given society may not be completely consistent. For example, U.S. culture tends to value both equality and freedom, but at a certain point, such as in regard to affirmative action programs that establish quotas to increase the representation of a particular racial or ethnic group in a given institution, those values may come into conflict.

One other point is important in regard to appeals to basic values. It obviously is essential to identify the dominant values that energize any particular culture or sub-culture, in order to explain how this strategy functions in a particular work of rhetoric. Values vary across culture. What is valued in one culture (or sub-culture) may not be valued in another.

Appeal to Self-interest ◆ In an appeal to self-interest, the rhetor essentially offers the audience something that they want. Throughout the 1980s and early 1990s, as the budget deficit of the United States increased and increased, both Republicans and Democrats continued to advocate tax cuts. Tax cuts remained popular throughout this period, despite the rising deficit, because everyone prefers low taxes. It is true that some conservatives believed that a tax cut would stimulate the economy, producing enough new growth to offset lost revenues (this did not happen in Reagan's first term). However, the appeal of the tax cut proposals was not based on a complex economic argument, but on the simple fact that people wanted their taxes to go down. The obvious conclusion is that people generally react favorably to positions that help them.

It is also important to understand that people don't tend to see themselves as selfish. Instead, they often perceive that their self-interest is the interest of the entire community. It would not be inaccurate, for example, to say that people define a "tax loophole," as a tax provision that helps "someone else." For instance, ordinary people do not tend to perceive the home mortgage deduction as a tax loophole, but of course in a technical sense that is precisely what it is. Instead, they see it as a sensible government policy that recognizes the importance of home ownership. Truthfully, the home mortgage deduction is both a loophole and a government policy that supports home ownership. The important conclusion is that people often interpret policies that aid them personally as principled attempts to accomplish a valid public purpose.

From the perspective of understanding how rhetoric produces a strong emotional response, the key judgment is that appeals to the self-interest are a very powerful way of motivating people. For example, in the 1988 election, Vice-President Bush appealed to self-interest by promising "No New Taxes." The ability of Bush and other Republicans to make Democrats look like supporters of high taxes, with the slogan "Tax and Spend Democrats" played a part in his victory in that election and the victories of many Republicans in campaigns for other offices.

Appeal to Guilt ◆ Guilt is a powerful motivating force in human society. It is easy to think of many instances in which someone felt guilt over some action (or inaction) and could not rest until that guilt was purged. On the other hand, there are many people who seem to be able to commit horrible acts and not feel the least bit guilty. The fact that some feel guilt so strongly and others apparently not at all makes it difficult to predict how guilt will function as a factor in any given work of rhetoric.

How is guilt created in rhetoric? One appeals to guilt in a speech or essay by pointing to a gap between the values and the actions of an individual or a group. Thus, for an audience that values opportunity for all, an advocate of civil rights might point to the gap between their economic situation and that of youths in the central city. Implicitly, the speaker would be saying the following: "You have enormous wealth and claim to value opportunity for all. But you aren't giving to this community in need. Either you are hypocrites or you should start giving now." Appeals using this strategy are found in a great deal of rhetoric. For example, advertisements asking for support for children in the Third World are another example of this strategy.

In relation to when appeals to guilt are likely to be successful, there are two key points to recognize. First, the strategy will not be successful unless the value is strongly held by the audience. It will not work to appeal to the sense of fairness of a racist. Second, the strategy is best applied via an enthymematic argument. A direct attempt to tap guilt in an audience may produce denial or backlash. In most situations a stronger approach is to make the appeal indirect, as in the examples cited earlier.

Appeal to History ◆ An appeal to history is a means of tapping into the basic stories that undergird any society. In a speech contained in the readings volume associated with this book,[7] President Clinton taps into the history of the civil rights movement as a means of motivating his audience. He uses the voice of Martin Luther King as a means of motivating his audience. Clinton actually tells the audience what King would say to them if he were there. The same strategy is present any time a rhetor uses the history of the larger society or a particular sub-set of the society as a means of tapping into strong emotion.

For an appeal to history to produce a strong emotional reaction, three conditions must be present. First, the history must be shared by the group members. If the story doesn't connect with the audience, there will be no emotional response. This is why stories about World War II work much more effectively with an older audience than a group from Generation X. Second, there must be a strong emotional resonance to the story. People feel strongly about history that made a difference for the group. A recounting of the efforts to pass the 1986 Tax Reform Act is unlikely to strongly motivate any group, but a recounting of the events leading up to Martin Luther King's "I Have a Dream" speech may produce very strong reactions.

Third, the historical reference must be relevant to whatever issue is being discussed. For example, many have used the history of U.S. involvement in Vietnam to oppose sending American troops into a foreign war. Clearly, this historical analogy has influenced several American presidents to be quite careful about sending ground troops into a conflict. But the same historical analogy would have no relevance to the use of troops in purely humanitarian missions. No one would have accepted the "No More Vietnams" position as a reason to stop U.S. Marines from helping hurricane victims.

In summary, shared history can be used in any society, organization, or group to produce an emotional reaction. By citing the history of the group, the rhetor draws on the way that history unifies the group. That is just as true of a social organization as it is of the United States.

Appeal to Religion ◆ An appeal to religion utilizes the power of religious dogma. The rhetor uses the principles at the heart of the faith as a means of energizing the audience. Alternatively, the rhetoric may cite a heroic figure within the religion, such as a saint or martyr, in order to tap the emotional power of faith.

The power of religion in producing a strong emotional reaction is obvious in history and the world today. For example, religion obviously plays a strong role in the conflict between Israelis and Arabs over Jerusalem. That city is not just real estate; it is a key religious site for Muslims, Jews, and Christians. As this example indicates, when people feel that their religion is threatened they may both have a strong emotional reaction and be motivated to act to protect their religious heritage. Religion also may be a powerful motivating force in cases where there is no threat to the group. For example, strong religious beliefs encourage many people to do volunteer work for the poor.

In summary, appeals to religion are a powerful specific type of value appeal and also may be a means of producing a sense of guilt in an audience.

Appeal to Myth ◆ When most people think of myth, they think of a false story. It is common to read articles with titles like, "The Myth of Gun Control." From a rhetorical perspective, however, this interpretation of myth is inadequate. In fact, the better argument is that myths are not false stories at all. Rather, myths are the most basic stories told in any society, stories believed to be absolutely true by the people who tell them.[8] In the United States, our most basic myths are the stories of the pioneers and of the founding of this nation.

Why are these stories so important? Myths in general, and the two stories I have mentioned, in particular, serve a definitional function. The stories of the pioneers and the Founding Fathers tell us what it means to be an American. More broadly, humans tell myths to answer big questions about the meaning of life, the nature of a good life or a good society, the chance for eternal life, and so forth. In this way, myths are anything but false stories. They are instead the most powerful stories that are perceived as true in any society.

It important to recognize, however, that not all myths are understood by the people who tell them as literally true. Instead, they may be interpreted as embodying a fundamental truth of some kind. In this way, a story about the pioneers may not literally have happened, but it still may contain a "truth" about what it means to be an American.

How are myths different from other stories? Myths possess a special rhetorical form that allows them to fulfill the functions I have mentioned.[9] Initially, before treating a story as a myth, the critic should make certain that the story is taken seriously by the people who tell it. Tales about Paul Bunyan, for instance, are not myths in the sense developed here, because they are stories told for fun. No one believes that Paul Bunyan and his ox Babe really existed. After making certain that the story is a serious one, it is important to identify the following characteristics.

Myths tell the stories of larger than life heroes, operating outside of normal space and time, and involve a theme that in some way answers a crucial question for the people telling the story.

The heroes in myth must be larger than life (Washington or Jefferson for instance), because their function is to provide a model for action. The hero solves the problem facing the society because he/she is greater than we are. And by solving the problem, the hero provides us with a model for how we should act in life. This is precisely how stories about both the pioneers and the founding of the nation continue to function in U.S. culture. The pioneer and revolutionary periods are long gone. But people who tell stories about these events, link them to contemporary life. Former President Reagan was a master at using our basic mythology to convince the American people that they could overcome whatever problem was confronting them at a given point in time.[10]

In relation to geography, myths occur in special places, places like Valley Forge, Gettysburg, Ellis Island, and so forth. These places are the proper site for a mythic narrative because of the crucial events that have occurred there. In essence, the function of the place is to add power to the story. For example, because of the heroic acts that occurred at Gettysburg, the place has great meaning in American history. The perfect example of proper mythic geography would be to place the story in Jerusalem, which as I noted earlier is sacred for three religions.

In terms of time, myths generally occur at the beginning or end of a society.[11] We tend to think of the beginning of anything as possessing special power. That is why the Supreme Court continues to consult the writings of the Founders in relation to Constitutional interpretation. It seems unlikely that Madison had much to say about the application of the First Amendment to the internet. However, the Supreme Court still consults his writing because he came first. A similar point can be made about the end of any society. That is one reason why so many religious myths focus on the "end times." In this country, our basic myths tell of the beginning of the nation and, in a sense, the new beginning provided by the frontier.

Finally, in relation to theme, myths speak to essential issues facing the group telling the story. In the case of the Founding Fathers and the pioneers, the myths provide the basic American story. They tell of a nation created out of many different cultures, drawing strength from both unity and diversity, which faces terrible obstacles and overcomes them through grit and determination. A rhetor can tap into that mythology by retelling a portion of it and in so doing draw on the power associated with the story.

Appeals to myth are related to the two previous strategies. Mythic stories are the most central stories told in a society. They are therefore even more basic than appeals to history. And myths also are tied to religion. It is the mythic narratives of the Old and New Testament, which undergird Christian and Jewish theology.

Elemental and Societal Symbols ◆ The final two sub-types of strategies that can be used to produce an emotional response relate to the "symbols" used by the rhetorician. Symbols are words or objects that represent an idea, need, value, or other principle. Elemental and societal symbols produce an emotional reaction by linking into one or more of the other categories for producing an emotional response. For example, a speaker can tap the value of patriotism, as well as both history and myth, by using the American flag as a symbol. Other examples of symbols include the Statue of Liberty, the Golden Gate Bridge, and blood as a means of representing sacrifice. By citing these symbols the rhetor draws on the emotional power associated with them.

There are two essential types of symbols: elemental (or natural) and societal. An elemental symbol (sometimes called an archetypal symbol)[12] has a single meaning regardless of culture. The best example of an elemental symbol is "blood," which, regardless of the culture (at least until the age of AIDS), represents life and sacrifice. To "shed your blood" is to risk death. Other elemental symbols include "fire," which represents both warmth and the threat of destruction, excrement, the sea and so forth.

It should be clear that there are not very many truly elemental symbols. Even in the case of some that I have mentioned, there may be some variation in usage. The "sea" seemed a lot more terrifying a thousand years ago than it does today.[13] Elemental symbols are tied to the basic structure of human existence on this earth. Since there are few universals across the planet, there are not many elemental symbols.

The use of societal symbols, symbols which have a particular meaning for a group or society, is far more common than the use of elemental symbols. For example, U.S. politicians often "wrap themselves in the flag" or make announcements concerning veterans benefits at the Tomb of the Unknown Soldier as ways of tapping into the power of societal symbols. In so doing, the rhetor uses the symbol as a means of getting at basic values, history, myth or other sub-strategy for producing an emotional response.

Summary of Strategy Categories

In the previous section, I identified the nine main sub-strategies for producing an emotional response in an audience. These nine sub-strategies are often found in combination together. In some cases, such as appeals to history, myth, and religion, it may be difficult to distinguish between the sub-categories. The important principle to keep in mind is that the sub-categories are a starting point for analysis. They should be used to identify the specific way that a speaker/writer attempts to create an emotional reaction in a given instance.

In the next section, I illustrate how the sub-categories can be used to produce a strong emotional response via an analysis of the "Common Ground" address which Jesse Jackson presented at the 1988 Democratic National Convention. Jackson had been a candidate for the Democratic nomination and had won more votes than anyone other than the eventual nominee, Michael Dukakis. In his address, Jackson appealed to both his constituency, the "Rainbow Coalition," and also to the entire party. Jackson's

1988 address was one of the most discussed and influential speeches of the decade of the 1980s. It is a fine example of how a rhetor can tap values, needs, and symbols representing those values and needs in order to produce a strong emotional response.

◆◆◆

Common Ground Address
1988 Democratic National Convention

Jesse Jackson

Tonight we pause and give praise and honor to God for being good enough to allow us to 1 be at this place at this time. When I look out at this convention, I see the face of America, red, yellow, brown, black and white, we're all precious in God's sight—the real rainbow coalition. All of us, all of us who are here and think that we are seated. But we're really standing on someone's shoulders. Ladies and gentlemen, Mrs. Rosa Parks.

The mother of the civil rights movement. 2

I want to express my deep love and appreciation for the support my family has given me 3 over these past months.

They have endured pain, anxiety, threat and fear. 4

But they have been strengthened and made secure by a faith in God, in America and in you. 5

Your love has protected us and made us strong. 6

To my wife Jackie, the foundation of our family; to our five children whom you met 7 tonight; to my mother Mrs. Helen Jackson, who is present tonight; and to my grandmother, Mrs. Matilda Burns; my brother Chuck and his family; my mother-in-law, Mrs. Gertrude Brown, who just last month at age 61 graduated from Hampton Institute, a marvelous achievement; I offer my appreciation to [Atlanta] Mayor Andrew Young who has provided such gracious hospitality to all of us this week.

And a special salute to President Jimmy Carter. 8

President Carter restored honor to the White House after Watergate. He gave many of us 9 a special opportunity to grow. For his kind words, for his unwavering commitment to peace in the world and the voters that came from his family, every member of his family, led by Billy and Amy, I offer him my special thanks, special thanks to the Carter family.

My right and my privilege to stand here before you has been won—in my lifetime—by 10 the blood and the sweat of the innocent.

Twenty-four years ago, the late Fanny Lou Hamer and Aaron Henry—who sits here 11 tonight from Mississippi—were locked out on the streets of Atlantic City, the head of the Mississippi Freedom Democratic Party.

From Congressional Quarterly, July 23, 1998, pp. 2057–2060. Reprinted by permission. Presented July 19, 1988.

But tonight, a black and white delegation from Mississippi is headed by [state party 12
Chairman] Ed Cole, a black man, from Mississippi, 24 years later.

Many were lost in the struggle for the right to vote. Jimmy Lee Jackson, a young student, 13
gave his life. Viola Liuzzo, a white mother from Detroit, called nigger lover, and brains blown
out at point blank range.

[Michael] Schwerner, [Andrew] Goodman and [James] Chaney—two Jews and a black— 14
found in common grave, bodies riddled with bullets in Mississippi. The four darling little girls
in the church in Birmingham, Ala. They died so that we might have a right to live.

Dr. Martin Luther King Jr. lies only a few miles from us tonight. 15

Tonight he must feel good as he looks down upon us. We sit here together, a rainbow, a 16
coalition—the sons and daughters of slaves sitting together around a common table, to decide the direction of our party and our country. His heart would be full tonight.

As a testament to the struggles of those who have gone before; as a legacy for those who 17
will come after; as a tribute to the endurance, the patience, the courage of our forefathers and
mothers; as an assurance that their prayers are being answered, their work has not been in
vain, and hope is eternal; tomorrow night my name will go into nomination for the presidency of the United States of America.

Common Ground at a Crossroads

We meet tonight at a crossroads, a point of decision. 18

Shall we expand, be inclusive, find unity and power; or suffer division and impotence? 19

We come to Atlanta, the cradle of the old south, the crucible of the new South. 20

Tonight there is a sense of celebration because we are moved, fundamentally moved, 21
from racial battlegrounds by law, to economic common ground. Tomorrow we will challenge
to move to higher ground.

Common ground! 22

Think of Jerusalem—the intersection where many trails met. A small village that became 23
the birthplace for three great religions—Judaism, Christianity and Islam.

Why was this village so blessed? Because it provided a crossroads where different people 24
met, different cultures, and different civilizations could meet and find common ground.

When people come together, flowers always flourish and the air is rich with the aroma of 25
a new spring.

Take New York, the dynamic metropolis. What makes New York so special? 26

It is the invitation of the Statue of Liberty—give me your tired, your poor, your huddled 27
masses who yearn to breathe free.

Not restricted to English only. 28

Many people, many cultures, many languages—with one thing in common, they yearn 29
to breathe free.

Common ground! 30

Tonight in Atlanta, for the first time in this century we convene in the South. 31

A state where governors once stood in school house doors. Where [former Georgia state 32
Sen.] Julian Bond was denied his seat in the state legislature because of his conscientious ob-
jection to the Vietnam War.

A city that, through its five black universities, has graduated more black students than any city in the world. 33

Atlanta, now a modern intersection of the new South. 34

Common ground! 35

That is the challenge to our party tonight. 36

Left wing. Right wing. Progress will not come through boundless liberalism nor static conservatism, but at the critical mass of mutual survival. It takes two wings to fly. 37

Whether you're a hawk or a dove, you're just a bird living in the same environment, in the same world. 38

The Bible teaches that when lions and lambs lie down together, none will be afraid and there will be peace in the valley. It sounds impossible. Lions eat lambs. Lambs sensibly flee from lions. But even lions and lambs find common ground. Why? 39

Because neither lions nor lambs want the forest to catch on fire. Neither lions nor lambs want acid rain to fall. Neither lions nor lambs can survive nuclear war. If lions and lambs can find common ground, surely, we can as well, as civilized people. 40

The only time that we win is when we come together. In 1960, John Kennedy, the late John Kennedy, beat Richard Nixon by only 112,000 votes—less than one vote per precinct. He won by the margin of our hope. He brought us together. He reached out. He had the courage to defy his advisors and inquire about Dr. King's jailing in Albany, Georgia. We won by the margin of our hope, inspired by courageous leadership. 41

In 1964, Lyndon Johnson brought both wings together. The thesis, the antithesis and to create a synthesis and together we won. 42

In 1976, Jimmy Carter unified us again and we won. When we do not come together, we never win. 43

In 1968, division and despair in July led to our defeat in November. 44

In 1980, rancor in the spring and the summer led to [President Ronald] Reagan in the fall. When we divide, we cannot win. We must find common ground as a basis for survival and development and change and growth. 45

Today when we debated, differed, deliberated, agreed to agree, agreed to disagree, when we had the good judgment to argue our case and then not self-destruct, George Bush was just a little further away from the White House and a little closer to private life. 46

Dukakis, Jackson: In the Same Boat

Tonight, I salute Governor Michael Dukakis. 47

He has run a well-managed and a dignified campaign. No matter how tired or how tried, he always resisted the temptation to stoop to demagoguery. 48

I've watched a good mind fast at work, with steel nerves, guiding his campaign out of the crowded field without appeal to the worst in us. I've watched his perspective grow as his environment has expanded. I've seen his toughness and tenacity close up. I know his commitment to public service. 49

Mike Dukakis' parents were a doctor and a teacher; my parents, a maid, a beautician and a janitor. 50

There's a great gap between Brookline, Massachusetts, and Haney Street, the Fieldcrest Village housing projects in Greenville, South Carolina. 51

He studied law; I studied theology. There are differences of religion, region, and race; differences in experiences and perspectives. But the genius of America is that out of the many, we become one.　52

Providence has enabled our paths to intersect. His foreparents came to America on immigrant ships; my foreparents came to America on slave ships. But whatever the original ships, we're in the same boat tonight.　53

Our ships could pass in the night if we have a false sense of independence, or they could collide and crash. We would lose our passengers. But we can seek a higher reality and a greater good apart. We can drift on the broken pieces of Reaganomics, satisfy our baser instincts, and exploit the fears of our people. At our highest, we can call upon noble instincts and navigate this vessel to safety. The greater good is the common good.　54

Expansion and Inclusion

As Jesus said, "Not my will, but thine be done." It was his way of saying there's higher good beyond personal comfort or position.　55

The good of our nation is at stake—its commitment to working men and women, to the poor and the vulnerable, to the many in the world. With so many guided missiles, and so much misguided leadership, the stakes are exceedingly high. Our choice, full participation in a Democratic government, or more abandonment and neglect. And so this night, we choose not a false sense of independence, but our capacity to survive and endure.　56

Tonight we choose interdependency in our capacity to act and unite for the greater good. The common good is finding commitment to new priorities, to expansion and inclusion. A commitment to expanded participation in the Democratic Party at every level. A commitment to a shared national campaign strategy and involvement at every level. A commitment to new priorities that ensure that hope will be kept alive. A common ground commitment for a legislative agenda by empowerment for the [Michigan Rep.] John Conyers bill, universal, on-site, same-day registration everywhere—and commitment to D.C. statehood and empowerment—D.C. deserves statehood. A commitment to economic set-asides, a commitment to the [California Rep. Ronald V.] Dellums bill for comprehensive sanctions against South Africa, a shared commitment to a common direction.　57

Common ground. Easier said than done. Where do you find common ground at the point of challenge? This campaign has shown that politics need not be marketed by politicians, packaged by pollsters and pundits. Politics can be a marvelous arena where people come together, define common ground.　58

We find common ground at the plant gate that closes on workers without notice. We find common ground at the farm auction where a good farmer loses his or her land to bad loans or diminishing markets. Common ground at the schoolyard where teachers cannot get adequate pay, and students cannot get a scholarship and can't make a loan. Common ground at the hospital admitting room where somebody tonight is dying because they cannot afford to go upstairs to a bed that's empty, waiting for someone with insurance to get sick. We are a better nation than that. We must do better.　59

Common ground. What is leadership if not present help in a time of crisis? And so I met you at the point of challenge in Jay, Maine, where paper workers were striking for fair wages;　60

in Greenfield, Iowa, where family farmers struggle for a fair price; in Cleveland, Ohio, where working women seek comparable worth; in McFarland, Calif., where the children of Hispanic farm workers may be dying from poison land, dying in clusters with cancer; in the AIDS hospice in Houston, Texas, where the sick support one another, 12 are rejected by their own parents and friends.

Common ground. 61

A Quilt of Unity

America's not a blanket woven from one thread, one color, one cloth. When I was a child   62
growing up in Greenville, S.C., and grandmother could not afford a blanket, she didn't complain and we did not freeze. Instead, she took pieces of old cloth—patches, wool, silk, gabardine, crockersack on the patches—barely good enough to wipe off your shoes with.

But they didn't stay that way very long. With sturdy hands and strong cord, she sewed   63
them together into a quilt, a thing of beauty and power and culture.

Now, Democrats, we must build such a quilt. Farmers, you seek fair prices and you are   64
right, but you cannot stand alone. Your patch is not big enough. Workers, you fight for fair wages. You are right. But your patch labor is not big enough. Women, you seek comparable worth and pay equity. You are right. But your patch is not big enough. Women, mothers, who see Head Start and day care and pre-natal care on the front side of life, rather than jail care and welfare on the back side of life, you're right, but your patch is not big enough.

Students, you seek scholarships. You are right. But your patch is not big enough. Blacks   65
and Hispanics, when we fight for civil rights, we are right, but our patch is not big enough. Gays and lesbians, when you fight against discrimination and a cure for AIDS, you are right, but your patch is not big enough. Conservatives and progressives, when you fight for what you believe, right-wing, left-wing, hawk, dove—you are right, from your point of view, but your point of view is not enough.

Reagan: 'Reverse Robin Hood'

We the people can win. We stand at the end of a long dark night of reaction. We stand   66
tonight united in a commitment to a new direction. For almost eight years, we've been led by those who view social good coming from private interest, who viewed public life as a means to increase private wealth. They have been prepared to sacrifice the common good of the many to satisfy the private interest and the wealth of a few. We believe in a government that's a tool of our democracy in service to the public, not an instrument of the aristocracy in search of private wealth.

We believe in government with the consent of the governed of, for, and by the people.   67
We must emerge into a new day with a new direction. Reaganomics, based on the belief that the rich had too much money—too little money, and the poor had too much.

That's classic Reaganomics. It believes that the poor had too much money and the rich   68
had too little money.

So, they engaged in reverse Robin Hood—took from the poor, gave to the rich, paid for by the middle class. We cannot stand four more years of Reaganomics in any version, in any disguise. 69

How do I document that case? Seven years later, the richest 1 percent of our society pays 20 percent less in taxes; the poorest 10 percent pay 20 percent more. Reaganomics. 70

Reagan gave the rich and the powerful a multibillion-dollar party. Now, the party is over. He expects the people to pay for the damage. I take this principled position—convention, let us not raise taxes on the poor and the middle class, but those who had the party, the rich and the powerful, must pay for the party! 71

I just want to take common sense to high places. We're spending $150 billion a year defending Europe and Japan 43 years after the war is over. We have more troops in Europe tonight than we had seven years ago, yet the threat of war is ever more remote. Germany and Japan are now creditor nations—that means they've got a surplus. We are a debtor nation—it means we are in debt. 72

Let them share more of the burden of their own defense—use some of that money to build decent housing! 73

Use some of that money to educate our children! 74

Use some of that money for long-term health care! 75

Use some of that money to wipe out these slums and put America back to work! 76

I just want to take common sense to high places. If we can bail out Europe and Japan, if we can bail out Continental Bank and Chrysler—and Mr. Iacocca makes $8,000 an hour—we can bail out the family farmer. 77

I just want to make common sense. It does not make sense to close down 650,000 family farms in this country while importing food from abroad subsidized by the U.S. government. 78

Let's make sense. It does not make sense to be escorting oil tankers up and down the Persian Gulf paying $2.50 for every $1.00 worth of oil we bring out while oil wells are capped in Texas, Oklahoma and Louisiana. I just want to make sense. 79

Leadership must meet the moral challenge of its day. What's the moral challenge of our day? We have public accommodations. We have the right to vote. We have open housing. 80

End Economic Violence

What's the fundamental challenge of our day? It is to end economic violence. Plant closing without notice, economic violence. Even the greedy do not profit long from greed. Economic violence. Most poor people are not lazy. They're not black. They're not brown. They're mostly white, and female and young. 81

But whether white, black or brown, the hungry baby's belly turned inside out is the same color. Call it pain. Call it hurt. Call it agony. Most poor people are not on welfare. 82

Some of them are illiterate and can't read the want-ad sections. And when they can, they can't find a job that matches their address. They work hard every day, I know. I live amongst them. I'm one of them. 83

I know they work. I'm a witness. They catch the early bus. They work every day. They raise other people's children. They work every day. They clean the streets. They work every day. They drive vans with cabs. They work every day. They change the beds you slept in these hotels last night and can't get a union contract. They work every day. 84

No more. They're not lazy. Someone must defend them because it's right, and they can-   85
not speak for themselves. They work in hospitals. I know they do. They wipe the bodies of
those who are sick with fever and pain. They empty their bedpans. They clean out their commode. No job is beneath them, and yet when the get sick, they cannot lie in the bed they
made up every day. America, that is not right. We are a better nation than that. We are a better nation than that.

War on Drugs

We need a real war on drugs. You can't just say no. It's deeper than that. You can't just get   86
a palm reader or an astrologer; it's more profound than that. We're spending $150 billion on
drugs a year. We've gone from ignoring it to focusing on the children. Children cannot buy
$150 billion worth of drugs a year. A few high profile athletes—athletes are not laundering
$150 billion a year—bankers are.

I met the children in Watts who are unfortunate in their despair. Their grapes of hope   87
have become raisins of despair, and they're turning to each other and they're self-destruct-
ing—but I stayed with them all night long. I wanted to hear their case. They said, "Jesse Jackson, as you challenge us to say no to drugs, you're right. And to not sell them, you're right. And
to not use these guns, you're right."

And, by the way, the promise of CETA [Comprehensive Employment and Training Act]—   88
they displaced CETA. They did not replace CETA. We have neither jobs nor houses nor services
nor training—no way out. Some of us take drugs as anesthesia for our pain. Some take drugs
as a way of pleasure—both short-term pleasure and long-term pain. Some sell drugs to make
money. It's wrong, we know. But you need to know that we know. We can go and buy the
drugs by the boxes at the port. If we can buy the drugs at the port, don't you believe the federal government can stop it if they want to?

They say, "We don't have Saturday night specials any more." They say, "We buy AK-47s and   89
Uzis, the latest lethal weapons. We buy them across the counter on Long Beach Boulevard."
You cannot fight a war on drugs unless and until you are going to challenge the bankers and
the gun sellers and those who grow them. Don't just focus on the children, let's stop drugs at
the level of supply and demand. We must end the scourge on the American culture.

Leadership in Pursuit of Peace

Leadership. What difference will we make? Leadership cannot just go along to get along.   90
We must do more than change presidents. We must change direction. Leadership must face
the moral challenge of our day. The nuclear war build-up is irrational. Strong leadership cannot desire to look tough, and let that stand in the way of the pursuit of peace. Leadership
must reverse the arms race.

At least we should pledge no first use. Why? Because first use begat first retaliation, and   91
that's mutual annihilation. That's not a rational way out. No use at all—let's think it out, and
not fight it out, because it's an unwinnable fight. Why hold a card that you can never drop?
Let's give peace a chance.

Leadership—we now have this marvelous opportunity to have a breakthrough with the 92
Soviets. Last year, 200,000 Americans visited the Soviet Union. There's a chance for joint ven-
tures into space, not Star Wars and the war arms escalation, but a space defense initiative.
Let's build in space together, and demilitarize the heavens. There's a way out.

American, let us expand. When Mr. Reagan and Mr. [Mikhail S.] Gorbachev met, there was 93
a big meeting. The represented together one-eighth of the human race. Seven-eighths of the
human race was locked out of that room. Most people in the world tonight—half are Asian,
one-half of them are Chinese. There are 22 nations in the Middle East. There's Europe; 40 million Latin Americans next door to us; the Caribbean; Africa—a half-billion people. Most people in the world today are yellow or brown or black, non-Christian, poor, female, young, and
don't speak English—in the real world.

This generation must offer leadership to the real world. We're losing ground in Latin 94
America, the Middle East, South Africa, because we're not focusing on the real world, that real
world. We must use basic principles, support international law. We stand the most to gain
from it. Support human rights; we believe in that. Support self-determination; we'll build on
that. Support economic development; you know it's right. Be consistent, and gain our moral
authority in the world.

I challenge you tonight, my friends, let's be bigger and better as a nation and as a party. 95
We have basic challenges. Freedom in South Africa—we've already agreed as Democrats to
declare South Africa to be a terrorist state. But don't just stop there. Get South Africa out of
Angola. Free Namibia. Support the front-line states. We must have a new, humane human
rights assistance policy in Africa.

To Hope and to Dream

I'm often asked, "Jesse, why do you take on these tough issues? They're not very political. 96
We can't win that way."

If an issue is morally right, it will eventually be political. It may be political and never be 97
right. Fannie Lou Hamer didn't have the most votes in Atlantic City, but her principles have
outlasted every delegate who voted to lock her out. Rosa Parks did not have the most votes,
but she was morally right. Dr. King didn't have the most votes about the Vietnam war, but he
was morally right. If we're principles first, our politics will fall in place.

"Jesse, why did you take these big bold initiatives?" A poem by an unknown author went 98
something like this: We mastered the air, we've conquered the sea, and annihilated distance
and prolonged life, we were not wise enough to live on this earth without war and without
hate.

As for Jesse Jackson, I'm tired of sailing my little boat, far inside the harbor bar. I want to 99
go out where the big ships float, out on the deep where the great ones are. And should my
frail craft prove too slight, the waves that sweep those billows o'er, I'd rather go down in a stir-
ring fight than drown to death in the sheltered shore.

We've got to go out, my friends, where the big boats are. 100

And then, for our children, young America, hold your head high now. We can win. We 101
must not lose you to drugs and violence, premature pregnancy, suicide, cynicism, pessimism
and despair. We can win.

Wherever you are tonight, I challenge you to hope and to dream. Don't submerge your   102
dreams. Exercise above all else, even on drugs, dream of the day you're drug-free. Even in the
gutter, dream of the day that you'll be upon your feet again. You must never stop dreaming.
Face reality, yes. But don't stop with the way things are: dream of things as they ought to be.
Dream. Face pain, but love, hope, faith, and dreams will help you rise above the pain.

Use hope and imagination as weapons of survival and progress, but you keep on dream-   103
ing, young America. Dream of peace. Peace is rational and reasonable. War is irrational in this
age and unwinnable.

Dream of teachers who teach for life and not for living. Dream of doctors who are con-   104
cerned more about public health than private wealth. Dream of lawyers more concerned
about justice than a judgeship. Dream of preachers who are concerned more about prophecy
than profiteering. Dream on the high road of sound values.

'Don't Surrender'

And in America, as we go forth to September, October and November and then beyond,   105
America must never surrender to a high moral challenge.

Do not surrender to drugs. The best drug policy is a no first use. Don't surrender with   106
needles and cynicism. Let's have no first use on the one hand, or clinics on the other. Never
surrender, young America.

Go forward. America must never surrender to malnutrition. We can feed the hungry and   107
clothe the naked. We must never surrender. We must go forward. We must never surrender to
illiteracy. Invest in our children. Never surrender; and go forward.

We must never surrender to inequality. Women cannot compromise ERA [Equal Rights   108
Amendment] or comparable worth. Women are making 60 cents on the dollar to what a man
makes. Women cannot buy milk cheaper. Women deserve to get paid for the work that you
do. It's right and it's fair.

Don't surrender, my friends. Those who have AIDS tonight, you deserve our compassion.   109
Even with AIDS you must not surrender in your wheelchairs. I see you sitting here tonight in
those wheelchairs. I've stayed with you. I've reached out to you across our nation. Don't you
give up. I know it's tough sometimes. People look down on you. It took you a little more effort to get here tonight.

And no one should look down on you, but sometimes mean people do. The only justifi-   110
cation we have for looking down on someone is that we're going to stop and pick them up.
But even in your wheelchairs, don't you give up. We cannot forget 50 years ago when our
backs were against the wall, [Franklin D.] Roosevelt was in a wheelchair. I would rather have
Roosevelt in a wheelchair than Reagan and [George] Bush on a horse. Don't you surrender
and don't you give up.

Don't surrender and don't you give up. Why can I challenge you this way? "Jesse Jackson,   111
you don't understand my situation. You be on television. You don't understand. I see you with
the big people. You don't understand my situation." I understand. You're seeing me on TV but
you don't know the me that makes me, me. They wonder why does Jesse run, because they
see me running for the White House. They don't see the house I'm running from.

The House He's Running From

I have a story. I wasn't always on television. Writers were not always outside my door. 112
When I was born late one afternoon, October 8th, in Greenville, S.C., no writers asked my
mother her name. Nobody chose to write down her address. My mama was not supposed to
make it. And I was not supposed to make it. You see, I was born to a teen-age mother who
was born to a teen-age mother.

I understand. I know abandonment and people being mean to you, and saying you're 113
nothing and nobody, and can never be anything. I understand. Jesse Jackson is my third
name. I'm adopted. When I had no name, my grandmother gave me her name. My name was
Jesse Burns until I was 12. So I wouldn't have a blank space, she gave me a name to hold me
over. I understand when nobody knows your name. I understand when you have no name. I
understand.

I wasn't born in a hospital. Mama didn't have insurance. I was born in the bed at the 114
house. I really do understand. Born in a three-room house, bathroom in the backyard, slop jar
by the bed, no hot and cold running water. I understand. Wallpaper used for decoration? No.
For a windbreaker. I understand. I'm a working person's person, that's why I understand you
whether you're black or white.

I understand work. I was not born with a silver spoon in my mouth. I had a shovel pro- 115
grammed for my hand. My mother, a working woman. So many days she went to work with
runs in her stockings. She knew better, but she wore runs in her stockings so that my brother
and I could have matching socks and not be laughed at at school.

I understand. At 3 o'clock on Thanksgiving Day we couldn't eat turkey because mama 116
was preparing someone else's turkey at 3 o'clock. We had to play football to entertain ourselves and then around 6 o'clock she would get off the Alta Vista bus when we would bring
up the leftovers and eat our turkey—leftovers, the carcass, the cranberries around 8 o'clock
at night. I really do understand.

Every one of these funny labels they put on you, those of you who are watching this 117
broadcast tonight in the projects, on the corners. I understand. Call you outcast, low down,
you can't make it, you're nothing, you're from nobody, subclass, underclass—when you see
Jesse Jackson, when my name goes in nomination, your name goes in nomination.

I was born in the slum, but the slum was not born in me. And it wasn't born in you, and 118
you can make it. Wherever you are tonight you can make it. Hold your head high, stick your
chest out. You can make it. It gets dark sometimes, but the morning comes. Don't you surrender. Suffering breeds character. Character breeds faith. In the end faith will not disappoint.

You must not surrender. You may or may not get there, but just know that you're quali- 119
fied and you hold on and hold out. We must never surrender. America will get better and better. Keep hope alive. Keep hope alive. Keep hope alive. On tomorrow night and beyond, keep
hope alive.

I love you very much. I love you very much. 120

Analysis of Jesse Jackson, "Common Ground: Address to the 1988 Democratic National Convention"

Jackson's 1988 Democratic Convention Address might be labeled a "dissident key-note" address. Jackson's speech was not the official keynote address of the 1988 convention, but it served much the same function as a keynote address. As I noted in reference to Cuomo's 1984 address, keynotes are primarily aimed at unifying and energizing the party faithful. To some extent they also aim at pulling undecided voters into the fold.

I label Jackson's address a "dissident" keynote because Jackson had been a candidate for the nomination and clearly was representing the liberal wing of the party. His purposes, therefore, included not only the general goals of any keynote, but also the aim of pulling the party to the political left so that it would better represent the interests for which Jackson had fought. Jackson also may have been using the address to set the stage for a possible run for the Democratic nomination in 1992. Of course, he later decided not to run for the nomination in that year.

The "dissident" nature of the speech is most evident in paragraphs 64 and 65, where he compares various interest groups within the Democratic party to the patches on a quilt. He begins the section by focusing on farmers, workers, women, students, Blacks and then Hispanics. In each case he calls for unity by saying "You are right. But your patch is not big enough." Then Jackson turns to what he calls "Conservatives and progressives," (the moderate wing of the party represented by people like Bill Clinton). In relation to this group he says: "when you fight for what you believe, right-wing, left-wing, hawk, dove—you are right, from your point of view, but your point of view is not enough" (65). While every other group in the party is simply "right," the moderate wing is only right "from your point of view." Of course, when someone says that you are right "from your point of view," what they really mean is that you are wrong.

Jackson did desire to unify and energize the party, but he also represented the agenda of his organization, the "Rainbow Coalition," and supported other liberal groups as well. Clearly, his address was concerned with supporting their position within the party.

Jackson faced significant rhetorical barriers and possessed one major rhetorical advantage in this address. His rhetorical advantage was that he was the second largest vote getter in the primaries and represented some of the largest constituencies in the Democratic party. In particular, Jackson was the most prominent Democrat who was associated with civil rights organizations and the African American community.

In relation to barriers, Jackson faced barriers similar to those faced by Cuomo. Like Cuomo, (see chapter six) he had to adapt to the constraints associated with a keynote address. In addition, Jackson faced barriers associated with his role as the most important spokesperson for the "Rainbow Coalition." Any time the representative of a particular group calls for national action that helps his/her group, there is the potential that the person may be perceived as self-interested. Jackson as the leader of the "Rainbow Coalition," supported initiatives that would aid people of color, women, gays, etc. Some, therefore, could perceive his remarks as self-interested.

Since Jackson is an African-American, one might expect that racism would be a barrier. However, given his message, racists are simply not in the implied audience. Jackson spoke to the Democratic party, which already was committed to strong support for civil rights for all Americans. As a consequence, outright racists or others who might feel some bias against Jackson because he is an African-American, simply were not in his audience.

Strategies in Jackson's "Common Ground," Address

Jackson relies on four major strategies in his 1988 address: narrative, credibility, language strategies, and various sub-strategies for producing an emotional response. Before discussing these strategies, it is important to note that Jackson does not rely heavily on rational argument. Jackson is, as the saying goes, "preaching to the saved." This religious metaphor expresses the fact that Jackson was talking to people who already agreed with him. In that context argument, evidence-oriented argument, is not necessary. This explains why in most cases in his 100 plus paragraph address, Jackson simply asserts claims. For example, in paragraphs 72–76 he calls for cutting defense spending in Europe and spending the money on education, health care, and slum redevelopment. In no case, does he support the effectiveness of the increased expenditures. Rational argument is not a core strategy in Jackson's address.

Narrative, Credibility, and Language Strategies

Instead of argument, Jackson relies on narrative, credibility appeals, language strategies, and all of the main sub-strategies for producing an emotional response.

The narrative strategy takes two forms. Throughout the address he briefly cites characters, whose story will be well-known to the audience. This strategy is used most extensively in the introduction, where he cites any number of heroes of the civil rights movement including Rosa Parks, Fanny Lou Hamer, Aaron Henry, and of course his mentor, Martin Luther King (paragraphs 11–16).

The second narrative strategy and Jackson's attempts to develop internal credibility are related. To some extent throughout the address, but most noticeably in the conclusion, Jackson uses his own life history as a model for others to emulate. From paragraph 112 to the conclusion of the address he develops this narrative/credibility strategy. In paragraph 112, he establishes his "credentials" as someone born into poverty. He concludes the paragraph by saying "I was not supposed to make it. You see, I was born to a teen-age mother who was born to a teen-age mother." In the following paragraph, he talks about how he did not live in a traditional nuclear family, but instead lived with his grandmother.

He continues with the theme that he was born into poverty in paragraph 114, where he notes that he was not born into a hospital, but at home in a house where wallpaper was not for decoration, but "for a wind breaker." In the next paragraph, he says that he "was not born with a silver spoon in my mouth. I had a shovel programmed for my hand." He then describes the sacrifices that his mother made for him and his brothers.

Paragraph 116 continues the theme that his mother sacrificed for him, but that the family still lived in utter poverty:

> I understand. At 3 o'clock on Thanksgiving Day we couldn't eat turkey because mama was preparing someone else's turkey at 3 o'clock. We had to play football to entertain ourselves and then around 6 'o'clock she would get off the Alta Vista bus when we would bring up the leftovers and eat our turkey—leftovers, the carcass, the cranberries around 8 o'clock at night. I really do understand.

It is the details in Jackson's description that make the passage so vivid. He remembers the specific bus his mother took and how she brought home the carcass of the rich folk's turkey.

Jackson uses the narrative to build his credibility, both as someone who can identify with the poor, and as someone who proved his mettle by escaping from poverty. He then uses both the credibility and the narrative to pound home his point that others can do what he has done. In the final four paragraphs of the address, he hits this theme again and again. In paragraph 117, he casts himself as a representative of all the downtrodden in our society: "Call you outcast, low down, you can't make it, you're nothing, you're from nobody, subclass, underclass—when you see Jesse Jackson, when my name goes in nomination, your name goes in nomination." Jackson then calls on these groups to reject the labels that others apply to them: "I was born in the slum, but the slum was not born in me. And it wasn't born in you. . ." Instead of accepting that label, they must fight, "Don't surrender. Suffering breeds character. Character breeds faith. In the end faith will not disappoint." In the next paragraph, he continues with this theme, almost screaming "Keep hope alive," before he concludes by again expressing his identity with the audience, "I love you very much."

In the final paragraphs of his speech, Jackson first builds his credibility as a poor kid who made it out of poverty, but still knows his roots. He then uses his personal narrative and credibility both to reaffirm identity with the groups within the Rainbow Coalition and to call on them to emulate his example. It is an extremely powerful passage.

In addition to his use of narrative and credibility, the Jackson address contains numerous language strategies. Jackson is a skilled rhetorician who relies primarily on language strategies to add interest to whatever specific point he is making. For example, in the concluding passages which I just cited, Jackson uses antithesis when he says, "I was born in the slum, but the slum was not born in me." His statement, "Suffering breeds character. Character breeds faith. In the end faith will not disappoint" has a natural rhythm that makes it memorable. "Never surrender" is a slogan that encapsulates a good portion of Jackson's message. He relies on parallel structure when he begins several passages in this section by saying "I understand."

The key point is that throughout the address Jackson relies on a wide variety of language strategies to invigorate his message. Jackson's use of multiple language strategies in combination with narrative, credibility, and various sub-strategies for creating an emotional response, which I will discuss in the next section, illustrates the point made in chapter seven that aesthetic strategies can be integrated into any work of rhetoric to add power to other strategies.

While Jackson primarily uses language strategies to make his message more vivid, there are four metaphors in the address that serve a more important function. At various points in the address, he compares the Democratic party to a "crossroads," to "common ground," to a "quilt," and of course to a "rainbow." The point of each of these metaphors is to define the party as composed of a number of different interest groups. The Democrats in Jackson's view are a diverse party including many groups in our society. Note that for Jackson the party is not a "melting pot" in which various groups are transformed and strengthened into a single group—Americans. Nor is the party, to borrow Ronald Reagan's phrase, an "empire of ideas." Instead, the party is a place (crossroads or common ground), an object (a quilt), or an image (a rainbow), in which different people come together to work in common cause, but maintain their different group affiliations.

Of these metaphors, Jackson develops the quilt theme in the most depth. He introduces the metaphor with a story about his grandmother:

> America's not a blanket woven from one thread, one color, one cloth. When I was a child growing up in Greenville, S.C., and grandmother could not afford a blanket, she didn't complain and we did not freeze. Instead, she took pieces of old cloth—patches, wool, silk, gabardine, crockersack on the patches—barely good enough to wipe off your shoes with
>   But they didn't stay that way very long. With sturdy hands and strong cord, she sewed them together into a quilt, a thing of beauty and power and culture. (paragraphs 62, 63)

In the following passage, which I cited earlier, he then compares the quilt to the various interest groups in the party. Jackson's powerful metaphor both adds interest to the address and provides a vision of the fundamental purpose of the Democratic party.

Jackson's 1988 convention address includes powerful narrative, credibility, and aesthetic strategies. It would have been an important speech with just these strategies, but the dominant strategy in the address is Jackson's use of various sub-strategies to produce a strong emotional response.

Emotion Producing Strategies in Jackson's Address

Jackson's address is literally a textbook example of how a rhetor can use various strategies to produce an emotional response from his audience. He also clearly recognizes the association between emotional response and vivid descriptive language. As I noted in the previous section, it is the details that Jackson provides, which makes the short narrative in the conclusion so powerful. We can imagine what it must have been like to wait until 8 p.m. to eat someone else's turkey carcass. Jackson clearly understands that graphic language is better adapted to producing an emotional response than abstract language.

Appeals to Basic Needs

Jackson cites basic human needs at several points in the address. For example, in paragraphs 81 and 82, he talks about the "Plant closings without notice, economic violence." He then refers to the effects of those plant closing. "But whether white, black or brown, the hungry baby's belly turned inside out is the same color. Call it pain. Call it hurt. Call it agony." Here, Jackson shows the effect of the relocation of manufacturing plants outside of the United States on ordinary people, in this case babies. He is arguing that basic human needs are threatened by what he calls "economic violence." This same strategy is found in other forms at several other points in the address.

Appeals to Basic Values

Throughout the address, Jackson draws on basic values including equality, opportunity, and diversity. For example, in paragraph 57, he says:

> Tonight we choose interdependency in our capacity to act and unite for the greater good. The common good is finding commitment to new priorities, to expression and inclusion. A commitment to expanded participation in the Democratic Party at every level.

He then uses the "common ground" metaphor to apply his call for inclusion to workers, teachers, hospital admissions, farmers, and others (paragraphs 59, 60).

Jackson also appeals to basic values in the conclusion. In this section, he taps into American values such as hard work, responsibility, and opportunity. For example, in a long passage, he calls on kids to reject drugs. He says "Do not surrender to drugs. The best drug policy is no first use" (paragraph 106). He then moves into the concluding narrative, which I cited earlier. The key point in relation to values that comes out of this narrative is that hard work and continued effort can produce opportunity. In essence, Jackson uses himself as the example proving that the American dream can be achieved.

Throughout the address, Jackson attacks Ronald Reagan and the values that he says Reagan stands for. The irony is that in the conclusion, Jackson endorses basic values very similar to the values at the core of Reagan's rhetoric—values like opportunity, hard work and personal responsibility. His rejection of drug use sounds very much like Nancy

Reagan's anti-drug slogan—just say no. I am not saying that Jackson is a hypocrite. My point is that basic American values, such as the ones Jackson draws on in the conclusion, are shared by nearly everyone in our culture. Those values are quite consistent with the messages of both Jackson and Reagan.

Appeals to Self-interest

Jackson clearly appeals to the self-interest of those Democratic constituencies, which he represents. His appeal to self-interest is most obvious in paragraph 64, where he uses the quilt metaphor to describe the party. "Farmers, you seek fair prices and you are right, but you cannot stand alone. Your patch is not big enough. Workers, you fight for fair wages. You are right. But your patch labor is not big enough. Women, you seek comparable worth and you pay equity. Your are right. But your patch is not big enough." He continues with this same theme in the following paragraph. The important point is that Jackson is appealing to the self-interest of each of the groups he references. He supports higher prices for farmers, better wages for labor, pay equity for women, and so forth. Note that in each case, he justifies an increased benefit for the group in terms of a universal principle, such as justice or equity.

Appeals to Guilt

Jackson's appeal to guilt is found most prominently in the section where he discusses the 1988 Democratic nominee for President, Michael Dukakis. After praising Dukakis for running a good campaign, Jackson comments on differences in their backgrounds. In four short paragraphs (50–53), he reminds the audience that unlike Dukakis, Jackson grew up in poverty and continues to suffer from the fact that his ancestors were slaves. In paragraph 53, he draws these themes together, "His foreparents came to America on immigrant ships; my foreparents came to America on slave ships. But whatever the original ships, we're in the same boat tonight." Here, and in several other passages, Jackson reminds the audience of the terrible treatment that African Americans received in the past and implicitly says to his audience, "Past treatment mandates action today."

In my earlier discussion of appeals to guilt, I noted that the strategy is best used when the guilt is implicit, rather than explicit. Jackson clearly understands this point. He does not come out and say, "past injustice mandates action today." Instead, he uses statements such as his reference to "the sons and daughters of slaves sitting together around a common table" (paragraph 16) to implicitly make that point to the audience.

Appeals to History

Jackson uses the history of the civil rights movement to tap the emotions of his audience. In the very first paragraph he uses antithesis to set up his historical reference. He says that the audience is not really seated, "we're standing on someone's shoulders." He then introduces Rosa Parks, who is famous for starting a protest against unequal treatment in transportation by refusing to go to the back of a segregated bus. Parks is used as a symbol of the civil rights movement as a whole. A little later in the address, but still in the introduction, Jackson refers to a number of heroes and martyrs of the civil rights movement. He speaks of Fanny Lou Hamer and Aaron Henry, who attempted to send an integrated delegation from Mississippi to the 1964 Democratic National Convention (paragraph 11). He then references martyrs of the civil rights movement including "[Michael] Schwerner, [Andrew] Goodman and [James] Chaney—two Jews and a black—found in a common grave, bodies riddled with bullets in Mississippi. The four darling little girls in the church in Birmingham, Alabama.[14] They died so that we might have a right to live" (paragraph 14).

Jackson's purpose in citing the history of the civil rights movement, especially the sacrifices of the innocent, is to draw on the emotion associated with the movement in order to support his cause. He makes that purpose clear in paragraph 10, immediately prior to his discussion of heroes and martyrs of the movement, when he says, "My right and my privilege to stand here before you has been won—in my lifetime—by the blood and sweat of the innocent."

Jackson also appeals to the history of the Democratic party. In paragraphs 41–46, he discusses past elections. His ultimate point is that Democrats can succeed if they are unified. In 1960 they were unified behind John Kennedy and they won "by the margin of our hope, inspired by courageous leadership" (paragraph 42). They also won in 1964 and 1976 (paragraphs 42, 43), but in 1968 and 1980 "division and despair" led to defeat (paragraphs 44, 45). "Today when we debated, differed, deliberated, agreed to agree, agreed to disagree, when we had the good judgment to argue our case and then not self-destruct, George Bush was just a little further away from the White House and a little closer to private life" (paragraph 46). In this section, Jackson uses history to support his call for Democratic unity. Of course, as I noted earlier, he wanted unity on his terms.

It is also important to recognize how he integrates the appeal to history with language strategies. In paragraph 46, which I cited earlier, he uses alliteration and antithesis in combination with the history.

Appeals to Religion

Jackson draws on Christian dogma at several points in the address. In paragraph 39, he notes that "The Bible teaches that when lions and lambs lie down together, none will be afraid and there will be peace in the valley." He then uses this biblical passage to call for common ground among Democrats. Even though "Lions eat lambs." And "Lambs sensibly flee from lions," "Neither lions nor lamb can survive nuclear war. If lions and lambs can find common ground, surely, we can as well, as civilized people" (paragraphs 39, 40). A little later, Jackson quotes Jesus, "Not my will, but thine be done" (paragraph 55) as support for his cause. Jackson is saying that in his own way, he is trying to do Christ's will.

Appeals to Myth

Jackson appeals to myth in conjunction with his historical narrative of the civil rights movement. At the end of the section in which he talks of martyrs of the civil rights movement, he says:

> Dr. Martin Luther King Jr. lies only a few miles from us tonight.
> Tonight he must feel good as he looks down upon us. We sit here together, a rainbow, a coalition—the sons and daughters of slaves sitting together around a common table, to decide the direction of our party and our country. His heart would be full tonight. (paragraph 15, 16)

King is a mythic figure, who in Jackson's description is looking down on the convention from heaven. Jackson draws upon the power associated with King as a hero to support his "rainbow coalition."

Appeals to Elemental Symbols

Jackson uses several elemental symbols in his address. In a passage I cited when discussing his appeals to history, Jackson refers to the "blood and the sweat of the innocent" (paragraph 10). Similarly, at the end of the main body of the address, Jackson uses elemental symbols as a way of showing that ordinary people are being harmed in this country. In discussing the effects of what he calls the "economic violence" brought on by the Reagan presidency, Jackson speaks of people who "work in hospitals" and "wipe the bodies of those who are sick with fever and pain. They empty their bedpans. They clean out their commode. No job is beneath them, and yet when they get sick, they cannot lie in the bed they made up every day. America, that is not right. We are a better nation than that" (paragraph 85).

In these passages, Jackson draws on symbols that are cultural universals. Blood means sacrifice. Sweat means effort. And in referencing those who wipe the bodies of the sick and clean out commodes, he is implicitly using "excrement" as a negative symbol. His point is that people who work so hard that they are willing to clean out excrement ought to have access to health care.

Appeals to Societal Symbols

In addition to his use of elemental symbols, Jackson cites any number of societal symbols, which in turn link to one of the other sub-strategies for producing an emotional response. For example, in paragraph 27 Jackson cites the inscription on the

Statue of Liberty—"give me your tired, your poor, your huddled masses who yearn to breathe free." In this passage, Jackson links the values of the Democratic party to the Statue of Liberty as a cultural symbol representing freedom and opportunity. The various heroes and martyrs of the civil rights movement and the Democratic party also function as societal symbols in Jackson's speech. They are symbols that represent values such as equality, justice, unity and sacrifice.

Summary of Jackson's Use of Emotion-Creating Strategies

Jackson masterfully draws upon all of the sub-strategies for producing an emotional response in the audience. Throughout the address, he combines these sub-strategies with language devices, narratives, and appeals to his own credibility. In so doing, Jackson brilliantly responds to the demands of the rhetorical situation. He unifies and energizes the Democratic party, but on his terms.

Jackson also implicitly responds to those who label him as the self-interested representative of a set of Democratic constituencies. Jackson both ties his message to fundamental values that unify the party and also shows that those core constituencies are essential to the party. In this way, he tries to have it both ways by saying on the one hand that he represents not special interests, but "justice." And on the other hand, his policies would help the very constituencies that he has linked to universal values.

While Jackson's address brilliantly adapted to the rhetorical constraints that he faced, his message had one weakness. The combination of universal values with appeals to specific constituencies works very well for unifying the "quilt" of groups that Jackson believes make up the Democratic party. But a strategy that works well for appealing to a number of interest groups might not be as strong a strategy for appealing to an entire nation.

Jackson's quilt metaphor can be used to illustrate this point. The metaphor masks the fact that the interests of each of the patches in the quilt are not fully consistent with those of the other patches. Higher prices for farmers mean higher food prices for the poor. More money for one group inevitably means less for another. The metaphor itself also has a weakness. A skillful moderate or conservative could argue that America is not a quilt of interest groups tied together. Nor is the nation a blanket of one color, as Jackson suggests. Rather, it is a multi-colored tapestry in which each of the groups that have come to the nation have become Americans. Although he did not use this metaphor, Ronald Reagan used essentially this strategy in two election victories in the 1980s.

Conclusion

An effective rhetor needs to do more than simply present a strong argument. He/she also needs strategies for energizing the audience to whom the argument is presented. This means that in order to motivate an audience to take action, it almost always will be necessary to utilize strategies that produce a strong emotional reaction. These strategies are not inherently inconsistent with also building a strong case. In The Declaration of Independence, Thomas Jefferson both built a strong case that Britain has usurped American liberty and also linked that case to basic values and needs, societal symbols, history and so forth.

At the same time, not all strategies producing an emotional response are ethical. Hitler relied on unethical means of producing an emotional reaction to take control of Germany. In discussion of "The Informed Citizen," I will develop criteria for distinguishing between ethical and unethical use of strategies that are aimed at producing an emotional response.

Notes

1. See Aristotle, *The Rhetoric* in *The Basic Works of Aristotle*, ed. Richard McKeon (New York: Random House, 1941), Book 1, Ch. 2, p. 1329.
2. Aristotle's analysis of the emotions is detailed in "Aristotle's View of Ethical Rhetoric," *Rhetoric Society Quarterly*, 15 (l985): 13–31, with Deanna Womack.
3. For example, a recent article in *The New Republic* referred to both former Senator Bill Bradley and Vice President Al Gore as "wooden orators." See, John B. Judis, "Journey Man," *The New Republic* 5 April 1999, p. 27.
4. See for example James MacGregor Burns, *Roosevelt: The Lion and the Fox* (New York: Harcourt, Brace & World, 1956), p. 477.
5. Franklin Delano Roosevelt, "First Inaugural Address," in Halford Ross Ryan, *Contemporary American Public Discourse*, 3rd edition (Prospect Heights, Illinois, Waveland, 1992), p. 13.
6. The classic essay on this point is Irving L. Janis, "Effects of Fear Arousal on Attitude Change: Recent Developments in Theory and Experimental Research," in *The Process of Social Influence: Readings in Persuasion*, Ed. Thomas Beisecker and Donn W. Parson (Englewood Cliffs, NJ: Prentice-Hall, 1972): 277–317.
7. William J. Clinton, "Remarks to the Convocation of the Church of God in Christ in Memphis, " *Weekly Compilation of President Documents* 13 November 1993: 2357–2362.
8. See Mircea Eliade, *Myth and Reality*, Trans. Willard R. Trask (New York: Harper & Row, 1963): 1.
9. A detailed analysis of how myth functions in rhetoric is developed in Robert C. Rowland, "On Mythic Criticism," *Communication Studies* 41 (1990): 101–116.
10. William Lewis, "Telling America's Story: Narrative Form and the Reagan Presidency," *Quarterly Journal of Speech* 73 (1987): 280–302.
11. See Eliade, especially pp. 71–78.
12. See Shirley Park Lowry, *Familiar Mysteries: The Truth in Myth* (New York: Oxford University Press, 1982).
13. See Michael Osborn, "The Evolution of the Archetypal Sea In Rhetoric and Poetic," *Quarterly Journal of Speech* 63 (1977): 347–363.
14. Jackson is referring to a church bombing that killed the four girls.

CHAPTER NINE

Confrontative Rhetoric and Social Movements

In this chapter, the focus of discussion is on two related subjects: the final strategy category, confrontative rhetoric, and a context area in which confrontation is often used, the advocacy of social movements. Confrontation is a rhetorical strategy in which the rhetor refuses to adapt to his/her audience, but instead intentionally attacks or offends them. Social movements advocate change on such subjects as the environment, civil rights, animal rights, and so forth, and include organizations such as the Sierra Club, the National Organization of Women, and many others.

Why combine the discussion of confrontation and social movements into a single chapter? The short answer to this question is that confrontation is a strategy most appropriately used by those who cannot use adaptive rhetorical strategies and lack the power to change society directly. While confrontation is used in a variety of contexts, it is most commonly associated with the rhetoric of certain social movements. In addition, it is appropriate to include a discussion of confrontation along with a consideration of social movements because use of confrontation creates certain rhetorical problems to which a movement must respond.

In the remainder of this chapter, I first define the nature of confrontative rhetoric. The next section considers when confrontation is an appropriate strategy and lays out the situation in which confrontation is likely to be effective. In the third main section, I discuss confrontation as it relates to social movement rhetoric and develop a typology of confrontative sub-strategies. Finally, I illustrate the use of confrontation in the context of a social movement by discussing an excerpt from one of the most famous speeches given by an American, Frederic Douglass', "What to the Slave is The Fourth of July."

It is important to note that while the focus of this chapter is on confrontation as it is used in social movements, the chapter is not intended to provide a complete theory of social movement rhetoric.[1] Rather, the goal is to provide an introduction to how social movements and others rely on confrontation as a rhetorical strategy.

Use of Confrontation as a Rhetorical Strategy

Going back to Aristotle, perhaps the single most basic principle of rhetorical strategy has been that the rhetor must begin with where the audience is.[2] In other words, to be successful, rhetoric must be adapted to the attitudes, values, and beliefs of the audience. This principle lies behind the standards for intrinsic evaluation of rhetorical effectiveness that I discussed earlier and also was assumed in the analysis of the first five strategy categories.

There is an old saying, however, that it "is the exception which proves the rule." The exception which proves the general rule that rhetoric should be adapted to an audience relates to the sixth strategy category, confrontation. There are rare circumstances in which the speaker or writer should not adapt to the audience, but confront that audience, sometimes offending or even attacking them. Confrontation is necessary in those instances to create the preconditions for successful rhetoric.

Traditional adaptive rhetorical strategies will not work in two particular situations. First, adaptive strategies generally will be ineffective if the position being supported would result in radical change in the society. Take the example of radical environmentalists who believe that the United States must reduce energy consumption by at least 75%. Such a policy would require dramatic changes in American society. It would devastate the auto industry, for instance. Normal adaptive strategies will not work on this subject because the public simply will reject the idea.

Second, adaptive strategies also may fail for groups that are outside of the system. In the 1950s, gay rights activists either were ignored or persecuted in our society. Writing letters to the editor or giving public speeches that adapted to dominant values was not going to accomplish much, because society labelled gays as deviant. This explains why gay activists in the 1960s often relied upon confrontation.

Therefore, confrontation may be a viable rhetorical option for groups calling for radical change or for groups that have been excluded from society. While I have focused on examples from the social movement context, there are other instances where confrontation may be the only option. Some therapists advocate use of what is essentially confrontative rhetoric to get the attention of a loved one or friend who has become addicted to drugs or alcohol or become a member of a cult. The cult member or addict cannot be reached through normal adaptive strategies because the person will deny that there is any problem. The alcoholic will say that he/she can quit at any time. The cult member will say that he/she is there of their own free will. In such a context, some psychologists believe that radical intervention by friends or family is needed to get the addict or cult member to change their life. While psychologists do not label that intervention as "confrontative rhetoric" in fact that is what it is.

The hypothetical example of the use of confrontation to deal with addiction or membership in a cult highlights an additional point, the risks associated with confrontation. When dealing with a drug addict or a cult member, there may come a time when there is no other alternative but to use radical confrontation to attempt to shake the person out of their lifestyle. However, there are obviously enormous risks associated with this choice. If you use confrontation with a friend who you believe has become an alcoholic, you may wake your friend up to the dangers of alcohol abuse, but you may lose the friendship. And you could spark a violent reaction from your former friend. In the next section, I consider the dangers associated with confrontation and the circumstances in which confrontation is an appropriate strategic choice.

Risks Associated With Confrontation

There are two primary risks associated with confrontation as a rhetorical strategy. First, the strategy may offend the audience and result in loss of credibility. By offending the audience, whether in an interpersonal context or in the larger society, the individual or the group may lose whatever credibility they had with the audience. For example, an environmental group that puts spikes in the tires of trash trucks as protest against the expansion of a landfill, may be perceived as a bunch of common criminals. In the mind of the public, this one act of confrontation may wipe out memory of a host of good works. In the interpersonal context, use of confrontation may lead a friend to simply shut you out of his/her life.

Second, use of confrontation can produce audience backlash and, in the case of social movements, societal repression. Remember, no one likes to be attacked. Throughout the history of this nation, groups that have used strong rhetoric to attack the system, often have faced police investigations, legislative restrictions, and even outright repression. For example, the FBI and other Federal agencies spent large sums to investigate both the peace and civil rights movements in the 1960s. In the interpersonal context, use of confrontation could provoke a (former) friend to respond in kind or even use violence.

Since confrontation can produce backlash and make things much worse, even if the issue falls into one of the two categories where adaptive strategies generally fail, confrontation may not be the proper option. This suggests that confrontation should be used only in the most serious situations and only if backlash seems unlikely.

As a general rule, confrontation is only an appropriate strategy in the following circumstances. First, confrontation should never be used if traditionally adaptive rhetoric is an option. It always makes sense to rely on a mixture of the first five strategy categories if it is possible that they could be used to achieve a particular rhetorical goal. Adaptation is much less risky than confrontation and generally more effective. Second, confrontation should be utilized only as a last resort. Even if it seems unlikely that adaptive strategies could work, the attempt should be made because the risks associated with confrontation are quite high.

Third, confrontation should not be utilized except on crucial issues. It is one thing to hold a sit-down strike over a fundamental issue of civil rights and quite another to hold the same protest because you don't like the landscaping in front of a building. In the interpersonal context, an intervention of some kind may be required if you fear that a roommate or close friend is about to harm themselves or someone else. But it would be silly to use confrontation because someone didn't put their socks in the clothes hamper.

Fourth, confrontation only works in a certain kind of society. Confrontative rhetorical strategies could not work in Hitler's Germany, Stalin's Soviet Union, or in Iraq, Iran, Libya, Syria, China, North Korea and many other places today. Confrontation only works in a democratic society, where rights are protected and a strong media exists that can cover the confrontative rhetoric. In a non-democratic society, use of a confrontative strategy simply results in punishment. For example, a sit-down strike in Stalin's Russia likely would have led to execution or, at best, long sentences to the prison camp system.

In addition to democratic rights, a strong media is necessary for confrontation to be effective. Martin Luther King, Jr., and others were able to use civil disobedience and other forms of confrontation to great effect in the United States because their acts generated great media coverage. The major television networks took pictures of the civil disobedience and, in many cases, of police violence against peaceful protesters. These pictures, along with written accounts, did a lot to convince millions of Americans of the morality of King's cause. Without the media coverage, the protests would have been much less effective.

In summary, rhetorical confrontation only works in a society which provides basic protection of human rights and which has a strong media. A similar point can be made about small group settings. Confrontative strategies would not work within a cult because there is no rhetorical space for them to function. In that context, rather than protest the cult's practices, the dissident cult member should simply leave and then go after the cult from the outside.

Finally, confrontation should be used only if there is nothing to lose. The dangers associated with confrontation are so high that it is too risky to use it unless the rhetor *cannot* be in a worse situation if the confrontation fails. In chapter three, I explained how Booker T. Washington adapted to Southern attitudes in the "Atlanta Exposition Address." Given the many lynchings of innocent Black people in that period, Washington was wise to make that choice. Confrontative rhetoric might have caused white backlash, which could have resulted in violence against Black Americans. Washington had something to lose; confrontation would not have been a good option for him.

A Brief Introduction to Social Movement Rhetoric

There is an enormous literature discussing the ways that social movements use rhetoric to achieve their aims.[3] Most of that literature is not relevant to this book, which introduces the ways in which rhetoric is used in a democratic society. However, a brief discussion of the role of social movements and the importance of confrontation in social movement rhetoric is needed.

Rhetorical theorists have proposed a number of different perspectives on social movements. In his original essay on movements, Leland Griffin took a largely historical approach. Later theorists have used other approaches including an emphasis upon the sociological constraints that groups lacking power face in calling for change in the larger society,[4] a treatment of movements as defined by rhetorical conflict within society,[5] and an analysis of movements as similar to drama.[6] Others have argued that social movement rhetoric is not always that different from the rhetorical practices of the establishment, noting that in many cases establishment leaders lack the power to simply implement an agenda and must rely on persuasion to accomplish their aims.[7]

In relation to the primary focus of this chapter, confrontation as a rhetorical strategy, there are two points about social movements that are important. First, in many instances social movements support radical actions, lack the power to implement change directly, and cannot adapt to dominant societal attitudes and values. This situation is not always the case. For example, Herbert Simons argues that social movements "are struggles on behalf of a cause by groups whose core organizations, modes of action, and/or guiding idea are not fully legitimated by the larger society."[8] Clearly, there are many social movements that fall within Simons' definition, which can rely on the five main adaptive rhetorical strategies.

However, there clearly are instances in which the movement has no real option other than confrontation. After presenting the definition cited above, Simons goes on to note that "the paradigm case of social movements continues to be an antiestablishment grassroots group spouting radical ideas in a manner calculated to get the attention but not necessarily the approval of those it opposes."[9] These groups cannot adapt to the dominant values of the society, because it is those very values that they are trying to change. For example, Martin Luther King could not adapt to racist attitudes and values; he was trying to eliminate a segregationist system. Thus, the first key point to understand about social movement rhetoric is that there are some movements, which are essentially forced into confrontation in order to have any chance of ultimate success.

The second essential point to understand about social movements relates to the two primary audiences of social movement rhetoric. Many rhetoricians speak to both an internal audience within the organization and an external audience composed of the larger society. To some extent both Jesse Jackson and Mario Cuomo, in the convention addresses considered earlier, spoke to an internal audience of Democratic loyalists and an external audience of undecided voters. The same is true in the area of organizational rhetoric. Any organization, whether a business, a governmental entity, a charitable group, or a social movement, speaks both to members of the organization and also to those outside the organization. It is sometimes difficult to satisfy both groups. Adapting to the larger public audience may offend the internal audience and vice versa.

However, the internal/external audience problem is often still more difficult for the leaders of social movements that lack social power and are forced to use confrontation. In such cases, movement leaders may have to overcome not only barriers present in the larger society, but also the way that group members or potential group members see themselves. In the discussion of metaphor in chapter seven, I mentioned the negative effects that labels can have on the self-concept of an individual. If a person is consistently told by society that he/she is inferior, it is inevitable that this labeling will have an effect.

This point applies most strongly to movements that attempt to gain rights for groups that previously have been labeled as inferior by the larger society. It is easily illustrated in relation to the civil rights movement, the feminist movement, and the gay rights movement. In each case, the larger society used words that "put down" members of the group. African Americans men often were called "boy," a label which denied their manhood. And both Black men and women were called still worse names. Similarly, grown successful women were referred to as "one of the girls" or by some other demeaning term. And gays were labeled as deviant. In each case, the effect of this labeling was to threaten the self-worth of the individual. Social movements that fight for the rights of oppressed groups face a particularly difficult "two audience" problem.

The movement must speak to the larger society, but also help members of the group discover and express their own identity. This was precisely what happened in the civil rights movement with the focus on "Black" power, "Black" history, "Black" studies, and so forth. Exactly the same point could be made about the feminist and gay rights movements.

Much of the advocacy of social movements looks very similar to the persuasion of government officials, business lobbyists and so forth. For example, the pro-environment rhetoric of the "Sierra Club," relies on a host of adaptive strategies including narrative, rational argument, credibility, and appeals to basic values and needs. In opposing the position of the Sierra Club, an oil company public relations campaign would rely on similar adaptive strategies, although from the opposite position.

However, there are two cases in which social movement rhetoric is quite different from other advocacy. Social movements sometimes have so little power and favor such radical action that confrontation is the only available primary rhetorical strategy. And movements that seek to liberate oppressed groups often face an extremely difficult "two audience" problem because of the negative effects of societal labeling on the self-worth of group members.

The next section fleshes out the two ways in which some social movement rhetoric differs from other advocacy by focusing on the functions fulfilled by confrontative rhetoric.

Functions of Confrontative Rhetoric

Confrontative rhetoric often is aimed at two audiences: an internal audience within a social movement or organization and an external audience composed of the larger society. Confrontative rhetoric does somewhat different work for the internal and external audiences.

For the internal audience, confrontative rhetoric serves two primary functions. First, confrontation can be used to create the perception that change is possible. Given the horrible oppression of people of color in this nation in the first half of this century, why was there not a more developed civil rights movement prior to the 1950s? One part of the answer is that people of color did not believe that change was possible. They saw a system in which African-Americans were lynched every year, a system in which they lacked significant political power, and a system in which segregation seemed to be totally entrenched, and concluded that protest was impossible. In this context, one of the key aims of the civil rights movement was to create the understanding that change could occur. Confrontative rhetoric often fulfills this function.

Second, confrontation may work for the internal audience as part of what might be called the rhetorical redefinition of self.[10] As I explained earlier, one of the terrible effects of oppression is to deny the selfhood of the individuals who are being oppressed. Through confrontative rhetoric, however, the oppressed people can assert their own independent identity. One of the most important aspects of the civil rights movement was that it fulfilled this identity re-creation function. Slogans like "Black is Beautiful," "Black Power" or "Black History," served both as language strategies and also as a means of redefining what it meant to be Black and American.

For the external audience, confrontation serves two additional functions. First, confrontative rhetoric is a means of getting the attention of the larger society. Without popular attention, the social movement can accomplish little. Gaining public attention usually requires use of strategies that make people mad. For example, animal rights activists spray paint women in mink coats as a way of bringing media attention to their cause. Other strategies may serve this function in an even more radical way. For example, in Great Britain, the Irish Republican Army (IRA) has used bomb threats (and real bombs) to bring attention to their cause.

In general, confrontative rhetoric gets the attention of the audience by doing or saying things that makes the audience angry. It is the anger which focuses attention on the issue. But this also illustrates the risk associated with confrontation. It is a dangerous thing to make your audience angry at you.

Second, confrontative rhetoric may be used to both create guilt and threaten the external audience. Oftentimes, different leaders of a social movement may utilize a sort of "good cop-bad cop" rhetorical strategy. In the 1960s, some radical Black nationalists threatened to use violence unless society changed. At the same time, people like Martin Luther King, Jr., drew on the Bible and the non-violent philosophies of Henry David Thoreau and Mahatma Gandhi to support civil disobedience in support of civil rights for all Americans. King and his followers called for radical action but did it in a less confrontative and more inclusive fashion than did the radical Black nationalists of the time. One result was that the threats of the radical nationalists made King's demands seem all the more reasonable.

In summary, to be effective confrontative rhetoric must fulfill two functions for each of the internal and external audience. For the internal audience, it must create the sense that change is possible and assist in the rhetorical redefinition of the self. For the external audience, it must gain public attention and both threaten and create guilt in the larger audience.

Strategies of Confrontative Rhetoric

There are eight sub-strategies for achieving the four functions of confrontative rhetoric, six of which deal primarily with the functions for the external audience and two of which relate to the internal audience.

Strategies for Confronting the External Audience

The first strategy for confronting the external audience is for the rhetor consciously to speak/write/act in order to shock or offend the audience. During the Vietnam era, anti-war protesters burned the American flag to achieve this effect. This garnered a great deal of public attention. Again, by shocking the audience, the rhetor at least gets the attention of the external public.

A second strategy is to attack the audience. Rather than adapt to them, the rhetor actually lashes out at them. This strategy is most appropriate when a rhetor is speaking to an audience that is in some sense sympathetic to the cause being advocated. The rhetor attacks this audience as a way of arguing that they really are not doing enough. If used against an audience that is unfriendly, the likely result is severe audience backlash.

The third strategy is closely related to the second. Oftentimes, movement leaders will attempt to create guilt in the larger audience. In essence, the speaker/writer says, "You claim to support our values, but you do nothing. That makes you worse than our opponents, who are at least honest in their views."

A fourth confrontative strategy is to threaten the audience. The effect of a threat to the audience may be to make more conservative advocates of a similar position seem more reasonable. Once again, in the 1960s threats of violence from radical Black Nationalists had the effect in the dominant white society of making Martin Luther King, Jr., seem quite reasonable.

The fifth confrontative strategy is to use civil disobedience. Civil disobedience occurs when an individual breaks a law in order to draw attention to a problem. The individual does not attempt to avoid law enforcement, but accepts his/her punishment as a means of proving moral superiority. From Thoreau to Gandhi and King, civil disobedience has been advocated as a means of opposing a repressive society. In rhetorical terms, civil disobedience works best if the society responds by punishing, even beating, the protesters. The willingness of people to suffer for their cause then, in a sense, proves the morality of the cause. And the repression also may bring media attention to the dispute.

The sixth confrontative strategy for dealing with the external audience is terrorism. Terrorism (or violence or disruption) is primarily a rhetorical strategy. The terrorist attacks the system in order to draw attention to whatever problem is at issue. One goal of the IRA has been to focus as much world attention on Northern Ireland as possible. Terrorist acts have been used by some in that group to get that attention.

Confrontative Strategies for Appealing to an External Audience

1. Shock or offend the audience.
2. Attack the audience.
3. Create guilt in the audience.
4. Threaten the audience.
5. Civil disobedience.
6. Use terrorism or other violence to draw attention to the cause. Note, this strategy is never appropriate in a democratic society that protects rights.

While terrorism inevitably gets public attention this does not mean that it is morally acceptable. Terrorism is never justified in a democratic society that protects rights because alternative rhetorical approaches are available.

Strategies for Confronting the Internal Audience

In addition to the six confrontative strategies for dealing with the external audience, there are two primary rhetorical strategies that are used for the internal audience of people within a movement. These two strategies are to draw on myth as a means of creating identity and to use rhetorical redefinition in order to create a strong sense of selfhood for members of the movement.

Movement leaders often draw on myth in order to energize their followers. In chapter eight, I explained that real societal myths are not perceived as false, but as fundamentally true stories. By telling or retelling a myth, movement leaders can connect a movement to great heroes and transcendent events. This explains why today, members of militia movements cast themselves as the heirs of the soldiers of the American Revolution, which they sometimes rather ominously call the "First" Revolution.

Mythic definition is especially important for movements representing those who perceive themselves to be oppressed. Via the myth, the individual no longer sees himself/herself as powerless, but rather as powerful. The myth also ties the goal of the movement to a higher ideal. In the case of religious myths, the movement can claim to be doing god's work.

The second primarily internal movement strategy is to use rhetoric to redefine the role of members of the movement. As I noted earlier, it was this process of rhetorical redefinition that was operating in the focus on Black Pride, Black History, and so forth in the 1960s and 1970s. By redefining what it meant to be a Black American, leaders of the movement sought to change all of the associations that went along with Black,

Negro, and other terms. Such redefinition also has been a prominent strategy in the feminist and gay movements. An example from popular culture clarifies this point. In her song "I am woman," Helen Reddy precisely states a message of rhetorical redefinition. Reddy redefines women from weak to strong in lines such as "I am woman, hear me roar." Such a message is needed before a social movement can take off because movement leaders and members must be able to overcome how a society defines their proper role.

Summary of Confrontation and Social Movements

Confrontation is a dangerous rhetorical strategy, both from the perspective of the rhetor and the society. It is dangerous for the rhetor because it may produce backlash. It is dangerous for society because it may result in increased conflict. Therefore, confrontation should be used as a last resort only.

To illustrate the dangers and sometime necessity of confrontation, in the next section, I focus on extended excerpts from one of the great speeches ever delivered by an American, Frederick Douglass' "What to the Slave is the Fourth of July," which was presented on July 5, 1852, in Rochester, New York. Douglass was the foremost American Black leader for almost half a century. The distinguished historian James M. McPherson has written of Douglass that he "strode across the stage of American history with a commanding presence equaled by few of his countrymen." Douglass, who based on his "gift of oratory, rose to international fame as a champion of freedom and equal rights" was a counselor to eight presidents.[11] There is no question about the influence of Douglass or the fact that the influence was traced to what McPherson called "the moral force of his language."[12] In a web page commemorating the 100th anniversary of Douglass' death, the Smithsonian Institution labeled him "the father of the civil rights movement," and noted that of his more than 1000 speeches opposing slavery, the most "powerful" was "What to the Slave is the Fourth of July."[13] In this address he confronts the difficulty of motivating generally anti-slavery white Northerners to take radical action in order to end slavery.

◆◆◆

Excerpt from "What to the Slave is the Fourth of July"

Frederick Douglass

Fellow citizens: Pardon me, and allow me to ask, why am I called upon to speak here today? What have I or those I represent to do with you national independence? Are the great principles of political freedom and of natural justice, embodied in that Declaration of Independence, extended to us? And am I, therefore, called upon to bring our humble offering to the national altar, and to confess the benefits, and express devout gratitude for the blessings resulting from your independence to us? 1

Would to God, both for your sakes and ours, that an affirmative answer could be truthfully returned to these questions. Then would my task be light, and my burden easy and delightful. For who is there so cold that a nation's sympathy could not warm him? Who so obdurate and dead to the claims of gratitude, that would not thankfully acknowledge such priceless benefits? Who so stolid and selfish that would not give his voice to swell the hallelujahs of a nation's jubilee, when the chains of servitude had been torn from his limbs? I am not that man. In a case like that, the dumb might eloquently speak, and the "lame man leap as an hart." 2

But such is not the state of the case, I say it with a sad sense of disparity between us. I am not included within the pale of this glorious anniversary! Your high independence only reveals the immeasurable distance between us. The blessings in which you this day rejoice are not enjoyed in common. The rich inheritance of justice, liberty, prosperity, and independence bequeathed by your fathers is shared by you, not by me. The sunlight that brought life and healing to you has brought stripes and death to me. This Fourth of July is *yours*, not *mine*. You may rejoice, I must mourn. To drag a man in fetters into the grand illuminated temple of liberty, and call upon him to join you in joyous anthems, were inhuman mockery and sacrilegious irony. Do you mean, citizens, to mock me, by asking me to speak today? If so, there is a parallel to your conduct. And let me warn you, that it is dangerous to copy the example of a nation whose crimes, towering up to heaven, were thrown down by the breath of the Almighty, burying that nation in irrecoverable ruin. I can today take up the lament of a peeled and woe-smitten people. 3

"By the rivers of Baylon, there we sat down. Yes! We wept when we remembered Zion. We hanged our harps upon the willows in the midst thereof. For there they that carried us away captive, required of us a song; and they who wasted us, required of us mirth, saying, Sing us one of the songs of Zion. How can we sing the Lord's song in a strange land? If I forget thee, O Jerusalem, let my right hand forget her cunning. If I do not remember thee, let my tongue cleave to the roof of my mouth." 4

Fellow citizens, above your national, tumultuous joy, I hear the mournful wail of millions, whose chains, heavy and grievous yesterday, are today rendered more intolerable by the 5

Presented in Rochester, NY, July 5, 1852.

jubilant shouts that reach them. If I do forget, if I do not remember these bleeding children of sorrow this day, "may my right hand forget her cunning, and may my tongue cleave to the roof of my mouth!" To forget them, to pass lightly over their wrongs, and to chime in with the popular theme, would be treason most scandalous and shocking, and would make me a reproach before God and the world. My subject, then, fellow citizens, is "American Slavery." I shall see this day and its popular characteristics from the slave's point of view. Standing here, identified with the American bondman, making his wrongs mine, I do not hesitate to declare, with all my soul, that the character and conduct of this nation never looked blacker to me than on this Fourth of July. Whether we turn to the declarations of the past, or to the professions of the present, the conduct of the nation seems equally hideous and revolting. America is false to the past, false to the present, and solemnly binds herself to be false to the future. Standing with God and the crushed and bleeding slave on this occasion, I will, in the name of humanity, which is outraged, in the name of liberty, which is fettered, in the name of the Constitution and the Bible, which are disregarded and trampled upon, dare to call in question and to denounce, with all the emphasis I can command, everything that serves to perpetuate slavery—the great sin and shame of America! "I will not equivocate; I will not excuse"; I will use the severest language I can command, and yet not one word shall escape me that any man, whose judgment is not blinded by prejudice, or who is not at heart a slave-holder, shall not confess to be right and just.

But I fancy I hear some of my audience say it is just in this circumstance that you and your   6
brother Abolitionists fail to make a favorable impression on the public mind. Would you argue more and denounce less, would you persuade more and rebuke less, your cause would be much more likely to succeed. But, I submit, where all is plain there is nothing to be argued. What point in the anti-slavery creed would you have me argue? On what branch of the subject do the people of this country need light? Must I undertake to prove that the slave is a man? That point is conceded already. Nobody doubts it. The slave-holders themselves acknowledge it in the enactment of laws for their government. They acknowledge it when they punish disobedience on the part of the slave. There are seventy-two crimes in the State of Virginia, which, if committed by a black man (no matter how ignorant he be), subject him to the punishment of death; while only two of these same crimes will subject a white man to like punishment. What is this but the acknowledgement that the slave is a moral, intellectual, and responsible being? The manhood of the slave is conceded. It is admitted in the fact that Southern statute-books are covered with enactments, forbidding, under severe fines and penalties, the teaching of the slave to read and write. When you can point to any such laws in reference to the beasts of the field, then I may consent to argue the manhood of the slave. When the dogs in your streets, when the fowls of the air, when the cattle on your hills, when the fish of the sea, and the reptiles that crawl, shall be unable to distinguish the slave from a brute, then I will argue with you that the slave is a man!

For the present it is enough to affirm the equal manhood of the Negro race. It is not as-   7
tonishing that, while we are plowing, planting, and reaping, using all kinds of mechanical tools, erecting houses, constructing bridges, building ships, working in metals of brass, iron, copper, silver, and gold; that while we are reading, writing, and cyphering, acting as clerks, merchants, and secretaries, having among us lawyers, doctors, ministers, poets, authors, editors, orators, and teachers; that while we are engaged in all the enterprises common to other men—digging gold in California, capturing the whale in the Pacific, feeding sheep and cattle on the hillside, living, moving, acting, thinking, planning, living in families as husbands, wives,

and children, and above all, confessing and worshipping the Christian God, and looking hopefully for life and immortality beyond the grave—we are called upon to prove that we are men?

Would you have me argue that man is entitled to liberty? That he is the rightful owner of   8
his own body? You have already declared it. Must I argue the wrongfulness of slavery? Is that a question for republicans? Is it to be settled by the rules of logic and argumentation, as a matter beset with great difficulty, involving a doubtful application of the principle of justice, hard to understand? How should I look today in the presence of Americans, dividing and subdividing a discourse, to show that men have a natural right to freedom, speaking of it relatively and positively, negatively and affirmatively? To do so would be to make myself ridiculous, and to offer an insult to your understanding. There is not a man beneath the canopy of heaven who does not know that slavery is wrong *for him.*

What! Am I to argue that it is wrong to make men brutes, to rob them of their liberty, to   9
work them without wages, to keep them ignorant of their relations to their fellow men, to beat them with sticks, to flay their flesh with the lash, to load their limbs with irons, to hunt them with dogs, to sell them at auction, to sunder their families, to knock out their teeth, to burn their flesh, to starve them into obedience and submission to their masters? Must I argue that a system thus marked with blood and stained with pollution is wrong? No; I will not. I have better employment for my time and strength than such arguments would imply.

What, then, remains to be argued? Is it that slavery is not divine; that God did not estab-   10
lish it; that our doctors of divinity are mistaken? There is blasphemy in the thought. That which is inhuman cannot be divine. Who can reason on such a proposition? They that can, may; I cannot. The time for such argument is past.

At a time like this, scorching irony, not convincing argument, is needed. Oh! Had I the   11
ability, and could I reach the nation's ear, I would today pour out a fiery stream of biting ridicule, blasting reproach, withering sarcasm, and stern rebuke. For it is not light that is needed, but fire; it is not the gentle shower, but thunder. We need the storm, the whirlwind, and the earthquake. The feeling of the nation must be quickened; the conscience of the nation must be exposed; and its crimes against God and man must be denounced.

What to the American slave is your Fourth of July? I answer, a day that reveals to him   12
more than all other days of the year, the gross injustice and cruelty to which he is the constant victim. To him your celebration is a sham; your boasted liberty and unholy license; your national greatness, swelling vanity; your sounds of rejoicing are empty and heartless; your denunciation of tyrants, brass-fronted impudence; your shouts of liberty and equality, hollow mockery; your prayers and hymns, your sermons and thanksgivings, with all your religious parade and solemnity, are to him mere bombast, fraud, deception, impiety, and hypocrisy—a thick veil to cover up crimes which would disgrace a nation of savages. There is not a nation of the earth guilty of practices more shocking and bloody than are the people of these United Sates at this very hour.

Go where you may, search where you will, roam through all the monarchies and despo-   13
tisms of the Old World, travel through South America, search out every abuse and when you have found the last, lay your facts by the side of the every-day practices of this nation, and you will say with me that, for revolting barbarity and shameless hypocrisy, America reigns without a rival.

◆◆◆

Analysis of Frederick Douglass, "What to the Slave is the Fourth of July"

In "What to the Slave is the Fourth of July," Douglass clearly identifies his ultimate purpose as the elimination of slavery. But unlike some abolitionists who believed that slavery could be ended via continuing political action, without a major crisis, Douglass recognized that major conflict was quite likely. Near the conclusion of the address, he essentially lays out the case for the necessity of radical confrontation. According to Douglass:

> At a time like this, scorching irony, not convincing argument, is needed. Oh! Had I the ability, and could I reach the nation's ear, I would today pour out a fiery stream of biting ridicule, blasting reproach, withering sarcasm, and stern rebuke. For it is not light that is needed, but fire; it is not the gentle shower, but thunder. We need the storm, the whirlwind, and the earthquake. The feeling of the nation must be quickened; the conscience of the nation must be exposed; and its crimes against God and man must be denounced. (paragraph 11)

Douglass clearly understood that radical action would be needed to eliminate slavery from American life. In paragraph 11 he justifies radical confrontation, what he calls "the storm, the whirlwind, and the earthquake," as the proper rhetorical approach to "quicken" the conscience of the nation.

Why was such a radical rhetoric needed? To answer this question it is important to consider the audience to whom Douglass spoke. Douglass gave the address at a meeting of an anti-slavery society in Rochester, New York on July 5, 1852. In one sense, he clearly was preaching to the "saved," to a group that already agreed with him that slavery was an abomination. But in another sense, he was trying to convince them that truly radical action, such as support for violence, even terrorism,[14] against slavery was needed.

In persuading the anti-slavery group that radical action would be needed, Douglass faced several barriers. First, he was speaking to a group in Rochester, New York, almost on the Canadian border. They were separated from slavery by a great distance, bore no personal responsibility for slavery, and could do little directly to attack slavery. Second, direct action against slavery clearly would require violence. It was obvious by 1852 that the South was not going to give up slavery in the near term without being made to do so. Thus, radical action clearly risked conflict and war, a point that later was reinforced by the Civil War.

Third, Douglass faced the expectations of the audience in regard to a speech on the Fourth of July. In the 19th century Fourth of July orations played a prominent role in American culture. Probably because the nation was so much closer to the first Fourth of July and because of the absence of an electronic media, public celebrations of the Fourth were far more important than they have become today.[15] Typically, speeches on the Fourth followed a very strict pattern. These addresses included an affirmation of basic American values, a discussion of the importance and meaning of patriotism, a reflection on the American Revolution and the history of the nation, and a prediction of greatness to come. These aspects of content were combined with a formal, serious, and sentimental style.[16] Audiences were familiar with a typical Fourth of July Oration and had strong expectations about what they would hear in any given speech.[17]

Audience expectations were a particular problem for Douglass because, given his purpose, he could not simply praise the nation and talk in reverential tone about American history. In order to rouse his audience to take radical action, Douglass had to convince them that there were serious evils that had to be confronted. Praise for America and patriotic sentiments would not do the trick and in all likelihood would be counterproductive.

Finally, Douglass faced the problem of racism. Even in Rochester, New York, Douglass confronted racist attitudes. For example, McPherson notes that Douglass' children were not allowed to attend the white public schools.[18] Racism created a double-barreled problem for Douglass. He had to overcome racist attitudes in order to persuade his audience of the justice of his cause. But he also had to be careful that he did not simply reinforce a sense of self-satisfaction in those who had chosen to come listen to a Black man talk. It would have been easy for Douglass to have given a speech in which he thanked the audience members for all that they had done and praised their work in the abolitionist movement. If he had taken this tact, his audience would not have been motivated to act. Instead, they would have had an increased sense of self-satisfaction. Thus, Douglass had little choice but to attack the audience.

Strategies in Douglass' Address

Clearly, the dominant strategy in Douglass' address was confrontation. He utilizes four of the sub-strategies for appealing to an external audience and both of the sub-strategies for dealing with the internal audience. In this case, of course, the external and the internal audiences are somewhat mixed together. Opponents of slavery are in one sense an internal audience for Douglass. In another sense, the white abolitionists are part of Douglass' external audience.

Throughout the address, Douglass both offends and directly attacks his audience. He begins the address with a rhetorical question, "why am I called upon to speak here today?" (paragraph 1). He then states that the "great principles of freedom and of natural justice, embodied in that Declaration of Independence" (paragraph 1) are not guaranteed to "us" (slaves and other Black Americans). From this introductory device, Douglass then notes "the immeasurable distance between us" (paragraph 3) and moves to a direct attack on "The Fourth of July" that must have seemed shocking to his audience. "This Fourth of July is *yours*, not *mine*. You may rejoice, I must mourn." (paragraph 3).

The pattern of both offending and attacking his audience that is evident in the first three paragraphs continues throughout the address. In paragraph 5, he says that he hears "the mournful wail of millions whose chains, heavy and grievous yesterday, are today rendered more intolerable by the jubilant shouts that reach them." He goes on to say "that the character and conduct of this nation never looked blacker to me than on this Fourth of July." Later in the same paragraph he says that "America is false to the past, false to the present, and solemnly binds herself to be false to the future."

And despite the sharpness of the language that I have quoted from the first half of the speech, Douglass is far harsher in the conclusion. In the final two sentences of the address Douglass makes his position quite clear:

> There is not a nation of the earth guilty of practices more shocking and bloody than are the people of these United States at this very hour.
>
> Go where you may, search where you will, roam through all the monarchies and despotisms of the Old World, travel through South America, search out every abuse and when you have found the last, lay your facts by the side of the very-day practices of this nation, and you will say with me that, for revolting barbarity and shameless hypocrisy, America reigns without a rival. (paragraph 12, 13)

Saying on the Fourth of July that the United States leads the world in "revolting barbarity and shameless hypocrisy" is not exactly audience adaptation.

Douglass also is adept at both creating guilt and, implicitly, threatening his audience. The guilt creation is obvious throughout the speech, but is most evident in the introduction. It is easy to imagine the audience settling into their chairs with the expectation that Douglass will praise them for their commitment to the anti-slavery cause. Instead, he speaks of the "sad sense of disparity between us. I am not included within the pale of this glorious anniversary! Your high independence only reveals the immeasurable distance between us" (paragraph 3). He continues that "You may rejoice, I must mourn. To drag a man in fetters into this grand illuminated temple of liberty, and call upon him to join you in joyous anthems, were inhuman mockery and sacrilegious irony?" Douglass then asks his audience, "Do you mean, citizens, to mock me, by asking me to speak today?"

Rather than the praise that they undoubtedly expected, Douglass points directly to the gap between them and him. In so doing, he also points to the gap between their values (opposition to slavery) and their actions. In this passage and at many other places, he attempts to create guilt in order to motivate truly radical action.

Douglass also threatens his audience. Here, he shows considerable rhetorical ingenuity. As part of a very small Black community in Rochester, Douglass has no way to threaten the audience directly. So, he invokes the threat of God's vengeance on them. At the end of paragraph 3, he warns his audience "that it is dangerous to copy the example of a nation whose crimes, towering up to heaven, were thrown down by the breath of the Almighty, burying that nation in irrecoverable ruin. I can today take up the lament of a peeled and woe-smitten people." Here, Douglass is alluding to the fate of the Babylonian Empire, after that nation forced the Jews of the Old Testament into exile.

He drives the point home in the following paragraph by quoting directly from the Old Testament to make certain that no one in his audience misses his allusion and argument.

It is important to recognize that in the 19th century, it is likely that every member of his audience immediately would have recognized this reference to the Bible and Douglass' implicit threat of divine retribution for the "sin" of slavery. In some ways, his comments foreshadow a similar statement in Abraham Lincoln's Second Inaugural Address.

While Douglass used four of the sub-strategies of confrontation for dealing with an external audience, he did not use civil disobedience or threaten violence. Of course, civil disobedience was not needed in the North and would have been counterproductive in the South. Slaves could not use civil disobedience; that would only get them beaten. In a sense, Douglass advocates violence, not against his audience, but against slavery. That was the implication of the paragraph in which he called for "the storm, the whirlwind, and the earthquake" (paragraph 11).

In summary, Douglass either uses or suggests the importance of using all of the sub-strategies of confrontation for dealing with an external audience, save civil disobedience, which does not fit the context.

Douglass also uses both sub-strategies for speaking to an internal audience. Abolitionists always faced the problem of race. It is important to recognize the unpleasant truth that even many committed abolitionists were racists, at least by the standards of the present day. Thus, it was important that Douglass both draw on myth to support the cause and redefine what it means to be a Black American.

In relation to myth, Douglass casts the slaves in the role of the Jews in the Old Testament. That is evident in the comparison of America to Babylon. Douglass' message goes like this. Babylon kept the Jews in chains. The United States keeps slaves in chains. Babylon was destroyed by God for harming his Chosen People. Therefore, the United States must either recognize that the slaves are the Chosen People of God or suffer the same fate as Babylon. As this example indicates, Douglass skillfully draws on religious myth in advocating radical action for abolition.

He also redefines what it means to be a slave. Douglass' redefinition is quite simple. A slave is a human. In five powerful paragraphs beginning at the mid-point of the speech, Douglass makes this point. In the first, he builds an argument for the personhood of slaves by noting that in Virginia there are 72 crimes that subject the slave to the death penalty. Douglass then says, "When you can point to any such laws in reference to the beasts of the field, then I may consent to argue the manhood of the slave" (6). Here, Douglass is essentially saying that slave states can't have it both ways. If they treat slaves as human by punishing them for wrongdoing, then they cannot deny that slaves are in fact human beings.

The following paragraph reinforces this theme. Although it is a long paragraph, it merits consideration in its entirety:

For the present it is enough to affirm the equal manhood of the Negro race. Is it not astonishing that, while we are plowing, planting, and reaping, using all kinds of mechanical tools, erecting houses, constructing bridges, building ships, working in metals of brass, iron, copper, silver, and gold; that while we are reading, writing, and cyphering, acting as clerks, merchants, and secretaries, having among us lawyers, doctors, ministers, poets, authors, editors, orators, and teachers; that while we are engaged in all the enterprises common to other men—digging gold in California, capturing the whale in the Pacific, feeding sheep and cattle on the hillside, living, moving, acting, thinking, planning, living in families as husbands, wives, and children, and above all, confessing and worshipping the Christian God, and looking hopefully for life and immortality beyond the grave—we are called to prove that we are men?

The first sentence in this paragraph clearly states the theme: We are human. The second proves it argumentatively by citing all the things that Black people are doing. But even more importantly, Douglass proves the equality of Black people with the sentence itself, which is more than 130 words long. Douglass' statement is filled with language strategies including rhythm, alliteration, assonance, parallel structure, repetition, and of course functions as a rhetorical question. The ultimate point of this sentence is to prove that a person who could utter it must be a human being. It is difficult to think of a contemporary political figure who could write such a sentence.

Douglass completes the redefinition in paragraphs 8, 9 and 10 with a series of rhetorical questions. "Would you have me argue that man is entitled to liberty? "Must I argue the wrongfulness of slavery?" "Is that a question for republicans?" (paragraph 8). He continues with questions in paragraphs 9 and 10, asking his audience if he should have to prove that slavery is wrong or prove that it is "not divine" (paragraph 10). The rhetorical questions are meant to drive home the point that he has established in paragraphs 6 and 7. If slaves are human then all morality demands that slavery be eliminated immediately. His redefinition of slaves as human leads him to conclude paragraph 10, "The time for such argument is past."

In "What to the Slave is the Fourth of July" Frederick Douglass brilliantly uses confrontation both to demand action from the external audience and to fulfill the needs of the internal audience for self-definition. Douglass clearly understood that given the South's economic and cultural commitment to slavery, the system was not going to simply wither away in the short term. Radical action was needed. History clearly proves that he was right.

Thus, Douglass knew that he needed to shock his audience out of its lethargy. He also knew that he could not adapt to the constraints associated with a traditional Fourth of July address and achieve his purpose. In this rhetorical situation, Douglass correctly chooses confrontation as the only sensible rhetorical option.

There is no evidence of the immediate reaction of his audience to the address. But we do know that the speech was widely reprinted and continues to speak to the American experience with race. Clearly, Douglass did a magnificent job of adapting to a difficult set of rhetorical barriers. He not only used confrontation, but even explained why that strategy must be used. It is a wonderful speech.

One other point is relevant about Douglass' address. It is important to recognize that a similar speech would not have been appropriate in the South. For even a white abolitionist to give such a speech in the South would have been foolhardy. Given the Southern commitment to slavery, the likely effect would have been immediate backlash against the speaker and possibly violence.

Conclusion

The focus of this chapter has been on the relationship between confrontative rhetoric and social movements. I identified the characteristics of confrontative rhetoric, explained the risks associated with the strategy, discussed the situations in which confrontation is an appropriate strategic option, laid out the relationship between social movements and confrontation, specified the functions served by rhetorical confrontation, identified sub-strategies of confrontation, and applied this system to Frederick Douglass'Address "What to the Slave is the Fourth of July."

Confrontation is a powerful, but extremely dangerous rhetorical strategy. In most situations, it should be rejected as a strategy, but in a few limited situations it is the only reasonable strategic response.

Notes

1. A good introduction to how rhetoric functions in social movements can be found in Charles J. Stewart, Craig Allen Smith, and Robert E. Denton, *Persuasion and Social Movements*, 2nd ed. (Prospect Heights, IL., Waveland, 1989).

2. In *Rhetoric,* Aristotle focuses on multiple means of adapting to the preconceptions of the audience. The *Rhetoric* is contained in *The Basic Works of Aristotle,* Ed. Richard McKeon (New York: Random House, 1941): 1325–1451.

3. A rhetorical approach to the study of social movements was first suggested by Leland Griffin in his essay "The Rhetoric of Historical Movements," *Quarterly Journal of Speech* 37 (1953): 184–188.

4. See Herbert W. Simons, Elizabeth A. Mechling, and Howard N. Schreier, "The Functions of Human Communication in Mobilizing for Collective Action from the Bottom Up: The Rhetoric of Social Movements," in *Handbook of Rhetorical and Communication Theory,* ed. Carroll C. Arnold and John Waite Bowers (Boston: Allyn and Bacon, 1984), 792–868.

5. See for example Robert Cathcart, "New Approaches to the study of Movements: Defining Movements Rhetorically," *Western Journal of Speech Communication* 36 (1972): 82–89.

6. Leland Griffin, "A Dramatistic Theory of the Rhetoric of Movements," in *Critical Responses to Kenneth Burke,* ed. William Rueckert (Minneapolis: University of Minnesota Press, 1969), 456–478.

7. One perspective on this position is found in David Zarefsky, "A Skeptical View of Movement Studies," *Central States Speech Journal* 31 (1980); 245–254.

8. Herbert Simons, "On the Rhetoric of Social Movements, Historical Movements, and 'Top-Down' Movements: A Commentary," *Communication Studies* 42 (1991), p. 100.

9. Simons, "On the Rhetoric of Social Movements, Historical Movements, and 'Top-Down' Movements: A Commentary," p. 100.

10. For a similar argument see Robert L. Scott and Donald K. Smith, "The Rhetoric of Confrontation," *Quarterly Journal of Speech* 55 (1969): 1–8.

11. James M. McPherson, "The Agitator," *The New Republic* 11 March 1991, p. 37.

12. McPherson, p. 37.

13. "Historians commemorate political reformer Frderick Douglass," http://www.si/edu/resour...ics/research/african.htm.

14. McPherson notes that Douglass "counseled violent resistance" to the Fugitive Slave Law and "supported John Brown's guerrilla warfare against slavery," p. 37.

15. See Howard H. Martin, "The Fourth of July Oration," *Quarterly Journal of Speech* 44 (1958), p. 398.

16. Klaus Lubbers, "Reinventing Native Americans in Fourth of July Orations," *Studies in the Literary Imagination* 27 (Spring 1994), p. 48.

17. See Martin p. 399.

18. McPherson, p. 37.

CHAPTER TEN

Generic Analysis

A genre is a category. In every area of human endeavor, categorization plays an important role in explaining and evaluating the object or concept. A good pop song will not meet the same standards as a symphony and vice versa. As this example indicates, it is almost impossible to judge anything without some knowledge of the larger category in which it fits.

There are many ways to categorize works of rhetoric. One could categorize a work based on its subject, the time or place where it was presented, the type of occasion, the situation, and so forth. Given the variety of possible categorical approaches, clearly there is need for guidance concerning appropriate and inappropriate categorization. For example, the category "Midwest" rhetoric would not seem to be very useful.

Why is it important to place a work of rhetoric in a category? The short answer is that in some cases knowing the category of the rhetoric helps the critic both describe and evaluate the rhetoric. There is, for example, a category of rhetoric called "the employment interview." In this situation, the job applicant wants to make a good impression and find out as much about the company or organization as possible. Given these purposes, most job applicants dress formally, try to present a positive demeanor, emphasize their skills and experience, and downplay weaknesses in their record. Knowing that these characteristics typify the employment interview, employers also know where to probe. For example, a two-year gap on a resume is a red flag that demands explanation.

Knowledge of the general characteristics of a typical employment interview also provides the employer with general standards for evaluating the interview. If the potential employee comes to the interview dressed for the beach and continually refers to the interviewer as "dude," there are good reasons to doubt whether he/she will fit into the culture of a big accounting or law firm. On the other hand, if the potential employee is applying for a job at a surf shop, he/she may fit in beautifully.

What does this example have to do with rhetoric? An employment interview is itself rhetorical. Both the interviewer and the potential employee rely on rhetoric in the interview. Knowledge of the category—employment interview—helps the rhetorical critic (a role played by both the interviewer and the interviewee) analyze and evaluate the exchange.

At this point, it should be clear that in some contexts (Midwest rhetoric), analysis of the category in which the rhetoric fits doesn't provide much assistance in analyzing that rhetoric. On the other hand, in some contexts (the employment interview), knowledge of the norms of that category of rhetoric is very helpful for both interviewers and interviewees. It would seem that sometimes, generic analysis is quite useful and sometimes it is almost useless. In the remainder of this chapter, I untangle this confusing situation. In the first section, I lay out the functions of generic analysis and more fully develop the potential problems with the approach. I then discuss a model for identifying useful rhetorical genres. In the final section, I apply that model to a common rhetorical genre, the eulogy.

Functions and Problems of Generic Analysis

The two primary functions of generic analysis are to reveal the nature of the category in order to: 1) aid in the description or analysis of the rhetoric and 2) provide standards for evaluating the rhetoric.

In many cases, an understanding of the category in which a given work of rhetoric falls can aid in explaining the nature of that rhetoric. Knowing the genre of the rhetoric can provide a shortcut in the analysis process. For example, later in this chapter, I identify seven characteristics that typically are found in eulogies. This list of the aspects of form, content, substance, and style that defines eulogies assists in the analysis process, because it gives the critic something for which to look.

The typical list of characteristics found in a eulogy essentially functions as a "recipe" for the normal eulogy. The analyst can use that list as a kind of "check-off" sheet to see if a given speech does what normal eulogies do. In that way, knowledge of the genre simplifies the analysis stage.

It is important to note, however, that the analyst does not stop with identifying the recipe for the eulogy or any other genre. After that recipe is identified, the analyst checks both for what is there and what isn't there in a given speech. In that way the generic recipe can help the analyst identify both typical characteristics and unique aspects of a given work of rhetoric.

The second function of generic analysis is to provide a shortcut in evaluating a work of rhetoric. Once the characteristics that define the genre have been identified, the critic can use that list as the first step in evaluating the effectiveness of rhetoric falling in the category. For example, in relation to eulogies, the critic would ask: "Does this speech do everything that a eulogy is supposed to do?" If one of the defining characteristics of the eulogy is absent that is a sign that the speech probably won't be successful. A second question is even more useful: "Does the speech violate any of the normal characteristics found in the eulogy?" For example, a good eulogy is personal in that it focuses on the human dimensions of the deceased and the relationship between the deceased and the person giving the eulogy. A eulogy, which violates this principle by presenting a resume of the person's accomplishments, is unlikely to achieve the general purposes served by all eulogies.

The two evaluative questions provide the analyst with a shortcut to evaluation. They do not, however, eliminate the need to consider the specific audience and other aspects of the situation that the rhetor faced. For example, despite the general principle that a eulogy should be somber, there are some eulogies that must include humor. A eulogy for Bob Hope, for example, would not be complete without humor, because of Hope's career as a comic.

In summary, knowledge of a genre can aid the analyst in both explaining and evaluating a work of rhetoric. That knowledge also can assist the practitioner in constructing a speech or essay. For example, it is much easier to create a good eulogy if you understand the characteristics of eulogies as a category of rhetoric.

While a generic approach is quite useful in many cases, there are other instances in which it is not useful at all. Take the category called "lecture." While all lectures serve the purpose of presenting information to an audience, many different tacts are taken. Some lectures are built around presentation of material in outline form. Others use audio-visual devices to add to the presentation. Some lecturers use various tricks to get the participation of the audience. Other lecturers take questions only at the end. Still others pepper the audience with questions as the lecture proceeds. And a few use questions to humiliate members of the audience. In relation to strategy types, some lecturers rely on argument. Others rely on narrative, credibility, aesthetic strategies and so forth. It is difficult to think of a single characteristic that applies to all lectures.

The key point is that while generic analysis is often useful, in some instances it is not useful at all. What are the problems associated with generic analysis? In the case of the lecture, the problem was that the category was too vague to tell us anything useful. Generic analysis also may fail if the critic tries to make the category too specific. A critic might argue that all lectures have X and Y characteristics. The problem is that there are no universal characteristics found in all lectures.

A third problem occurs if the critic mis-identifies the category. I once attended a presentation which the speaker thought was supposed to be a detailed highly academic lecture for graduate students. The problem was that it in fact was designed to be a lecture for the general public. The speech was a disaster because the academic lecture did not fit the public audience. This example supports the point that mis-identification of the category may lead to a radical misunderstanding of the rhetoric.

At this point, we are faced with a problem. It is clear that in some cases generic analysis is quite useful. It is equally clear that in many other instances generic analysis is not only not useful, but is positively misleading. The answer to the difficulty is to develop a model for understanding generic constraints that helps the critic distinguish between the *useful* and the *useless* generic categories.

A Model for Generic Analysis[1]

The place to start in building a model for generic analysis is with the factor that makes a category like "employment interview" useful and the category "lecture" so useless. What factor is that? The obvious answer is that for a variety of reasons there are strict limitations on what is acceptable in an employment interview, but no such limitations on the lecture. It is important to consider how these limitations work and from where they come.

In a useful genre, the rhetor will feel constrained to choose from a narrow range of strategies, themes, and so forth. The characteristics defining the content, form, strategy, theme and so on of the genre will be limited by his/her perception that the rhetoric has to be done in a given way or it will fail. That is why job interviewees behave as they do; they know that other rhetorical choices will prevent them from getting the job.

At this point, two-thirds of a model for identifying useful genres can be described. The characteristics of the rhetoric—the form, content, style, and substance of a useful genre—are produced because the rhetor perceives strategic constraints that limit what he/she can say. So far the model looks like this:

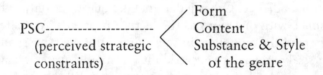

The problem is to determine what brings into existence the perceived strategic constraints.

The perceived strategic constraints are created by the interaction of three forces that operate broadly in the situation in which the rhetoric is presented. The first of these forces is the recurrent problem confronted by the rhetoric. The recurrent problem faced in a job interview is the need to get a job. The recurrent problem faced by a speaker giving a eulogy is the death of someone close to the audience. If a given type of rhetoric does not respond to an easily definable recurrent problem that type of rhetoric probably cannot be defined as a useful genre. This explains why the category "Midwest rhetoric" is valueless. There is no limiting problem associated with being in the Midwest and thus no force that limits what rhetors can say about the subject.

The second force is the purpose of the rhetor. In the job interview situation, the potential employee wants to get the job. That purpose constrains what the interviewee can say. Occasionally, someone will go on a job interview just because they are curious about the firm. They already have a good job and just want to check things out. That person may behave quite differently from a normal interviewee because his/her purpose is different.

The same point can be made about any useful genre. In a useful genre, rhetors will share a purpose that constrains what they can say. An example of a speech type that is related to but not the same as a eulogy may make this point clear. If Saddam Hussein were to die, a given Senator might comment on the event, but he/she would not present a eulogy. The Senator would not give a eulogy because his/her purpose would not be to honor Hussein's memory. Because his/her purposes would not be those which are found in a normal eulogy, the Senator would not present a eulogy at all.

The third force creating the perceived strategic constraints is the limitation on acceptable rhetoric established by the society in which the rhetoric is presented. Societal limitations define what is appropriate in a given context. For example, in a job interview, formal business clothes are appropriate; shorts and a t-shirt are not. Social forces limit other types of rhetorical action as well. In the 19th century it was common for politicians to speech for hours at a time. Today, audiences would not accept such long-winded speakers.

The combination of the recurrent problem, the purpose of the rhetor, and the societal constraints facing the rhetor together create the perceived strategic constraints that in turn produce the characteristics of form, content, substance, and style that define the rhetoric in a useful genre. The complete model looks like this:

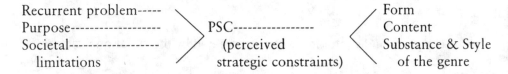

Recurrent problem-----
Purpose------------------
Societal------------------
    limitations

PSC-----------------
(perceived
strategic constraints)

Form
Content
Substance & Style
   of the genre

At this point, it is possible to distinguish between useful and useless generic analysis. It will be useful to identify the genre in which a work of rhetoric is operating if the combination of recurrent problem, purpose, and societal limitations is stable across rhetoric in the category *and* those characteristics produce narrow perceived strategic constraints to which the rhetor must adapt if he/she is to successfully persuade an audience.

If these conditions are met then the critic can use the characteristics of form, content, substance, and style that define the category as a starting point for analyzing any particular work of rhetoric in the category. As I noted earlier in this section, the characteristics of form, content, substance, and style also can be used to evaluate rhetoric. A speech or essay that does not contain the required characteristics in all likelihood will be an ineffective work.

One other point is important in application of the system. If a work that appears to fall in a particular category does not share the same recurrent problem, purpose or societal constraints with other works in the category, there is good reason to doubt that the work in fact falls into the genre. This aspect of the model provides a check against inappropriate application of generic analysis.

In summary, in order to identify a useful rhetorical genre, the critic should identify the recurrent problem, purpose(s), and societal constraints influencing works in the category. From those characteristics, the critic can infer the perceived strategic constraints and identify the form, content, substance, and style that defines a given category of rhetoric. Using this approach, the critic also can discover whether the perceived strategic constraints are narrow or broad. It is only when the perceived strategic constraints are both consistent across the category and quite narrow that generic analysis is likely to be extremely useful. A summary of this process is included below.

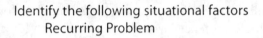

Genre Analysis

Identify the following situational factors
    Recurring Problem

    Constraining Purpose

    Societal Constraints

Identify the perceived strategic constraints created by the situational factors

Identify the characteristics of form, content, substance, and style required by the perceived strategic constraints

Generic evaluation:
1. Does the rhetoric contain all of the defining characteristics of the genre?
2. Does the rhetoric violate any of the defining characteristics of the genre?
3. Are there specific circumstances or purposes that demand adaptation of the genre?

A Case-Study of Generic Analysis: The Eulogy

To illustrate the value of generic analysis, it is helpful to apply the system to perhaps the most limited category of rhetoric, the eulogy. The recurrent problem faced in a eulogy is the death of a person close to us. When someone important to us dies grief is created. In addition, the death also reminds us that we are going to die. And death also may shock the organization or community in which the deceased lived. For example, the assassination of President Kennedy brought this nation to a standstill.

There are four purposes fulfilled by an effective eulogy, all of which are closely related to the recurrent problem. The first purpose of a eulogy is to directly confront the death of the person. There is a psychological principle that healing cannot begin until the pain has been confronted. A good eulogy forces us to directly confront the death of someone important in our lives. Second, eulogies fulfill the purpose of bringing closure to our relationship with the deceased. The eulogy tells us the meaning of the person's life in relation to our own. Third, eulogies help the audience confront the inevitability of their own mortality. The death of someone close to us always reminds each of us that someday we will die. Finally, an effective eulogy pulls the community back together. Just as individual healing cannot occur until the death has been confronted, the organization cannot move on until the community has been reestablished.

In terms of societal limitations, eulogies are governed by the culture of today's society. In the 19th century, religious references would have been mandatory. Today they aren't. Similarly, in an earlier era a longer and more flowery address would have been the norm. Today the style is more subdued.

In the case of the eulogy, the combination of recurrent problem, purpose, and societal limitations creates extremely narrow perceived strategic constraints. In essence, there is only one way to give a good eulogy.

An effective eulogy is defined by seven characteristics of form, content, substance & style. First, in an effective eulogy the rhetor begins by acknowledging and confronting the death, usually by stating what a sad day it is. Again, the pain must be confronted before it can be transformed. The second and third characteristics of an effective eulogy are both related to linguistic tone. A good eulogy possesses a somber tone, especially at the beginning. The somber tone is demanded by the occasion of the eulogy, the death of someone close to us. At the same time, a good eulogy is personal. It tells the audience about the relationship between the deceased and the living. It isn't a recital of accomplishments, but a reflection on the person who has died.

The fourth characteristic of a good eulogy is that it tells us who the deceased was. A eulogy is not a resume. Rather, it is a description of the essence of the person. Oftentimes, the eulogist will pick out two or three qualities of the deceased and illustrate those qualities with personal examples.

Fifth, a good eulogy can be thought of as a kind of rhetorical journey. It begins in darkest night with the pain of the person's death. It then gives us an understanding of the person's life and ends with emotional catharsis. The eulogy has brought closure to the crisis created for the community by the death; that community now can go on. In that way the journey is from pain to emotional release.

Sixth, a good eulogy comforts the living by telling us that the deceased lives on in some way. One can live on in heaven, in the memory of the audience, or in the work of the audience. The fact that the deceased lives on helps us face the loss of the individual and our own mortality.

Finally, a good eulogy is shaped around the character of the person who has died. As I noted earlier, when Bob Hope dies, the person giving the eulogy will need to use humor to make the eulogy effective, despite the fact that humor is not normally used in eulogies. Why? Hope was one of our very best comedians for decades and the message of his life is that humor can help us deal with even the most difficult situation. He used humor to entertain hundreds of thousands of American soldiers and sailors in his Christmas tours. An appropriate eulogy for Hope will have to use humor as a way of paying tribute to his life and service.

The important point is that the eulogy must meet the general characteristics I have outlined, but also be adapted to the particular individual. So, for example, all of the eulogies for Richard Nixon that are included in the readings volume associated with this book make reference to the Watergate affair. Senator Robert Dole, former Secretary of State Henry Kissinger, Governor Pete Wilson, and President Bill Clinton all knew that Watergate was in the back of everyone's mind, so they all dealt with the problem in one way or another.

The critic can apply the system I have developed to analyze and evaluate any eulogy. The first step is to identify the recurrent problem, purpose, and societal limitations to make certain the work falls into the category of eulogy. Recall that I noted earlier that a speech by a Senator following Saddam Hussein's death would not be a eulogy. At this point, the reason should be obvious. An American Senator would not be fulfilling the four eulogistic purposes in speaking after the death of Hussein. Therefore, he/she might speak about Hussein, but would not give a eulogy.

Form, Content, Substance, and Style of the Eulogy

1. The eulogy must confront the death of the person.
2. The tone of the eulogy should be somber, especially at the beginning of the speech.
3. The content of the eulogy should be personal.
4. The eulogist should tell us the meaning of the life of the person who has died and not give us a resume of their life.
5. A good eulogy is a rhetorical journey from pain to catharsis.
6. In a good eulogy, the deceased lives on in some way.
7. The eulogy must be adapted to the specifics of the person's life.

The second step is to compare the speech to the seven characteristics of an effective eulogy. This should help in breaking the speech down into analysis categories. A comparison of the speech to the seven characteristics also can be used to evaluate the eulogy. If the eulogy met all seven characteristics that is a strong indication that it was a good speech. If it violated one or more of the seven characteristics, it probably failed as a work of rhetoric.

In order to illustrate application of the system, I next use it in judging a eulogy presented by Ronald Reagan, following the Challenger accident.

Reagan's Challenger Eulogy in Houston Texas

The Houston eulogy was presented a few days after the tragic death of the Challenger Seven in the explosion of the space shuttle. President Reagan spoke to the families of the astronauts and also to workers at NASA.

Memorial Service for the Crew
of the Space Shuttle *Challenger*
Ronald Wilson Reagan

We come together today to mourn the loss of seven brave American, to share the grief that we all feel, and perhaps in that sharing, to find the strength to bear our sorrow and the courage to look for the seeds of hope.   1

Our nation's loss is first a profound personal loss to the family and the friends and the loved ones of our shuttle astronauts. To those they left behind—the mothers, the fathers, the husbands and wives, brothers and sisters, yes, and especially the children—all of America stands beside you in your time of sorrow.   2

What we say today is only an inadequate expression of what we carry in our hearts. Words pale in the shadow of grief; they seem insufficient even to measure the brave sacrifice of those you loved and we so admired. Their truest testimony will not be in the words we speak, but in the way they led their lives and in the way they lost their lives—with dedication, honor, and an unquenchable desire to explore this mysterious and beautiful universe.   3

The best we can do is remember our seven astronauts, our *Challenger* Seven, remember them as they lived, bringing life and love and joy to those who knew them and pride to a nation.   4

Delivered in Houston, TX, January 31, 1986

They came from all parts of this great country—from South Carolina to Washington   5
State; Ohio to Mohawk, New York; Hawaii to North Carolina to Concord, New Hampshire. They
were so different; yet in their mission, their quest, they held so much in common.

We remember Dick Scobee, the commander who spoke the last words we heard from the   6
space shuttle *Challenger*. He served as a fighter pilot in Vietnam earning many medals for
bravery and later as a test pilot of advanced aircraft before joining the space program. Danger was a familiar companion to Commander Scobee.

We remember Michael Smith, who earned enough medals as a combat pilot to cover his   7
chest, including the Navy Distinguished Flying Cross, three Air Medals, and the Vietnamese
Cross of Gallantry with Silver Star in gratitude from a nation he fought to keep free.

We remember Judith Resnik, known as J.R. to her friends, always smiling, always eager to   8
make a contribution, finding beauty in the music she played on her piano in her off-hours.

We remember Ellison Onizuka, who as a child running barefoot through the coffee fields   9
and macadamia groves of Hawaii dreamed of someday traveling to the Moon. Being an Eagle
Scout, he said, had helped him soar to the impressive achievements of his career.

We remember Ronald McNair, who said that he learned perseverance in the cotton fields   10
of South Carolina. His dream was to live aboard the space station, performing experiments
and playing his saxophone in the weightlessness of space. Well, Ron, we will miss your saxophone; and we *will* build your space station.

We remember Gregory Jarvis. On that ill-fated flight he was carrying with him a flag of his   11
university in Buffalo, New York—a small token, he said, to the people who unlocked his future.

We remember Christa McAuliffe, who captured the imagination of the entire nation, in-   12
spiring us with her pluck, her restless spirit of discovery; a teacher, not just to her students, but
to an entire people, instilling us all with the excitement of this journey we ride into the future.

We will always remember them, these skilled professionals, scientists, and adventurers,   13
these artists and teachers and family men and women; and we will cherish each of their stories, stories of triumph and bravery, stories of true American heroes.

On the day of the disaster, our nation held a vigil by our television sets. In one cruel mo-   14
ment our exhilaration turned to horror; we waited and watched and tried to make sense of
what we had seen. That night I listened to a call-in program on the radio; people of every age
spoke of their sadness and the pride they felt in our astronauts. Across America we are reaching out, holding hands, and finding comfort in one another.

The sacrifice of your loved ones has stirred the soul of our nation and through the pain   15
our hearts have been opened to a profound truth: The future is not free; the story of all human progress is one of a struggle against all odds. We learned again that this America, which
Abraham Lincoln called the last, best hope of man on Earth, was built on heroism and noble
sacrifice. It was built by men and women like our seven star voyagers, who answered a call beyond duty, who gave more than was expected or required, and who have it little thought to
a worldly reward.

We think back to the pioneers of an earlier century, the sturdy souls who took their fam-   16
ilies and their belongings and set out into the frontier of the American West. Often they met
with terrible hardship. Along the Oregon Trail, you can still see the grave markers of those
who fell on the way. But grief only steeled them to the journey ahead.

Today the frontier is space and the boundaries of human knowledge. Sometimes when   17
we reach for the stars, we fall short. But we must pick ourselves up again and press on despite

the pain. Our nation is indeed fortunate that we can still draw on immense reservoirs of courage, character, and fortitude; that we're still blessed with heroes like those of the space shuttle *Challenger*.

Dick Scobee knew that every launching of a space shuttle is a technological miracle. And he said, "If something ever does go wrong, I hope that doesn't mean the end to the space shuttle program." Every family member I talked to asked specifically that we continue the program, that is what their departed loved one would want above all else. We will not disappoint them.   18

Today we promise Dick Scobee and his crew that their dream lives on, that the dream lives on, that the future they worked so hard to build will become reality. The dedicated men and women of NASA have lost seven members of their family. Still, they, too, must forge ahead with a space program that is effective, safe, and efficient, but bold and committed.   19

Man will continue his conquest of space. To reach out for new goals and ever greater achievements—that is the way we shall commemorate our seven *Challenger* heroes.   20

Dick, Mike, Judy, El, Ron, Greg, and Christa—your families and your country mourn your passing. We bid you goodbye: we will never forget you. For those who knew you well and loved you, the pain will be deep and enduring. A nation, too, will long feel the loss of her seven sons and daughters, her seven good friends. We can find consolation only in faith, for we know in our hearts that you who flew so high and so proud now make your home beyond the stars, safe in God's promise of external life.   21

May God bless you all and give you comfort in this difficult time.   22

◆◆◆

Since Reagan's speech clearly responded to the situational factors that define a eulogy (recurrent problem, purpose, and societal limitation), there is no question that it was a eulogy. The next step in the generic analysis is to consider whether it possesses the characteristics of form, content, and substance of an effective eulogy. A brief description of the development of the speech will aid in this effort.

In the first paragraph Reagan confronts the death of the astronauts. He says that "We come together today to mourn the loss of seven brave Americans." This theme is continued in the second paragraph where he refers to "Our nation's loss" and then talks of the "personal loss to the family and the friends and the loved ones of our shuttle astronauts." The somber tone continues in the third paragraph where he says that "Words pale in the shadow of grief."

At the end of the third paragraph, Reagan begins a transition to a personal discussion of the character of the astronauts. He refers to "the way they led their lives," which was "with dedication, honor, and an unquenchable desire to explore this mysterious and beautiful universe."

The following paragraphs then tell us who they were. Reagan begins by emphasizing that they came from all over this nation. In so doing, he features their character as Americans, a theme he will return to a few paragraphs later. He then devotes one paragraph to each of the Challenger Seven (paragraphs 6 through 12). In so doing, he tries both to give the audience a personal detail about each individual and also to put the person's life into perspective. At the end of this section, he pulls together the description of the Challenger Seven and labels them "American heroes" (paragraph 13). Throughout this section, Reagan emphasizes that the crew members of the Challenger Seven were both different and the same. They had individual characteristics, but they all were typical American heroes.

In the following paragraphs, Reagan puts their heroism into perspective. He labels the astronauts as pioneers who sacrificed in order to pull this nation into the future. Reagan says that "The future is not free" (paragraph 15). It has to be earned with hard work and sacrifice. And that sacrifice will not have been in vain. Reagan promises that the dream of the Challenger Seven "lives on" (paragraph 19). He adds that "the future they worked so hard to build will become a reality" (paragraph 19).

In the final paragraphs, Reagan calls for this nation to "commemorate" the astronauts by continuing the "conquest of space" (paragraph 20). He then adds that the nation "will never forget you" and concludes by stating that those "who flew so high and so proud now make your home beyond the stars, safe in God's promise of eternal life" (paragraph 21).

Reagan's Houston eulogy is a near perfect example of what a eulogy is supposed to do. Reagan begins by directly confronting the death of the astronauts. He uses a somber tone in the introduction, a tone that will gradually change as the eulogy progresses. He next provides a personal detail relating to each of the Challenger Seven and then pulls them back together to tell of the meaning of their lives. In this section, he makes particular reference to Christa McAuliffe, the teacher who was on the mission. In the conclusion, Reagan states that the Challenger Seven live on in the space program, our memory and in heaven.

Reagan's speech clearly contains all seven characteristics of form, content, and substance that define an effective eulogy. He does an especially good job of adapting to the specifics of the situation, in this case the fact that he is eulogizing seven people in one speech. Reagan adapts to this problem by discussing each astronaut in turn, but also treating them as a group. It is a brilliant speech.

Reagan's Commemoration of the Challenger Seven on the Night of the Accident

Reagan's eulogy for the Challenger astronauts in Houston did a terrific job of doing everything that a eulogy is supposed to do. But it isn't the speech that we remember Reagan giving about the explosion of the space shuttle. On the night of the accident, President Reagan made a very moving five-minute speech about the shuttle accident. The primary author of that speech, Peggy Noonan, reports that there was an outpouring of public response to Reagan's brief comments, and that Reagan himself called the next day to thank her for her "wonderful remarks."[2] If this is the famous "eulogy" the generic system that I have developed should explain its success as well.

Address to the Nation on the Explosion of the Space Shuttle *Challenger*

Ronald Wilson Reagan

Ladies and gentlemen, I'd planned to speak to you tonight to report on the state of the Union, but the events of earlier today have led me to change those plans. Today is a day for mourning and remembering. Nancy and I are pained to the core by the tragedy of the shuttle *Challenger*. We know we share this pain with all of the people of our country. This is truly a national loss. 1

Nineteen years ago, almost to the day, we lost three astronauts in a terrible accident on the ground. But we've never lost an astronaut in flight; we've never had a tragedy like this. And perhaps we've forgotten the courage it took for the crew of the shuttle. But they, the *Challenger* Seven, were aware of the dangers, but overcame them and did their jobs brilliantly. We mourn seven heroes: Michael Smith, Dick Scobee, Judith Resnik, Ronald McNair, Ellison Onizuka, Gregory Jarvis, and Christa McAuliffe. We morn their loss as a nation together. 2

For the families of the seven, we cannot bear, as you do, the full impact of this tragedy. But we feel the loss, and we're thinking about you so very much. Your loved ones were daring and brave, and they had that special grace, that special spirit that says, "Give me a challenge, and I'll meet it with joy." They had a hunger to explore the universe and discover its truths. They wished to serve, and they did. They served all of us. We've grown used to wonders in this country. It's hard to dazzle us. But for 25 years the United States space program has been doing just that. We've grown used to the idea of space, and perhaps we forget that we've only just begun. We're still pioneers. They, the members of the *Challenger* crew, were pioneers. 3

And I want to say something to the schoolchildren of America who were watching the live coverage of the shuttle's takeoff. I know it is hard to understand, but sometimes painful things like this happen. It's all part of the process of exploration and discovery. It's all part of taking a chance and expanding man's horizons. The future doesn't belong to the fainthearted; it belongs to the brave. The *Challenger* crew was pulling us into the future, and we'll continue to follow them. 4

I've always had great faith in and respect for our space program, and what happened today does nothing to diminish it. We don't hide our space program. We don't keep secrets and cover things up. We do it all up front and in public. That's the way freedom is, and we wouldn't change it for a minute. We'll continue our quest in space. There will be more shuttle flights and more shuttle crews and, yes, more volunteers, more civilians, more teachers in space. Nothing ends here; our hopes and our journeys continue. I want to add that I wish I could talk to every man and woman who works for NASA or who worked on this mission and tell them: "Your dedication and professionalism have moved and impressed us for decades. And we know of your anguish. We share it." 5

Delivered January 28, 1986.

There's a coincidence today. On this day 390 years ago, the great explorer Francis Drake   6
died aboard ship off the coast of Panama. In his lifetime the great frontiers were the oceans,
and an historian later said, "He lived by the sea, died on it, and was buried in it." Well, today
we can say of the *Challenger* crew: Their dedication was, like Drake's, complete.

The crew of the space shuttle *Challenger* honored us by the manner in which they lived   7
their lives. We will never forget them, nor the last time we saw them, this morning, as they
prepared for their journey and waved goodbye and "slipped the surly bonds of earth" to
"touch the face of God."

◆◆◆

Reagan begins his commemoration of the Challenger seven by explaining to the national audience that the State of the Union Address had been postponed. As in any good eulogy, he expresses his grief over the loss, stating that "Nancy and I are pained to the core by the tragedy. . ."(paragraph 1).

In the second paragraph, he puts the accident in a larger frame, noting that while astronauts had been killed before, "we've never had a tragedy like this." He then labels the Challenger astronauts as "heroes" and adds that "We mourn their loss as a nation together."

The theme of mourning is continued in the third paragraph, where he speaks to the families of the astronauts. At the end of this paragraph, he labels the Challenger astronauts as "pioneers."

In paragraphs four and five, he shifts his focus to school children and NASA. Paragraph four speaks to the many school children who had been watching the shuttle launch live because of the teacher, Christa McAuliffe, who was a member of the shuttle crew. He explains that "sometimes painful things like this happen" but that "It's all part of the process of exploration and discovery." According to Reagan, "The *Challenger* crew was pulling us into the future, and we'll continue to follow them."

Paragraph five shifts the focus to NASA. Reagan expresses his admiration for the space program and inserts a jab at the Russians by saying "We don't keep secrets and cover things up. We do it all up front and in public. That's the way freedom is, and we wouldn't change it for a minute." He promises "more shuttle flights and more shuttle crews" and then praises the "dedication and professionalism" of those who work at NASA.

In paragraph six, Reagan compares the shuttle crew to the famed explorer Sir Francis Drake, who died 390 years before on the same day. He concludes in paragraph seven by quoting a selection from the poem "High Flight, "We will never forget them, nor the last time we saw them, this morning, as they prepared for their journey and waved goodbye and 'slipped the surly bonds of earth' to 'touch the face of God.'"

There is no question that the speech is one of the most famous and admired of Reagan's presidency. Reagan himself chose to include it, and not the Houston eulogy, in the collection of speeches that he published after the conclusion of his presidency.[3] However, the speech raises questions about using a generic system to evaluate a work of rhetoric. The problem is that this highly praised speech doesn't look like a normal eulogy.

In some ways the speech does possess the characteristics of a typical eulogy. Reagan begins by confronting the deaths of the astronauts and he uses a somber tone throughout. He certainly adapts to the unique characteristics of the situation by explaining why the State of the Union had been delayed and speaking directly to school children and NASA.

In other ways, however, the speech is not a typical eulogy. For example, Reagan says little about the Challenger astronauts themselves. He labels them heroes and pioneers, but gives us no personal details. In fact, he focuses more on NASA than on the astronauts. And it is decidedly odd to see an attack on the Soviets in a eulogy. Nor does Reagan clearly say that the Challenger astronauts will live on in our memory, our work or heaven. In the last line, he does say that they touched the "face of God," but he certainly does not develop the theme that the astronauts live on.

Finally, the speech lacks the emotional progression typically found in eulogies. Reagan does not move us from pain to catharsis. Instead, he talks about the nation's pain in virtually every paragraph. And the touching concluding quotation reinforces that point.

The clear conclusion is that the speech that Reagan gave on the night of the Challenger accident isn't a very good eulogy. But both public reaction and expert commentary label it as one of his most successful speeches. Does this contradictory state of affairs undercut generic analysis of rhetoric?

The reason that Reagan's first Challenger speech could be so successful, while not fulfilling the requirements of a typical eulogy, is that it wasn't a eulogy at all. This point is obvious when the speech is analyzed from the perspective of the generic model I discussed earlier in this chapter. While the speech had the same recurrent problem and cultural constraints of a typical eulogy, it did not have the same purposes. It is obvious from the address that two of Reagan's main purposes were to help school kids cope with their grief and to protect NASA from political fallout from the accident. That is why he spends roughly 1/3 of the address dealing with these subjects. In addition, it is clear that Reagan's purpose was not to move the nation to catharsis, but to hold the pain in.

On the night of the accident, it was too soon to give a normal eulogy that moves us to acceptance and almost joyful remembrance of the deceased. It was still time to feel the pain of the accident. Reagan's speech was designed to help us feel that pain, but to make certain that the anguish did not overcome school kids or create a political backlash that harmed NASA.

When the real purposes served by the speech are considered, it is immediately obvious that the address was not a traditional eulogy. It thus makes no sense to evaluate it by applying the defining characteristics of eulogy. In addition, a consideration of the purpose of the speech helps make clear why the public found it so comforting. Reagan did exactly what he needed to do on the night of the accident. He was comforting and eloquent about the sacrifice of the astronauts. And he spoke directly to America's school children and NASA. The speech did exactly what was needed, which was not a traditional eulogy.

In a memoir of her time as a speech writer for Reagan, Peggy Noonan reports that she sensed that the President was dissatisfied with the Challenger speech that he gave on the night of the accident. She quotes him as saying, "And I got off the air and I thought, Well, not so good. But then I got these calls and telegrams. . ."[4] Although it is impossible to know for sure, it seems likely that Reagan's disquiet with the speech draft was because he knew it wasn't a good eulogy. However, Noonan's draft was right on target, because she correctly realized that a eulogy was not what was needed. That was why the public responded with those calls and telegrams.

Conclusion

The analysis of Reagan's two Challenger speeches indicates both the value of generic analysis and the difficulty of carrying it out. When a work of rhetoric fits clearly into a narrow genre, as Reagan's Houston eulogy did, generic analysis is very useful for explaining the functioning of the work and evaluating it. But there are also severe dangers associated with generic analysis. Mis-categorization of the speech on the night of the accident as a eulogy would produce a wildly inaccurate evaluation of the speech. The best way to minimize the problems associated with generic analysis and to maximize the benefits is to utilize the system for identifying narrow, limiting genres, which I laid out earlier in this chapter.

Further examples of rhetorical genres are found in the genre section of the readings volume associated with this work.

Notes

1. The analysis of genres and the model for applying generic analysis were developed in my essay "On Generic Categorization," *Communication Theory* 1(1991): 128–144.
2. Peggy Noonan, *What I Saw At the Revolution: A Political Life in the Reagan Era* (New York: Random House, 1990), p. 258.
3. Ronald Reagan, *Speaking My Mind: Selected Speeches* (New York: Simon and Schuster, 1989), pp. 290–293.
4. Noonan quoting Reagan, p. 258.

CHAPTER ELEVEN

The Informed Citizen

The blood of any democracy is rhetoric. It is through the rhetorical circulation of ideas that decisions get made. Just as a disease of the bloodstream can harm the body, so can sickness in rhetoric harm the body politic. If the rhetorical blood does not circulate properly, the result inevitably will be either poor decisions or decisions which ignore the wishes of many citizens.

Unfortunately, the leaders at every level in society have tremendous incentives to mislead and deceive us. If they don't have good reasons for their proposals, deceptive rhetoric may allow them to get their way. This means that effective democracy depends upon the ability of citizens to distinguish between good reasons and bunk, between honest appeals to basic values and needs and deceptive attempts to irrationally manipulate our emotions. In the following section, I develop a system, which I call the "Informed Citizen" that a truly informed citizen can use to protect himself or herself in from such unethical rhetoric.

The "Informed Citizen" provides a system for "rhetorical self-protection." Through its use, people can identify manipulative or deceptive rhetoric. There are four stages in the Informed Citizen.

Stage One: Determining the Need for Critical Self-protection

The first stage in becoming an "Informed Citizen" is to determine the need for self-protection. While it is important that citizens be critical thinkers, not all situations call for application of rigorous standards. For example, most family gatherings do not call for application of stringent standards of critical analysis. Therefore, before moving to the following stages of the Informed Citizen, the critic should ask two questions:

1. Is a major claim on beliefs/attitudes/values or actions being made?
2. Is the person merely relaying information or is he/she strategically presenting the material?

If no claim is being made or if the rhetoric is merely informational, there is probably no reason to apply rigorous analytical standards to it. But if the rhetoric asks you to change your actions or beliefs or if the material is being presented in a persuasive fashion, there may be a very good reason to apply the further tests in the "informed citizen" system. And if the rhetoric both calls for action and presents material strategically, then it certainly makes sense to apply the remaining steps in the system.

Stage Two: Identifying the Claim Being Made

The second stage in the informed citizen is to identify the claim on action/belief/attitude that is being made and to lay out the strategies that are used in support of that claim. Data for this stage comes from the application of the analysis categories discussed in chapter two. This stage is necessary because one cannot fairly evaluate a position without knowing exactly what has been said.

Stage Three: Testing the Claim

The third stage in the Informed Citizen is to evaluate the case made in the rhetoric. The essence of this stage is to consider whether the rhetor provides strong reasons to back up his/her conclusion. Of course, it is not possible to know or check every fact in the world. And on many issues there is no consensus about the facts. Who shot JFK? Would gun control be effective? But the Informed Citizen can demand that those who want us to do something provide strong reasons in support of their positions.

By demanding strong evidence and good reasoning before a claim is accepted, a person can increase the chance that he/she will not be deceived and will be able to make good and sensible decisions. There undoubtedly are instances in which the better arguments are on one side, but truth on the other side. No one expected the U.S. Olympic hockey team to beat the Russians in 1980. But in most cases, testing the case being made gives you a good chance to uncover the stronger position and the likely outcome of a given action.

In the third stage the critic should apply a series of five main questions to test the case being made.

1. Does the rhetor provide evidence and reasoning for every claim?
2. Does the support material meet the tests of evidence?
3. Is the reasoning consistent?
4. Does the reasoning lead to the conclusion directly or could there be alternative factors that invalidate the conclusion?
5. Are there counter arguments or facts that invalidate the conclusion?

These sub-stages are important for identifying strengths and weaknesses in the position being advocated.

Presence of Evidence and Reasoning

If the rhetor does not back up every claim with evidence and reasoning, then he/she is asking the audience to accept that claim on faith. Thus, it is very important to see if every claim in a given work is supported. Without support, a claim is merely a statement of personal opinion, not a rational argument.

If the analyst discovers that a given claim or set of claims is not supported with evidence and reasoning, he or she then should ask if the rhetor is himself/herself an expert on the subject. If that is not the case, then the claim should be treated as merely an unsubstantiated personal opinion. There is no reason to give significant credibility to such opinions.

Tests of Evidence

Even if evidence is presented that does not mean that the data is adequate. Fortunately, there are general questions that can be applied to test each of the four main types of evidence: examples, statistics, comparisons, and authoritative material.

Examples ◆ In relation to examples, it is important to consider the following:

1. Are there enough examples to support the conclusion?
2. Are the examples from a relevant time/place/culture?
3. Are the examples typical?
4. Are there counter-examples?

Each of the four questions gets at an important point. First, it is important that there be sufficient examples to support a given claim. Sports provides an excellent example of the importance of this principle. On any given day in baseball, for instance, an average player may hit three home runs. One good day, however, does not make a season. Over time, the average player is likely to return to his normal performance.

The second, third, and fourth questions all get at the degree to which an example is typical. The second question forces the critic to think about whether the example comes from a relevant place and time. For instance, an example of how college students behave at an extremely conservative religious school would not necessarily reveal how students behave at a secular, liberal place like the University of California, Berkeley. The third question also is aimed at testing representativeness, in this case by asking whether the example was typical of the factual situation.

Finally, it is important to ask about counter-examples. One occurrence of a given incident may not prove much if there are many counter-examples indicating that the occurrence happens only very rarely.

Taken together, these questions allow the critic to determine whether there are enough relevant examples supporting a conclusion and to judge whether those examples are typical.

Statistics ◆ In relation to statistics, it is important to consider the following:

1. Is the sample large enough in order to draw a conclusion?
2. Is the sample representative of the population being studied?
3. Are alternative variables allowed for in the statistics?
4. Did the research follow appropriate statistical procedures?

The first question is a way of considering whether the results might be accidental. Early in an NBA season, for example, some obscure player may well be averaging 20 points a game. But by season's end that player will be down near his historical average. It is likely that he had such a high average at the beginning of the season, simply because of random factors. Over time, the player almost certainly will return to his normal level of success.

The second question is a way of making certain that the sample in the statistics is representative of the larger society. For example, if one were interested in how average Americans were coping with inflation, it would not make sense to survey Lexus owners. Since the Lexus is an extremely expensive car, almost all owners are (at minimum) upper middle class. In this case, the sample of Lexus owners would not necessarily be representative of all U.S. citizens.

The third question notes that in some cases a statistical finding may relate more to alternative factors than to the main point being claimed. For example, it might not be sensible to make national policy toward teen pregnancy based on the experience of the State of Utah. Utah is one of the most conservative places in America and many residents of the state are Mormons, a conservative religious group. A public policy that would work in Utah might not work at all elsewhere.

The fourth question focuses on the statistical procedures followed in the study. It is important, for example, that researchers consistently apply the same definition of terms in all aspects of a study. There is one problem with applying this test, however. In many cases, the details concerning the statistics may not be presented. If this is the case, the Informed Citizen carefully should test the credentials of the source of the research against the standards for authoritativeness, which will be discussed in a moment.

The four tests of statistics provide a means of distinguishing between statistics that powerfully support a point and misleading statistical data.

Comparisons ◆ In relation to comparisons of all types it is important consider the following questions:

1. Are there enough points of similarity to back up the conclusion?
2. Are the similarities relevant to the issue being considered?
3. Are there important differences between the two objects being compared?

Comparisons are generally believed to be the weakest form of proof. Through application of the above questions, it is possible to test whether a comparison is adequate to support a point.

Obviously, if the two objects/ideas/people being compared are not similar in important ways, the comparison probably isn't valid. That is why it is important to check a comparison for points of similarity between the items being compared. A comparison of Michael Jordan and Larry Bird would contain many points of similarity. They were, after all, both great basketball players who dominated the sport and led their teams to NBA titles. A comparison of Michael Jordan to Michael Dukakis, on the other hand, would seem to be based only on one point of similarity, each has the same first name.

The Jordan versus Dukakis comparison illustrates the other questions as well. Clearly, the similarity in first names is unlikely to be important; it isn't a relevant point of similarity. And there are obviously many differences between Jordan and Dukakis. One is probably the greatest basketball player of all time; the other is a failed Democratic nominee for President.

Thus, it is important to consider the points of similarity between two items being compared, the relevance of those points of similarity, and relevant differences. By applying these three tests, it should be possible to distinguish between strong and weak comparisons as a form of rational support.

Authoritative Evidence ◆ In relation to authoritative evidence, there are three important questions to consider:

1. Does the source have expertise or experience in the area under consideration?
2. Is the source in a position to know the conclusion being developed?
3. Is the source biased?

The first question tests whether the person is actually an authority. If he/she does not have either special expertise or relevant experience on the subject then there is little reason to treat his/her views with any special deference. If a famous actor or actress talks about acting, I listen. When he/she testifies about foreign policy, I say "pass the popcorn."

The second question relates to the degree to which the source could know the conclusion being drawn. During the Cold War, both liberals and conservatives sometimes speculated about the motivations of the leaders of the Soviet Union. But these sources were not in a good position to know Soviet goals. The Soviet Union was a closed society in which no one had direct access to the views of the leadership. Rather than expert opinion, a statement about the motives of Soviet leaders more accurately could be considered to be an informed guess.

The third question gets at the motivation of the source. The key point to consider is whether the source is in any way self-interested. For example, it makes sense to doubt testimony of a scientist employed by the tobacco industry that smoking is not that harmful. There is good reason to believe that the scientist takes that position because he/she is paid to defend it.

The three questions for testing authoritative evidence provide simple rule of thumb standards for distinguishing between real authorities and those who either lack the proper credentials to be considered an authority or who possess a substantial bias that makes their comments untrustworthy.

Summary of Testing Evidence ◆ In sum, in the second sub-stage of stage three, the informed citizen should check the adequacy of the evidence presented. This may seem a daunting task, but in fact it is simply a matter of considering each individual bit of evidence in relation to the specific tests of evidence that have been discussed.

Testing Consistency

The third sub-stage asks whether the reasoning presented in support of the claim is consistent. An example may make clear the importance of testing the reasoning for consistency. Many conservatives oppose social programs as handouts that destroy personal initiative. At the same time, some of them favor government programs that provide support for business development. But the business development program and the social program would seem to have very similar goals. It is hard to see why it is ok to support rich companies, but not ok to provide a training program for a poor person. The existence of this inconsistency suggests that one or the other position may not be sensible. If it is appropriate to support big companies, then maybe some programs for the poor can be justified. On the other hand, if programs aiding the poor are wasteful then perhaps big companies don't need the support either.

Of course, it is possible that the inconsistency is only apparent, that there is a relevant distinction that can be drawn between the two situations. Still, the presence of an apparent inconsistency is important. If you see smoke billowing out of your house, it makes sense to investigate. The presence of a major inconsistency is a lot like that smoke. It may mean nothing, but it would be wise to check—and quickly.

Testing Reasoning

In the fourth sub-stage, the informed citizen considers whether the reasoning leads to the conclusion directly. Recall that it is reasoning which "links" the evidence to the conclusion. In some cases, however, the reasoning does not perform that linking function adequately. The best way to test the adequacy of the linkage is to mentally test whether the reasoning present in the argument *necessarily* leads to the conclusion.

Consider the following example: "Joe Jones has friends who have been convicted of drunk driving. Therefore, he should not be elected to the City Council." In this example, the conclusion is that Jones should not be elected to the City Council. The data is that he has friends who have been convicted of drunk driving. The implied reasoning is that someone who has friends who drink and drive is not an appropriate member of the Council. More specifically, the thinking appears to be that someone who associates with a convicted drunk driver must be either immoral him/herself or a drunk. This reasoning seems obviously specious. The fact that a friend drove drunk says little about the behavior of the candidate. In fact, remaining loyal to a friend might be a sign of high personal morality.

Note that the conclusion drawn in relation to the above example could have been quite different had the data been different. If the friends had been convicted of multiple acts of racist violence, our judgment would have been changed. Someone who remains friends with an individual who commits racially motivated violent acts is not an appropriate representative of the people.

It is traditional in books on argument and logic to label the flaw in reasoning in the above example as "guilt by association." In guilt by association, one person is judged guilty of some act based on his/her association with someone else. Along with guilt by association, these books tend to list a host of other fallacies including the following: ad hominem (a personal attack), slippery slope (some action will push us down the slippery slope to a disastrous result), and many others. The question then is why not use these specific fallacies, rather than a general focus on whether the reason links directly the claim and the conclusion.

The answer to this question is that the specific fallacies are not fallacious in all cases. For example, personal attacks are often irrelevant to a claim being made, but not always. If the issue is the person, then the personal attack may be completely relevant. The underlying point behind each of the fallacies I have mentioned is the principle that reasons must directly link the evidence and the conclusion. It is for this reason that I focus on the linkage itself. The key point, therefore, is that the informed citizen should ask whether the reasoning leads to the conclusion directly or whether there might be an exception that would invalidate the reasoning.

Considering Alternative Data

In the fifth sub-stage, the informed citizen considers whether there are counter arguments that might deny the conclusion. No work of rhetoric can present the entire story. It makes sense to weigh other available material before accepting a claim and consider counter-arguments against those presented by the rhetor.

For example, at the end of the 1990s both President Clinton and some Republicans talked a great deal about the new budget surplus for the United States. Predictably, they disagreed about what to do with that surplus. The Republicans wanted tax cuts and Clinton wanted to save most of it to strengthen Social Security and Medicare. In considering the arguments of both sides, however, one of the most important points is that the United States, in fact, did not have a real budget surplus at all. Rather, the United States had a net surplus when you took into account revenues paid into the Social Security system.[1] Without the Social Security surplus, there was a net deficit on the Federal books. But that Social Security money will be needed someday to pay for the retirement of baby boomers. The upshot is that in fact the United States had no surplus at all.

The discovery that the United States was not, in fact, running a surplus in turn cast doubt on the proposals of both the Congressional Republicans and President Clinton. Since there was no real surplus, there would seem to be little reason to cut taxes. And President Clinton's call to hold the majority of the money for Social Security must be seen as politically self-serving since that is where the money already was.

As the budget surplus example makes clear, it is important to consider counter-arguments and counter-evidence to whatever has been presented. By considering this material, the analyst can make a better judgment concerning whatever claim has been made.

Summary of Stage Three

At the end of the third main stage in the informed citizen system, the critic should be in a good position to evaluate the strength of the claim being made. In drawing this judgment, it makes sense to list the strengths and weaknesses of the case being presented and then make an on-balance conclusion about the quality of the argument. Possible conclusions include the following:

1.   There are good reasons to accept the judgment of the rhetor.
2.   There may be something in the claim, but there isn't enough support without more data.
3.   The claim is totally flawed. I am being deceived.

Through the application of the third stage, any citizen can protect him/herself from deceptive rhetoric.

Stage Four—Testing Rhetoric for Manipulation

Rhetoric may be used to unify and motivate us, but it also can be used to divide society and create hate. In the fourth stage, the critical analyst asks questions to protect himself/herself and society from divisive and hateful rhetoric.

There are three important questions to be considered:

1.   Does the rhetoric attempt to prevent other voices from being heard?
2.   Does the rhetoric attempt to overwhelm our reason?
3.   Does the rhetoric attack groups or individual people, rather than their ideas or actions?

These questions are tied to the function of rhetoric in a democratic society. Rhetoric is the vehicle through which various groups in society negotiate their disagreements and work to solve problems. Rhetoric that violates one of these three principles cannot fulfill its function.

First, rhetoric that denies someone the right to speak is unethical because it prevents the democratic society from functioning. For any democracy to work, the people must be able to speak both directly to each other and via their representatives. If that opportunity to speak is denied the democracy has failed.

It is important to understand that people rarely say explicitly "Don't listen to X." At the same time, they often do that implicitly by labeling the other side as immoral. When someone says that X group should be excluded from the debate because of their extreme views on some issue this cuts that group out of the democratic dialogue. If we don't listen to the other side, we will never hear their views and there is a greater chance of making an inappropriate decision.

Of course, there are exceptions to this rule. It makes sense to prevent someone from putting directions for making a nuclear bomb on the internet. But the exception, in a sense, proves the rule. As a rule, rhetoric which implicitly or explicitly labels an individual or group in such a way that they are ignored is quite dangerous.

Second, some rhetoric is unethical because it is dominated by strategies that are designed to overwhelm our reason. As I explained earlier, narratives, appeals to value and so forth are not necessarily irrational. Sometimes, rhetoric can produce a strong emotional reaction *and* also build a powerful rational case for a position. On the other hand, the strategies for producing an emotional response may be used to distract us from the best case that can be made for a position. When anti-abortion advocates show pictures of aborted fetuses or pro-choice advocates show pictures of "women in chains," both sides are trying to overwhelm rational thought. The issue is not whether a fetus had blood; the question is whether the fetus had a soul. The picture cannot speak to that issue. Nor does the picture of a "woman in chains" relate to an issue such as whether a regulation requiring a 24 hour waiting period following consultation with a physician prior to having an abortion is reasonable. The waiting period in fact may be a bad idea, but it hardly places a woman in "chains" to require her to think for a day before having an abortion.

In both cases, the point of the rhetoric is to overwhelm the reason of the audience with emotional reactions. On an issue such as abortion, we need the power of "sweet reason" in order to talk to each other. An over emotional rhetoric drowns out rational discussion.

Third, rhetoric, which attacks groups or individuals, rather than their ideas, is extremely dangerous in a democratic society. Rhetoric is a powerful force for unification. Many presidents and others have used rhetoric to pull together all the people of this nation. But rhetoric also can be used to divide us and create hate. Hitler did that. Rhetoric that creates hate or divides society into the just and unjust, the moral and the evil, threatens the very fiber of democratic action.

In the 1996 presidential campaign, ultra-conservative Pat Buchanan presented several speeches in which he referred to illegal immigrants to the United States with the name "Jose."[2] Buchanan's reference implicitly devalued all Americans of Hispanic origin. What difference would it make whether the illegal immigrant was named Sven or

Olaf or any other name? In using the name Jose, Buchanan drew on stereotypes of Hispanic Americans. Such rhetoric threatens our democratic system both because it creates hate and because it says that some citizens of this nation are "real" Americans and some are not.

By applying the three questions in stage four, the informed citizen can protect him/herself from unethical rhetorical practice.

Summary of Stages in the Informed Citizen

I.   Determine the need for critical self protection by asking:

    1.   Is a major claim on beliefs/attitudes/values or actions being made?

    2.   Is the person merely relaying information or is he/she strategically presenting the material?

II. Identify the claims that are being made

III. Test the Quality of the Case for the Claims

    1.   Does the rhetor provide evidence and reasoning for every claim?

    2.   Does the support material meet the tests of evidence?

    3.   Is the reasoning consistent?

    4.   Does the reasoning lead to the conclusion directly or could there be alternative factors that invalidate the conclusion?

    5.   Are there counter arguments or facts that invalidate the conclusion?

IV. Test the Rhetoric for Manipulation

    1.   Does the rhetoric attempt to prevent other voices from being heard?

    2.   Does the rhetoric attempt to overwhelm our reason?

    3.   Does the rhetoric attack groups or individual people, rather than their ideas or actions?

Application of the Informed Citizen

The informed citizen system should be applied in the same way that a virus protection program operates on a hard drive. A good virus protection program is always running in the background. It doesn't effect the computer user until a virus is detected. At that point, the program identifies and destroys the virus.

The informed citizen system can serve a similar function. It can be running in the mental background, always ready to help the individual identify deceptive or manipulative rhetoric.

The Importance of Being an Informed Citizen

Other than abortion, gun control probably has generated stronger reactions than any other issue facing the country today. Proponents of gun control have labeled gun manufacturers and sellers as the "murder" industry. And the NRA and others who oppose gun control have attacked gun control advocates for wanting to take away our basic civil liberties. Sometimes passionate debates on an issue such as gun control can generate useful discussion and sensible decisions. In this case, however, more heat than light has been created. One of the reasons for this result is that some of the rhetoric produced on the issue has been misleading and even deceptive.

A classic anti-gun control advertisement produced by the National Rifle Association illustrates this point.[3] The advertisement, which opposes all forms of gun regulation, includes a picture of a shattered cameo locket. It asks the readers to imagine the horrors that might be inflicted on your own mother or grandmother by vicious thugs. "The next few minutes of mindless cruelty will leave her beaten, broken, perhaps silenced forever. It is grueling to imagine. But we ask you to imagine it for a moment for a reason. Because it *does* happen so often it no longer makes headlines."

The ad also argues that advocates of gun control and others, including media, police chiefs and judges don't care anything about ordinary citizens. It even implies that politicians care more about criminals than the public. The ad states in answer to the question "Who Cares? "*Not Certain politicians,* who'll see that her attackers get lawyers, psychiatrists and warm beds." The implication is that only the NRA cares enough to protect your "constitutional freedom to make that choice [to protect yourself with a gun]."

There is no question that this advertisement is designed to distract the people from the core issues involved in the debate about gun control and thus fails to meet the standards contained in the Informed Citizen. First, the advertisement wants us to feel terrible about how elderly women are beaten up by uncaring thugs, but not to think about how those beatings relate to gun control. As terrible as such violence is, it has nothing to do with gun control, unless the NRA is suggesting that elderly women systematically should arm themselves. It is unsurprising that the NRA does not cite any evidence that such position would be effective. Second, there are obvious potential problems with arming any group to prevent crime. It is certainly possible that the nice elderly woman with the locket would be more vulnerable if she were armed. The criminal might become enraged by the gun and kill her or he (statistics say almost all thugs of this type are men) might take the gun away from her and use it himself. Alternatively, the elderly woman might be worse off with a gun because of the risk of a gun accident or use of the weapon in a crime of passion.

Third, the NRA violates principles in both stages three and four by suggesting that politicians care more about criminals than ordinary citizens. The reason that politicans guarantee minimum living conditions for prisoners is not some great love for felons (remember convicted felons cannot vote), but that the Supreme Court has required them to do so. The statement that politicians don't care about ordinary citizens also represents both an attack on politicians as members of a group and an attempt to overwhelm our reason. The last thing the NRA wants with this ad is a careful consideration as to whether your mother or grandmother would be safer if she were "packing."

My point in dissecting the NRA advertisement is to show that there is a great deal of misleading rhetoric in American society. Any number of other examples could be cited. To make this point clearer (and in a spirit of balanced analysis), I will illustrate the application of the informed citizen system, by applying it to a Handgun Control advertisement featuring former Reagan press secretary James Brady, who was seriously injured in the attempted assassination of President Reagan. The advertisement was printed in a number of newspapers and magazines as part of a campaign in support of the Brady Bill. That legislation was passed into law early in the Clinton Administration.

Application of the Informed Citizen to Handgun Control Inc. Advertisement

The first stage is to consider whether the Informed Citizen system should be applied. In this case, there is no doubt that both parts of the test are met. The advertisement clearly asks for action on the part of the audience, both in the form of a monetary donation to the organization and also general support for the Brady bill. There is also no doubt that the advertisement selectively presents material. For instance, the picture of Brady in his wheel chair is designed to elicit a strong emotional response.

The goal in stage two is to identify the main claims being made and supporting materials, including strategies, that are used to back up those claims. In this case, the advertisement makes three main claims. First, it argues that gun violence is a significant problem. The advertisement cites Brady as an example of this point, along with examples of students killed in a high school and drivers killed on the highway. It also notes that 220,000 people have been killed by handguns since Brady was shot.

The second claim is that the Brady Bill would be effective. This claim is implied by the reference to the act as "common sense" and also by statements that the "cooling

-- James S. Brady --
President Reagan's Press Secretary
Shot on March 30, 1981 by John Hinckley

Please Help Me Save Lives

"Add your voice to mine. Help stop random gun violence.

I know firsthand the daily pain of a gunshot wound. And I'm one of the lucky ones. I survived a bullet to the head. Since I was shot eleven years ago, more than 220,000 men, women and children have been killed in handgun fire. Each night's news seems to bring a more horrible story. Shots fired in a classroom. Two students killed in a high school hallway. Woman shot in the head while driving on a freeway. America's epidemic of random gun violence rages on.

I'm calling on Congress to enact a common sense law -- the Brady Bill -- requiring a "cooling-off" period before the purchase of a handgun so police can run a thorough background check on the buyer. Time to cool off a hot temper. Time to screen out illegal purchasers. Every major police group in America supports this public safety measure.

So why hasn't Congress passed the Brady Bill? Because too many Members of Congress are either afraid of the hardcore gun lobby or pocket the gun lobby's PAC money. Like Senator Phil Gramm (R-TX) who has received more than $349,000 in campaign support from the NRA since 1984.

Right now, the Brady Bill is being blocked from final passage by Senator Gramm and a few others controlled by the gun lobby. We need to send these politicians a message. It's time to put public safety ahead of politics. If our legislators really care about saving lives, they will pass the Brady Bill.

Let your Senators know you want action on the Brady Bill now -- before you or someone you love becomes a victim."

Help free the Brady Bill in the Senate. It's real easy. Here's how.

Just call **1-900-860-8787**

The cost of the call is $3.75, and will appear on your phone bill. We'll send letters in your name to your Senators urging them to help free the Brady Bill. We'll also send you copies.

Call anytime -- our lines are open 24 hours a day!

Help me "cool-off" gun violence and make America safer.

JIM, I've called 1-900-860-8787. But, I want to do more.

☐ I'm enclosing a check so you can run this ad nationwide:

☐ $15 ☐ $25
☐ $50 ☐ $100
☐ Other $_____

Name_____

Address_____

City_____ State____ Zip____

JBKY

HANDGUN CONTROL

Because we lobby full time for common sense laws, contributions are not tax deductible.

This public safety message sponsored by Handgun Control, Inc. 1225 Eye Street, N.W. Washington, D.C. 20005 (202)898-0792

Keep the Peace!

Join Our Campaign to Fight Gun Violence!

Did You Know?

- Every day, 15 children, aged 19 and under, are killed with firearms.
- Every six hours, a youth aged 10 - 19 commits suicide with a firearm - 1,426 in all in 1992.
- In 1992, 3,336 children and teenagers were murdered with guns and 501 died in unintentional shootings.
- An estimated 1.2 million elementary-aged, latch-key children have access to guns in their homes.
- The presence of a gun in the home triples the risk of homicide in the home.
- Firearm homicide is the leading cause of death for black men aged 15 - 24.
- There are more than 222 million firearms in the possession of private citizens in the U.S. 76 million of the firearms in circulation are handguns.
- At least $1 billion is spent annually on hospital costs associated with the treatment of firearm injuries.

> *"Gun violence is out of control. Don't get lost.*
> *Join HCI today."*
> **- Michael Stipe, REM**

Michael Stipe joins HCI Chair Sarah Brady and Jim Brady.

Join Jim and Sarah Brady and HCI in our important fight to stop gun violence.

My check, payable to Handgun Control, Inc., is enclosed for:

☐ $15 ☐ $30 ☐ $50
Other $ _____

Name _____
Address _____
City _____ State _____ Zip _____

Mail to: HCI, 1225 Eye Street, NW, #1100, Washington, DC 20005 • (202) 898-0792.

Because we lobby full-time for stronger gun laws, your contribution is not tax-deductible.

off" period in the bill would allow time for the tempers of individual buyers to cool (thus preventing crimes of passion). The cooling off period also would allow the police to check out potential purchasers and prevent criminals from purchasing weapons. The advertisement also cites authoritative evidence in the form of support for the legislation from police organizations.

The third claim is that the bill has not passed previously because of opposition from the NRA. The advertisement says that a few Senators who are "controlled" by the gun lobby are blocking the bill. It cites the example of Senator Gramm of Texas, who received almost $350,000 from the NRA in campaign contributions.

It is also important to note that the advertisement relies on an appeal to the basic values of life and safety, with the picture of Brady in his wheel chair as the major means of using these values to tap an emotional response.

Stage three in the application of the Informed Citizen is to test the quality of the case being made. The first question to be considered is whether evidence is cited for all of the claims. Clearly, the answer is yes. There is data supporting each of the three main positions in the rhetoric. The second question is to consider whether the evidence cited meets the tests of evidence. Again, there would not seem to be major problems. The examples of harmful gun violence cited by Handgun Control Incorporated are not detailed but they seem representative of the gun violence problem. The other evidence appears to be strong as well.

In applying the third sub-step, the test of consistency, however, problems arise. One major difficulty is that the action advocated by the advertisement, passage of the Brady Bill, would do little about the gun violence problem specified in claim one. The Brady Bill could reduce deaths by giving the police time to identify convicted felons, who then would not be allowed to purchase guns. The legislation also might prevent a few deaths with the required cooling off period. However, the vast majority of gun deaths are tied to use of guns by citizens who already own them, use of guns by citizens who legally can buy them, or illegal use of guns by people who would ignore the law. It is quite telling that two different police organizations that testified in favor of the Brady Bill before a Congressional Committee both emphasized that the legislation would help, but that it was by no means a solution to the gun violence problem. A representative of the Fraternal Order of the Police, Tim Mullaney, noted that "The legislation. . . will not, if enacted, by itself solve problem of handgun violence." He went on to defend the value of the legislation for providing a "valuable tool" that could be used by law enforcement. Similarly, David Mitchell of the International Association of Chiefs of Police, admitted that "this legislation cannot stop guns from getting into the hands of criminals, but it will in fact, prevent an appreciable number from getting into the hands of criminals."[4] It seems clear that the vast majority of the 220,000 gun fatalities cited in the advertisement could not have been prevented by the legislation. Therefore, the discussion of the magnitude of the problem in the first claim and the discussion of the solution in the second are not consistent.

There also are problems with the advertisement in relation to the fourth question. Clearly, there are alternative factors that could invalidate some of the reasoning. For example, the fact that Phil Gramm accepted large donations from the NRA does not necessarily mean that he is controlled by that organization. Perhaps the NRA contributes to Gramm because he is a strong advocate for their views. After all, Gramm is from Texas, where there are few proponents of gun control.

And application of the fifth question also reveals difficulties. For example, it seems unlikely that criminals would follow the law. They will not fill out the necessary paper work and wait for the police to find them. Rather, they will procure guns illegally. Even advocates of gun control agree that five of six criminals buy their weapons on the street.[5]

On balance, the advertisement does not do a good job of supporting the claim that the Brady Bill would make a major dent in handgun murder. It might slightly reduce the rate, but the bulk of the problem would remain. And in fact that is exactly what happened after the Brady Bill was passed.[6] For example, Handgun Control Incorporated claimed that in California, the bill prevented about 2400 people from purchasing illegal guns. Unfortunately, that was only one percent of gun purchases.[7]

The application of stage four to the advertisement reveals problems relating to the second and third questions. In comparison to the first question, the advertisement does nothing to cut off debate. Yes, it attacks the NRA, but clearly the NRA has had adequate access to the public forum. In relation to the second question, however, there is a major problem. The advertisement clearly uses the picture of Brady, the statistic on the number of gun deaths, and the examples of random gun violence to produce a strong emotional reaction in favor of gun control. The trouble is that the legislation would do little to deal with any of the gun problems upon which the advertisement focuses. Brady's example illustrates this point. The Brady Bill would have done nothing to stop the man who shot Brady and Reagan, John Hinckley, from purchasing a gun, because he was a legal purchaser at the time. Thus, the advertisement seems to use strategies that could prevent us from truly understanding the gun violence issue.

A similar point can be made in relation to the third question. The statement that Senator Gramm is "controlled by the gun lobby," is a personal attack, rather than a discussion of the issues. It may be that Senator Gramm is controlled by the NRA, but clearly that position needs more support. Personal attacks as opposed to discussion of the issue should be avoided unless there is overwhelming support for them. In this case, it is clear that reasonable people oppose gun control. Perhaps Senator Gramm is one of those people.

Overall, Handgun Control Incorporated makes a strong case that the Brady Bill might somewhat reduce gun violence, but it does so in a somewhat misleading fashion. The advertisement seems designed to convince the reader that the Brady Bill could make a major dent in gun murders when it clearly could not do so.

I introduced the application of the Informed Citizen system with an illustration drawn from the rhetoric of the NRA. I then applied the system to an ad by Handgun Contorl Incorporated. These two examples illustrate two points. First, the system can be applied to any work of rhetoric in order to test whether a strong case is made and whether deceptive strategies are used. Second, the fact that both the NRA and Handgun Control Incorporated used strategies that were quite questionable is indicative of the need for the Informed Citizen system to protect us from deception and manipulation.

Conclusion

President Abraham Lincoln is reported to have said that "You can fool all the people some of the time, and some of the people all the time, but you can not fool all the people all of the time."[8] For Lincoln's aphorism to remain true in this media-saturated age, people need to become "Informed Citizens." Through the use of the system I have described they can do that.

At the beginning of this chapter, I noted the importance of being able to distinguish between strong ethical argument and utter bunk. The four stages of the Informed Citizen system can be thought of as a sort of "bunk detector" to aid in this process. By systematically testing the claims, evidence, and reasoning, people can distinguish between strong argument and utter deception, between honest appeals to our values and attempts to mislead or deceive us.

Notes

1. A press release from the New Democrat Coalition, a group of moderate Democrats in Congress made this point clear. They cite Congressional Budget Office numbers indicating that in 1998 the United States had a $29 billion deficit, when Social Security surpluses were excluded from the budget calculation. See New Democrat Coalition, "Fiscal Discipline and Debt Reduction Must be Top Priority," 1999, p. 1.
2. See James Bennet, "Candidate's Speech is Called Code to Controversy," *New York Times* 25 February 1996: A22.
3. The ad was published in *The New York Times* 26 January 1988, A9. It appeared in other publications as well.
4. The testimony of the two police organizations is found in *Brady Handgun Violence Prevention Act,* House Hearings Before the Subcommittee on Crime and Criminal Justice of the Committee on the Judiciary, 30 September 1993 (Washington: Government Printing Office, 1994), pp. 193, 206–207.
5. See Cable News Network, "Gun Control and the Brady Bill," www.cnnsf.com.
6. After the Brady Bill was passed the rate of gun murders dropped, but so did other murders and all crime. In the same period, the percentage of murders committed with handguns rose from roughly 50% to 54%. See United States Department of Commerce, *Statistical Abstract of the United States 1998* (Washington: Government Printing Office, 1998), chart 339.
7. Handgun Control Incorporated is cited in Cable News Network, "Gun Control and the Brady Bill," www.cnnsf.com.
8. See the *Oxford Dictionary of Quotations* (New York: Oxford University Press, 1979), p. 314